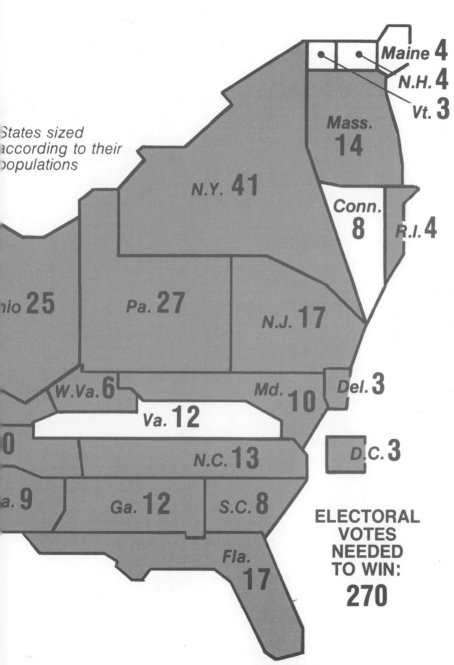

Bartle

▽ **W9-BKO-247**

Maine **4**

N.H. **4**

Vt. **3**

Mass. **14**

States sized
according to their
populations

N.Y. **41**

Conn. **8**

R.I. **4**

hio **25**

Pa. **27**

N.J. **17**

W.Va. **6**

Md. **10**

Del. **3**

Va. **12**

N.C. **13**

D.C. **3**

0

a. **9**

Ga. **12**

S.C. **8**

**ELECTORAL
VOTES
NEEDED
TO WIN:
270**

Fla. **17**

Base map from the Ohio Bureau of Employment Services

we almost made it

we
almost

made it

BY MALCOLM D. MACDOUGALL

CROWN PUBLISHERS, INC. NEW YORK

Printed in the United States of America

Published simultaneously in Canada by
General Publishing Company Limited

Designed by Ruth Kolbert Smerechniak

Library of Congress Cataloging in Publication Data

MacDougall, Malcolm.
  We almost made it.

  1. Presidents—United States—Election—1976.
2. Ford, Gerald R., 1913-   I.   Title.
E868.M3 1977   329'.023'730925   76-57959
ISBN 0-517-52933-5

To Ina Brown MacDougall Treat,
who secretly prayed
that I would someday turn out
to be a Republican.

CONTENTS

ACKNOWLEDGMENTS

I would like to thank the patient clients and personnel of Humphrey Browning MacDougall for generously lending me to the Ford campaign for two and a half months. I also owe a debt to John Deardourff, Doug Bailey, and Bob Teeter, for their advice, and for their willingness to be quoted through the haze of memory. Also to Joan Turco, for many extra hours spent above and beyond her already invaluable secretarial duties. Finally, to Larry Freundlich, who diagnosed and discreetly cured my lapses of objectivity.

part one

How would you like to do a Presidential Campaign?

1
STARTING FROM SCRATCH

The night before I got the phone call I knew for sure that Carter was going to win the election. I'd been listening to "Sports Huddle," Boston's most popular radio talk show. Lillian Carter called in from Plains, Georgia. She said that she was a wrestling fan and had heard that Eddie Andelman, the show's host, knew more about wrestling than just about anyone in the whole country. She talked about her favorite wrestlers. She admitted she hated midgets. I was spellbound. One little phone call and 100,000 avid Boston sports fans had undoubtedly fallen in love with Jimmy Carter's mother. I pictured her hanging up the phone and dialing city after city, talk show after talk show, a smiling campaign worker at her shoulder, sliding typewritten notes under her elbow. Her deep Southern accent, just slightly cracked with age, drawling into the telephone—and into a million homes a night.

The election was over as far as I was concerned. And it was only August 7. The Republicans hadn't even decided who they wanted to run against Jimmy Carter. Why bother?

Later that night I was watching the "Tonight" show when Barbara Howar appeared as a guest. She didn't want to talk about her new book. She wanted to talk about her trip to Plains, Georgia. In the beginning she wasn't a believer, she said. No, sir. She had been just as cynical as a lot of us liberals. But she'd talked with Jimmy Carter for hours. Just sat there on the porch, the two of them, talking about life and government and religion. And now she was a believer. Jim Carter is real, she said. (Note: it was "Jim" now, not "Jimmy.") He is going to save our country. He is going to make us all better people. And then she reminded us—millions of us—that President Ford eats tamales with the wrapper on.

I remember my thoughts clearly. I was in absolute awe of the sheer political genius behind Jimmy Carter. I wanted to find out who this mastermind was. I understood the strategy, and to me it was sheer genius. Every talk show, every panel show, every game show, every quiz show. It hadn't cost a nickel to bring "the real" Jimmy Carter into every living room in America. He was part of the furniture before Ronald Reagan or Jerry Ford entered the fight. And the networks still didn't know that they were being had.

Slick. That's the word that came to mind as I headed for bed. Maybe to you, that's a nasty word. But not to me. I'm an advertising guy. Nobody admires a great selling job more than I do. I hoped only that Jimmy Carter was a reasonably good product.

I got the phone call the next morning.

"How would you like to do a Presidential campaign?"

He didn't even say "Hello." It was John Deardourff calling from Washington. I hadn't heard from him in five years. I knew that he and his best friend, Doug Bailey, had formed a political consulting firm eight years ago. Deardourff and Bailey. They were both Liberal Republicans, and I knew that they worked only on campaigns for Liberal Republicans. Ford? A Liberal compared to Reagan, maybe. I couldn't imagine Deardourff and Bailey running Ford's campaign. It was an ideological mismatch.

"I gave up political advertising," I told him. "I couldn't give up cigarettes or booze, so I gave that up instead."

"I'm serious," John said. "They want us to run the advertising. And we may do it if the conditions are right. You're one of the conditions."

"Why me?"

"Because we only want to work with people we know."

I'd been hoping that he'd say he had heard about the success of our agency in Boston, that he knew about all the creative awards we'd won, that the President himself had said, "Get MacDougall!" But no. I was an old friend. And in times of trouble . . . .

"Who's doing the advertising now?" I asked. I'd been vaguely following the Ford campaign in *Advertising Age,* the trade journal of our business. I'd read about several people doing the ads for Ford in the primaries, including Jim Jordan, President of Batten, Barton, Durstine, & Osborn—my old boss, my old friend, my old rival.

"Nobody," John said.

"But the campaign is just about to begin," I said. "They must have *started* work on the commercials."

"You wouldn't believe it," John said. "There is no plan. There is no strategy. There are no people. There is nothing."

"I thought they had an in-house agency. What's it called?"

"Campaign '76," said John. "It consists mostly of empty offices in a building in Washington."

"Well, they must have bought the media," I said, knowing that all the television time for the coming fall season had been sold out for the last six months. "If they haven't bought the time, the campaign is over. There are no spots left. Anywhere."

"That's the only thing they did right," John said. "They reserved the time last January. They start paying for it after the convention."

"If he wins the convention," I said.

"When he wins the convention," John said.

"You said there were other conditions. What are they?"

"Ford has to come out strongly for the Equal Rights Amendment for one thing."

"Why is that so important?"

John laughed. "Because both my wife and Doug's wife are involved in the Republican platform fight for E.R.A."

"What are the other conditions?"

"We have to have complete control of the advertising campaign, with direct access to the President."

"Good," I said. "What about Connally? I'm damned sure you guys wouldn't do it if he's on the ticket."

"Don't worry," said John. "He won't be."

"What do you want me to do?" I asked.

"We want you to be the creative director."

"You mean you want to hire the agency?"

"We don't care how you do it. We want you to do the ads. You can use the people in your agency. You can hire free-lancers. Whatever you want."

Humphrey Browning MacDougall is a medium-sized agency. We bill thirty million dollars. We have twenty-five clients. I knew that handling a Presidential campaign, even a losing one (and I had no illusions about that), would be fairly good for the agency's image. I also knew that the fall was our busiest season, and I couldn't possibly add a ten-million-dollar Presidential campaign on top of the burden the creative people already had to carry. We would probably end up losing half of our regular clients.

"My partners would kill me if I used the agency," I said.

"There are plenty of good people around. You'll probably need three or four writers. And a couple of TV producers. And a couple of art directors."

"Nothing to it," I said. "Just pick 'em up off the street. Were you serious when you said nothing has been done? Nothing?"

"Nothing."

I was stunned. We usually allow about six months to get a thirty-second commercial on the air. We have strategy sessions with the client. We test concepts with the public. Then there are bids from production companies, pre-production meetings, casting sessions, location hunting. And then we normally allow six weeks from the time the camera rolls to the time the finished commercial emerges from the film laboratory. John was suggesting that we do an entire Presidential campaign, with God knows how many commercials, in ten weeks. No! It was ten weeks to election day. The first films would have to be ready in three weeks.

"What do you think they'll need?" I asked.

"We'll need a couple of thirty-minute films. Six or seven five-minute spots. And a bunch of thirty-second spots. Oh, yes. We've got some one-minute spots too. And some two-minute spots."

"Oh."

"And we're going to want to make different commercials for different parts of the country."

"Oh."

"Why don't you come to Washington tomorrow. Doug and I will fill you in."

"I have to be in New York tomorrow. Oldsmobile is unveiling its new cars. I have to be there. They're a paying client."

"Meet us Tuesday then. For lunch. We told the Ford Committee that we'd let them know by Tuesday night."

I said, "Do you think they'll definitely hire you if you agree to do the job?"

"They will if they can swallow our last condition," John said.

"What's that?"

"Doug and I have other commitments. We're doing nine other campaigns. All big campaigns. It's been a very good year for us."

"You're going to add this on top of nine campaigns?"

"We can promise only the President two days a week—at the most."

"Do they know that?"

"Not yet."

"Oh," I said. "What makes you think they'll buy that?"

"They don't have much choice."

"Oh."

"Anyway," John said. "You'll be there full time."

"I'd like to do it," I said. "But it's been a good year for me too. And this is the worst possible time for me to leave."

"Well, you don't have to make up your mind right now," John said. "You can call me back in an hour. By the way. How have you been?"

"Fine."

"We'll see you Tuesday. The Federal Club in the Sheraton-Carlton Hotel. Twelve-thirty."

"Sure," I said. I put the receiver down very slowly.

Mimi had walked into the kitchen while I was on the phone. She'd been out buying the Sunday *Times*. She was reading the theater section when I hung up. Mimi used to be an actress. And like me, she's a New Yorker at heart. We'd been married just six months, and since our marriage we'd never been separated for more than two consecutive nights.

"Who was that?" she asked, not looking up from the paper.

"An old friend of mine. John Deardourff."

"Never heard you mention him."

"He wants me to do the Ford advertising campaign."

Mimi looked up from the paper. "That's great." She paused. "But how can you do Ford? Don't you already have Oldsmobile?"

"Not that Ford. The other Ford."

"The President Ford?"

"Until November second, yes."

"Are you going to do it?"

"How can I? I can't leave the agency for two and a half months."

Her eyes sparkled. "You're going to do it, aren't you."

"I can't *possibly* do it," I said.

Mimi did a little dance step and grinned at me. "You're going to do it!" she said.

Mimi and I are exactly alike. One of our most pronounced traits is that neither of us has ever let practical considerations stand in the way of a possible adventure.

"Now wait a minute," I said, disentangling myself from an exuberant hug. "If Rick, Frank, and Ed aren't for this, I'm definitely *not* doing it."

I meant that. Rick Humphrey, Frank Browning, and Ed Eskandarian were my partners. We'd built the agency together. Every major decision we'd made had been unanimous. This was not going to be the exception.

Mimi looked worried. "They'll have a thousand reasons why you can't do it," she said.

"Good reasons, too," I said. "But let's see."

I called Rick first. He was stunned. He didn't come up with a thousand reasons why I couldn't do it. Only five or six good ones. But a funny thing happened. The more I agreed with his solid good reasoning, the more solutions he found to the problems. By the time I hung up, Rick was trying to convince me I should do it.

Frank Browning is our chairman and treasurer. The first question he would ask me, I was sure, was how much money the agency would make. A reasonable question. It occurred to me as I was dialing his number that John and I hadn't discussed money.

I hung up from my chat with Frank with a confused look on my face.

"What did he say?" asked Mimi, with just a hint of belligerence in her voice.

"He didn't even ask about the money," I said flatly. "He said it was an honor for the agency to be asked and that we should do it."

Mimi beamed. "I told you Frank Browning was the smartest one of 'em all," she said.

Ed Eskandarian would have the toughest pill to swallow if I walked out of the agency for two months. He was already badly overworked. My absence would almost double the burden. But Ed, too, was for it.

"Just don't blow the goddamned election," he said. "That won't make HBM look too good."

When I hung up, one more problem began to gnaw at me. I wasn't really sure how I felt about Gerald Ford. It worried me.

"I don't really know anything about Ford," I told Mimi. "I don't even know whether you spell his first name with a "G" or a "J.""

"That's why you have to take the job," Mimi said. "Everybody knows Jimmy Carter. Everybody knows he's a little ol' peanut farmer. Everybody knows Lillian and Rosalynn. Everybody knows that he's found Jesus. The only thing people know about Ford is that he bumps into things."

"And eats tamales with the wrapper on."

Mimi looked at me seriously. "Carter scares me to death," she said.

I thought about what Mimi had said. Her reaction to Jimmy Carter was intuitive. Politically, she was exactly like me. Independent. She voted her instincts. My own instincts told me that Jimmy Carter was the product of a smart pollster and a slick advertising man. That didn't necessarily mean that Carter was bad. That didn't mean he wouldn't make a good President. It just meant that he was a consummate politician. But Mimi's instincts had apparently spotted something else. There was something about the man. The big grin, the sharp eyes, the smooth tongue, the casual hair.

I trusted Mimi's instincts.

"You know we can't possibly win, don't you?" I said finally.

"The only thing that can keep you from winning," Mimi said, "is dumb statements like that."

I decided she was right.

2

...BUT WOULD
I VOTE FOR FORD?

The houselights dimmed in the magnificent new Uris Theater in Manhattan. The first-nighters tinkled little silver bells that had been placed on each seat. They were five hundred Oldsmobile dealers and their wives who were here to watch what to them was unquestionably the most wonderful musical of the year: the unveiling of the 1977 Oldsmobiles.

The orchestra struck up the overture. All the songs were familiar: "Old Black Magic," "Yankee Doodle Dandy," "It's a Grand Old Flag." Soon the curtain would go up and freshly scrubbed, rosy-cheeked singers and dancers would put meaningful new words to those songs.

"That new Olds magic has me in its spell . . . "

"It's a brand-new Olds, it's a high-flying Olds . . ."

The dealers would cheer and whistle and tinkle their silver bells as each gleaming new car would appear magically on stage. It was all magnificently expensive, magnificently corny. And I loved every minute of it. This was my world. Marketing show biz. A part of Americana that no foreigner could ever hope to comprehend.

How could I leave all this wonderful silliness to help elect a President of the United States?

I had my first serious doubts about my ability to help Ford as a troop of twenty girl scouts emerged singing from the rear of the new, roomier Vista Cruiser station wagon.

10

I had always felt that when you create advertising, you have some responsibility to the public. I had never lied about the products I sold. But I had certainly danced on the edge of the truth for dramatic effect. My job seemed quite simple to me. I'm a salesman. I'm hired to sell products to millions of consumers. I'm judged on how well those products actually sell.

But what about a President? Who am I to tell people that they should vote for Gerald Ford? Who am I to say he's a better man than Carter? What right do I have to spend ten million dollars on television ads to tell *other* people they should vote for Ford?

Hell, I didn't even know if *I* was going to vote for the guy.

Another disturbing thought occurred to me.

What if I blow it? What if people hate our commercials? What if it's a close election after all, and in the final analysis the experts decide that it was those dumb Ford commercials that put Carter over the top?

Talk about looking silly. I'd go through life as the man who cost President Ford his job.

I tried to focus my thoughts back to the show on stage. The chorus was dancing in front of a giant backdrop of a drawing by Leonardo daVinci. Now they were lowering another backdrop from the ceiling. It was an engineer's sketch of the new Olds 98. I got the message, but my mind was going back to Ford.

If I wasn't *sure* about Ford, if I wasn't *enthusiastic* about him, should I be doing his advertising? Was it *right* to do his advertising? After all, I owned an Olds Cutlass. I was convinced it was the best car for the money on the road. I played Titleist golf balls. I used Stanley tools. I drank Salada tea and A & W root beer. I played Parker games with my kids. And I was sure that a Lionel train was the best toy a kid could get on Christmas. It was easy for me to be enthusiastic about the products our agency advertised.

I didn't think about the question from a moral point of view. I looked on it as a professional problem. Could I do my best job if I was uncertain about the man?

I thought about President Ford. Why did I sort of laugh when John first told me that he wanted me to work on the campaign? Probably because the first thought that popped into my mind was that President Ford bumped into things. The press had done that to him. As I thought about it, I felt that here was a guy who had been given a bum rap. Here was a guy with a real image problem. If there ever was a candidate who needed good advertising, it was President Ford. Maybe I didn't know the product too well, I thought. But I could spot a fascinating advertising problem when I saw one. If I was really a professional, here was a real challenge.

I was beginning to get enthusiastic, when I thought about the hacks I had known in political campaigns. The egomaniacs. The sycophants. The cronies. The cigar-chewing old pols who tell you the only way to win is to convince the public that the other guy is a crook or a fag.

I'd been in enough political campaigns. A mayor's race. A couple of gubernatorial campaigns. Some congressional campaigns. I'd seen enough fools with an ear to the candidate to make me quit politics. I could imagine what it would be like in a Presidential campaign. If by some miracle I did manage to come up with an honest, effective advertising campaign for Ford, how could I possibly get it through a maze of committees manned by self-serving hangers-on who had all the answers long before I joined the campaign?

Six beautiful girls in bathing suits were waving at me from an Olds Toronado when I made my decision to call Deardourff and tell him I wasn't interested.

I pushed my way past some Oldsmobile dealers and left the hall. I decided to have a cigarette in the vestibule before I made the call. I thought about John Deardourff as the relaxing smoke curled around my badly abused lungs.

John was a politician. He was also everything that all those other people were not. He was a brilliant political tactician. I knew that as a fact. I had worked closely with him in two campaigns. We had won both of them—and both times against seemingly impossible odds.

I knew, too, that he believed deeply in the business of making the American political system work. His cause was the liberal wing of the Republican party, and if there was ever a dying cause, it was his. I had heard that he turned down the Nixon campaign the first time around with one disdainful laugh. I knew that his partner, Doug Bailey, was the same kind of guy. They would not be in this thing if they didn't believe in this thing.

And didn't John say that we would be completely in charge and have direct access to the President?

I made my way back to my seat just as a James Cagney imitator was singing "I'm a Yankee Doodle Dandy" and tap-dancing around the new 1977 Olds Cutlass. He gestured with his hands to the audience, and I found myself singing along with the five hundred Olds dealers and their wives.

"I'm a Yankee Doodle Dandy,
Yankee Doodle do or die. . . ."

3
STORM WARNING

That night I got the first taste of what the next two and a half months would be like. Hurricane Belle hit the East Coast. I couldn't get home to Mimi and our summer house in Gloucester. The house is on the ocean. I tried to sound calm and masculine over the phone.

"Get lots of candles. Get some extra flashlight batteries. Make sure the transistor radio is working. Get lots of masking tape. Don't sleep in our room. Too many windows. Sleep in the middle room. Bring the kids in with you. Bring the dog and the cat, too."

"Can't find the cat," Mimi said. "I think she's gone off to the woods to have her kittens."

"Well, go out and find her. She can't have her kittens in a hurricane!"

"We'll find her. Don't worry. We'll be all right. What do I need the masking tape for?"

"The windows. It's an old house. The windows will probably break if you don't tape them to the sill."

"But we have hundreds of windows. I can't tape them all!"

"Make the kids help you."

"I don't have time, damn it. The storm is supposed to hit in a couple of hours. And I have to transplant the morning glories."

"You have to *what*?"

"The garden will be ruined if I don't get the flowers inside."

"You're kidding. There's a hurricane coming and you're worried about the flowers."

"Well, I like the flowers better than your stupid cat."

"Mimi," I said calmly, "I think we're having our first fight."

"Well, I've never had to face a hurricane alone before," she said just a little contritely.

"And I've never had to face a Presidential campaign before," I said apologetically.

We called each other twice more that night. The hurricane veered out to sea and only a heavy rain hit Gloucester.

4
THE SCORE: 62–29

The Federal City Club began as a luncheon club for Democrats when blacks in the Kennedy administration were barred from the Metropolitan Club. Reluctantly, they allowed a few Republicans to join, including Deardourff and Bailey. They were *liberal* Republicans after all. The women didn't make it until a couple of years ago.

We spent the first part of the luncheon telling each other how much older we looked. Actually, John and Doug had hardly changed at all in the five years since I'd last seen them. John was still the tall, handsome, self-assured Midwesterner, the kind of guy who always leads the way to the table when you enter a dining room. And I was pleased to notice that he still started every sentence with a little laugh. John finds something funny in almost everything. In a tough political campaign, that can be a priceless asset. The years had put no bulges in his midsection.

Doug's hair had gotten no grayer. It couldn't. I'm sure it had grayed out when he got his Ph.D. at Harvard. Doug was the academic politician. The intellectual half of the Deardourff-Bailey team. John was the one who got things done. Doug was the guy who made sure they thought about it before they did it. When he spoke, there were deliberate pauses in his sentences, as if his mind was carefully sorting out a catalogue of facts. But he had a sense of humor, too. A dry, academic sense of humor with a professor's love of bad puns.

We were halfway through the main course before we got down to the matter at hand.

"What's the real situation?" I asked.

"Grim," said Doug.

"Gloomy," said John.

"We are precisely where Goldwater was on this very date in 1964," Doug added.

"62–29," John said. "The latest Gallup poll. And Teeter doesn't dispute it."

"Who's Teeter?" I asked.

"The ace up our sleeve," Doug said. "You'll be seeing lots of Bob Teeter."

"The President listens to Teeter," John said.

"Will he listen to us?" I asked.

"What do you want for dessert?" Doug asked.

I gently spelled out some of my conditions during lunch. I couldn't involve the agency. I had to be free to hire anybody I felt I needed. All my expenses had to be covered. My salary had to be covered. The agency had to be paid a modest fee to cover the back-up people that would be needed in my absence. My partners and I had agreed earlier that we didn't want to make any money on the campaign. We just wanted to make sure we didn't lose any.

John and Doug just smiled at my conditions and I realized that I should have sounded less like a willing bedmate. Money was no problem. The Federal Elections Commission was going to turn over twenty-two million dollars to Ford the minute he got the nomination. The only problem was finding someone rash enough to agree to pull their irons out of the fire.

"When do the Ford people make the decision?" I asked finally.

"After our meeting with them tonight," John said.

After lunch we walked the four blocks from the Sheraton-Carlton Hotel to Deardourff and Bailey's offices. I'd been in Washington before, but I'd never felt a part of Washington before. The city has a way of making you feel more like a stranger than any city I've known. All those sturdy, important-looking buildings intimidated me. But today, instead of feeling like part of the audience, I felt like one of the actors. Someone with a humorous bit part. A George Plimpton walk-on role, a political guru for a day.

I felt a little disappointed when I came to the building that housed Deardourff and Bailey. It wasn't important-looking at all. It was a dingy, thirties office building advertised by only a number. I noticed a dirty movie theater next door. It was playing "Misty Beethoven."

I remember thinking that I'd rather spend the afternoon seeing "Misty Beethoven" than be cooped up in this old office building.

We rode a slow elevator to the eleventh floor. There was no big sign heralding "Deardourff and Bailey" in gold letters. Just two doors marked 1120.

I walked into the reception area and immediately tripped over a pile of suitcases standing just inside the door.

"When you run a political consulting business," Doug explained, "you always have to be ready to go on the lam."

The image of a company on the run was heightened by the two receptionists. Both were talking on the phone, running their fingers across the pages of the Airlines Guide. They were making plans to get John to St. Louis that night, Detroit the next day, New York the next, Kansas City the next. And they were smoothing the way for Doug's trip to Vermont, then to Detroit, and on to Kansas City.

Phil Angell, Deardourff and Bailey's assistant, greeted us with a sheaf of urgent messages about political campaigns all over the United States and in Puerto Rico. I had been there two minutes when one fact became extremely clear to me.

The firm of Deardourff and Bailey couldn't possibly add a Presidential campaign to the work they'd already contracted to do.

But what the hell, I thought. Neither could the firm of Humphrey Browning MacDougall.

I wandered around the office, feeling left out, while John and Doug picked up various telephones, putting out various political fires. I caught snatches of conversations.

"My advice to Kit Bond," John barked into the phone, "is to take the Vice-Presidency if it's offered to him." Then he smiled. "Of course it's not likely to be offered to him but it will make him feel good for a few days."

Doug on the phone to someone at Ford's headquarters:

"I read it. I read it. It is the single worst acceptance speech ever written. Is that the best they can do?"

Holding his hand over the receiver, Doug asked his secretary to "hurry in with the speech."

"What speech?" she asked.

"*The* speech," Doug ordered.

I wandered out of Doug's office while he was reading a passage from his own version of the acceptance speech.

I didn't belong here. I wanted to find a small corner where I could hide. I can sell Salada Tea. I'm good at that sort of thing. Just let me handle Acushnet Titleist golf balls in a good head-to-head ad battle with the Spaulding Top Flite. That's my style. I have no business in the middle of a Ford-Carter fight.

If I could have gotten either of them off the phone for a minute I would have resigned right then and there. Instead, I called my own office in Boston and tried to get interested in problems I could understand. No one in the office, except for my partners, knew about the Presidency thing yet. They couldn't understand why I wasn't in the office where I belonged. It seemed that at least six people had creative problems that demanded my immediate attention. It made me feel better.

I had called the office from a phone in the reception area, and while I talked my eyes roamed over the political posters that lined all the walls in the room. Deardourff and Bailey's trophies. At least thirty big smiling faces glued to the walls. Each one carrying a political slogan.

"Vote Proudly for Percy."

"Re Pete DuPont."

"Let's go to work for Senator Schweiker."

"Stand Tall for Big Jim Thompson."

"John Chaffee—he's his own man."

"Cahill gets things done."

It occurred to me that soon there'd be a big smiling Jerry Ford glued to those walls. I wondered what the poster would look like. I wondered what the slogan would be. And then I realized I was the guy who had to make the poster. I was the guy who had to write the slogan.

Doug and John finally got off their respective phones, but before I could tell them I was backing out they were hurrying me through the door.

"C'mon," John said. "We're already late."

"Where's the meeting?" I asked.

"Just down the street."

I grabbed my suitcase in one hand, my attaché case in the other. I threw my raincoat over my arm. I felt foolish with the raincoat. It was a beautiful day. I hurried down the street, the suitcase bumping against my legs. I had trouble keeping up with them. They had longer legs.

"I have a slogan," Doug said as we hurried along.

We didn't give him the benefit of a response.

"Ford has more cures," Doug said in an announcer's voice, "than Carter has ills."

Well, Doug hadn't changed.

5

A NICE PLACE TO VISIT

After about a block and a half of scurrying along with the suitcase banging against my leg, and listening to three more of Bailey's slogans which I have mercifully forgotten, we turned a corner and there was the White House. I slowed down. There were a cluster of people standing in front of the fence, taking turns having their picture taken. I looked at the White House lawn. It needed cutting.

John hurried me along. I asked him how much farther we had to go to get to this damn meeting. He and Doug suddenly turned left, and I followed.

We were at a guard house. There were three big men staring at us from behind a glass partition. I knew, or at least I thought I knew, that we were still in the general vicinity of the White House. In fact that was the White House right smack in front of me. I heard one of the guards say something through a loudspeaker.

"May I have your identification?"

I reached quickly for my wallet, took out my driver's license, and put it in a slot in the window. It was like making a deposit at a drive-in teller's window.

Then I remembered my suitcase and attaché case. Surely they were going to go through everything, item by item, paper by paper, underwear, dirty shirts, everything. I wondered if I had anything incriminating. I was ready to kill John and Doug for dragging me into this place without any warning. I at least could have combed my hair. My hair isn't long, but it's long enough. Haldeman would have had me investigated on the spot.

Then I remembered the copy of *Emmanuelle* I'd bought at the airport. I thought Mimi would be amused. Now they'll find it. Right on top of my attaché case.

The man looked at our drivers' licenses, nodded, and pushed a button. A gate to our left swung open. As we started down the path, one of the guards came out of the house. He looked at my suitcase.

"You can leave those here if you don't need them inside," he said politely.

I knew what he meant. He meant leave them here. Period. So we can take our time looking for the bomb. I handed him the two bags, then draped the raincoat over his arm. I was going to go in clean.

It was about one hundred yards from the guard house to the entrance of the White House offices. I felt as if I were walking into a picture postcard. I didn't say a word. I just hoped that I wouldn't bump into the President, or get bitten by one of his dogs. I just wanted to get inside—and out again.

The receptionist in the first waiting room had been expecting us. We were the only ones in the room. As I sat down on a sofa, the room reminded me distinctly of the lobby of a Treadway Inn I'd once visited. Everything was a little too neat, too perfect. All early American reproductions, with the slight smell of the factory still lingering in the wood. Then I realized that this was the room the Treadway people had been trying so very hard to copy.

Doug lit a cigarette. I wanted one desperately, but I didn't have his nerve. All the ashtrays were clean. They looked as if they'd never been used. I was damned if I was going to be the first person in history to dirty one of those ashtrays.

A very young, skinny man in glasses entered through a side door and walked purposefully towards us. He had to be still in his twenties. He greeted John and Doug enthusiastically. John introduced him to me. Foster Chanock. He apologized for keeping us waiting, though Doug had had time for just one puff of his cigarette. He led us through the door he'd entered, and down a long, narrow corridor past rows of magnificent American primitives. Jackie must have hung them, I thought.

We entered a small anteroom, where a pleasant secretary told us that Mr. Cheney was on the phone with Kansas City. Now I knew whom I was going to see. Mr. Cheney. Whoever Mr. Cheney was.

While we were waiting, Foster Chanock asked us if we wanted a beer or a Coke. I wanted a beer. I ordered a Coke. Foster was the only one who had a beer. He took the beer out of an ice chest that

was near a man-sized safe that had a big sign across it saying
"LOCKED." I remember thinking that the sign had a certain silly
significance. To get the Cokes, Foster had to go down the hall and
feed quarters into a machine in another closet. Interesting, I noted
mentally. Free beer, but you pay for your own Cokes.

I liked Foster immediately. He was clearly one of those brilliant,
enthusiastic former child prodigies that always seem to pop up at the
elbow of politicians. He reminded me of a classmate who had
graduated from Harvard summa cum laude when he was fourteen.
Foster, I learned later, was twenty-three. He escorted us into a
third waiting room, a little living room with a TV set, and announced
that this represented "an extended foreplay."

We had been in the White House about ten minutes in all when
Cheney opened the door and greeted John and Doug like old friends.
After the introductions, Dick Cheney, whom I later learned was
Ford's chief-of-staff, led us into a large, comfortable office that was
furnished like a living room. A disturbing thought occurred to me as
I looked around this dignified office with a modest view of the White
House lawn. Bob Haldeman had worked here.

I still had my Coke in my hand when I sat down in an easy chair
facing Dick Cheney, and I didn't know where to put it. I was damned
if I was going to be the one who left the white ring on Thomas
Jefferson's old coffee table. Foster rescued me. He spilled his beer
on the rug. I don't know how it happened, but there it was. A can of
Schlitz gushing its contents out on the white rug. My reaction was an
instinct left over from a traumatic experience I'd had with my third-
grade teacher at Madison Elementary School.

"I didn't do it!" I blurted out.

Chaeney looked at me. Then he looked at the spreading puddle of
beer on his rug. Then he laughed and sat down. Foster rushed out for
paper towels. John said something about Foster having had too
many beers. I put my Coke in an empty ashtray and leaned back in
the big chair. I decided that I would just look casual.

We chatted about the convention, which now was just five days
away. The newspapers and networks were talking of nothing else but
the great Ford-Reagan battle in Kansas City. No one was predicting
a Ford victory. But if there was any real concern among the Ford
staff, Dick Cheney certainly didn't show it. He told me some amus-
ing anecdotes about balky delegates, and he and John reminisced
about the time Nelson Rockefeller spent a million and a half in advertising in an unsuccessful effort to win the Ohio delegation.

"Christ," said Cheney. "He could have bought the entire delegation for half that."

"Well," said John, getting down to the business at hand, "how bad is it?"

"Well, right now," Dick said with a smile, "we have no plans beyond next week. Except to go to Vail, for a short vacation."

We laughed. I hoped the laugh was appropriate.

Cheney then touched briefly on some of the tactical plans for the final campaign. The electoral vote strategy, the key states, some critical voting groups, the timing of the advertising, how the President could campaign from the White House. Apparently the President had slipped in some of the polls when he left the White House to campaign during the primaries. They had decided to keep him in the White House throughout most of the first phase of the final campaign, signing bills, giving news conferences, fighting Congress, running the country. It seemed like pretty good strategy to me.

Cheney thought that the President would not officially start to campaign until after Labor Day. That would allow just over two weeks, after the Convention, to set up the new campaign organization, hire the staff, prepare the logistics, and set the advertising plan.

Cheney paused. "I don't want to sound stuffy," he said, "but it's not appropriate for me to talk politics here. Even though it *is* after hours. I want you guys to meet with Bob Teeter as soon as you can. He'll give you the answers you want. We've got some problems, sure, but with a tight organization and some great advertising, we can win. I really mean that. Our advertising in the primary was a disaster. It didn't show people the kind of man this President is."

He paused again. He got up from his chair. He looked as if he wanted to tell us something that meant a lot to him.

"You know," he said finally, "this is such a good, decent man. He is so respected and admired by everyone he meets, by everyone in government, by everyone who works for him, by everyone he has to deal with. He's got so much character. He's so genuine. If we could only, somehow, find a way to portray the kind of man he really is."

"I think one of the troubles," said John, "is that he just doesn't come across very well on camera."

"Know what the problem is?" Cheney said. "He freezes on camera. "When the light goes on, he goes rigid. It's a reflex. I think it's because he's been a politician from Grand Rapids for twenty-five years. When he sees a camera, he automatically turns from a person into a politician. He stops talking and starts making a speech. That's going to be one of your most interesting problems."

Then he told us about the money problem. The Ford campaign was broke. Dead broke. They had been limited to spending ten million dollars for the primary campaign, and every last penny was gone. There would be no more money, to pay for anything we might want to do, until after the convention.

"I'll tell you how bad it is," Cheney explained. "I have to pay my own way to Kansas City. *That's* how bad it is!"

"We don't even have money for balloons," Foster said. "How can you have a convention without balloons?"

John casually mentioned that it would be easy to arrange some kind of loan. Cheney laughed.

"We're not just obeying the letter of the law," he said. "The *spirit* of the law. This will be the first time in history that the Republicans aren't going to have a financial advantage."

Then he ticked off some of the other problems that he saw ahead of us. He stretched out a finger of his left hand each time he mentioned a problem. When he was through, he had all five fingers in the air.

"They have twice as many voters as we do."

"They have a six-month headstart."

"They're ahead 3–1 in the polls."

"They have a united party."

"They have a candidate who is far better known."

"But we have the President," I argued. "He's pretty well known."

"He's known as the President. The post-Watergate President. He's known as a former Republican Congressman." Cheney's voice sounded disgusted. "Everybody knows that Carter is a peanut farmer—even though he isn't a peanut farmer. He's a peanut wholesaler. Everybody knows about Plains, Georgia. And Lillian. Nobody really knows Ford. He never had a hometown. He never had a mother. He never had a childhood, as far as the American people are concerned."

"What about his record?" I asked.

"We can't beat it to death. Nobody cares what he did yesterday. People only vote on the promise of the future."

I said that I agreed with him, because I did agree with him. Strongly.

Cheney got up, went to the shelf, and pulled out a manuscript in a plain blue ring binder. It looked as if it contained about two hundred pages.

"Only three people have seen this. It's the plan. It's also the toughest document that's ever been shown to a President of the United States. There are no punches pulled."

John took the plan. He didn't open it.

"I don't have to tell you not to . . . ''

"No, you don't," interrupted John.

Cheney looked at me. "I hear you're from Boston," he said.

"Right," I said, ready to launch into my prepared pitch about the agency. I had decided to make it short, simple, accurate. "Our agency is headquartered in Boston, but we have a New York office for TV production," I started.

"Good," said Cheney. "Now. I want you guys to get together with Teeter tomorrow."

I realized that my pitch was over.

"Wait till you hear what he's found out about the religious issue," Cheney said. "It's the goddamnedest thing you ever heard."

John looked hard at Cheney. "Do you know about all our conditions?

"I heard some nonsense about you only being in the office two days a week."

"We've already contracted for nine other campaigns. We can't let them down."

"If the President doesn't win, *they're* in trouble. Ford is going to call them to see if they'll free up some of your time."

"Fine," said John. "What's our authority going to be? I'd like to hear it from you."

"Complete authority. Campaign '76 is your show."

"Will we have direct access to the President?" Doug asked.

"Damn right you will," Cheney said. "We don't have time for anything else. You three guys will be meeting with him Friday afternoon, the day after the nomination. He wants to review the advertising plan before he goes to Vail."

"What's he going to do about E.R.A.?" asked Doug.

"You know how he feels about that," Cheney said. "He feels almost as strongly about it as Mrs. Ford."

"But is he going to help us get it through the platform committee?"

"Are those nuts trying to shoot it down?" I asked.

"Those aren't nuts," said Cheney. "They're delegates."

I got the idea they wouldn't become 'nuts' until after the nomination.

"Is Ford going to issue a statement on E.R.A.?" asked Doug.

"He'll do it tomorrow," Cheney said.

John smiled conspiratorially at Cheney. "Who's the Vice-President?" he asked.

"Only one man knows," said Cheney. "And he's right down the hall. Ask him if you want."

The meeting was over. As I got up to leave I looked at the blue book tucked under John's arm. I knew it meant that we had the account. It was the goddamnedest pitch I had ever made. But then—it was the goddamnedest account I had ever pitched.

As I walked back down the hall, past the primitives, I saw a tall, familiar figure chatting with someone about fifty feet away. When I saw him, something important occurred to me. If he can take two and a half months off the job to run a political campaign, certainly I can. He's got a pretty important job too.

See you Friday, I said to myself.

6

HOW NOT TO WRITE A POLITICAL AD

Detroit. If they'd asked me to go to any city but Detroit, I would have had my first serious conflict of the campaign. But I had to be in Detroit.Wednesday morning anyway. I had an important meeting in Battle Creek with the president of Kellogg. My luck was running strong. I could feel it as I flew from Washington to Detroit that night. It was the same feeling I'd once had when I rolled thirteen straight passes at a dice table in Las Vegas. This was the beginning of a lucky streak. The president of Kellogg was going to love our new campaign for Salada tea. President Ford was going to win the nomination next week. The Republican Party was going to surprise everyone and unite behind him. Ford was going to find new fire in his veins and suddenly start waging a good old give-'em-hell campaign. The polls were going to start swinging our way. My ads were going to go through the committees unchanged. Little old ladies were going to watch our commercials and say, "I've changed my mind, I'm going to vote for that nice man Jerry Ford after all." Ford wins! Landslide! Hurrah! I could feel it.

The stewardess brought me two bourbons. Before I had finished the first one, I took out my Pentab and some notepaper and began to violate the first rule of advertising.

Advertising is supposed to be a disciplined business. All good marketing people will tell you that successful ads invariably come out of sound research which produces hard facts about the product, the market, the prime prospects. It takes two years to begin to learn the discipline at the Harvard Business School.

The trouble is, good creative people aren't disciplined. They will tell you in meetings, in speeches, in books, and especially at cocktail parties that it is impossible to create successful advertising until you have all the facts, and understand all the facts completely. But they don't really believe it for a second. They won't admit it, they *can't* admit it, but every good creative person in the business knows that the best advertising springs full-blown from their own imagination.

I didn't need facts. I knew we had the election won as I finished my drink and wrote my first slogan. I wrote it in big letters across the top of the notepaper.

"President Ford. He'll Give America Her Four Greatest Years."

There it was. The big promise that David Ogilvie said was the very essence of successful advertising. I liked the ring of it. "*Her* four greatest years." That was a nice touch. America as a woman. I began to write the script for a thirty-second commercial. It was about the new mood of America. No. The new *spirit* of America. The spirit Jerry Ford had given us. I saw faces on the Fourth of July. Young people hugging one another and singing "God Bless America." And then I wrote:

"You can feel the new spirit of America in your heart. And it's just the beginning." *(Shot of young people singing at July Fourth celebration.)*

"You can feel a new kind of peace in the world. And it's just the beginning." *(Shot of President Ford with his arm around Russian leader.)*

"You can see your hard-earned dollars beginning to bring you more of the better life." *(Shot of family on Thanksgiving.)*

"We are at peace with ourselves, we are at peace with the world, our country is stronger than it has ever been. And it's just the beginning." *(Quick cuts of happy Americans.)*

"You know the job he has done. It's the prelude to America's four greatest years." *(Dramatic shot of the President.)*

Super Slogan: "He'll give America Her Four Greatest Years."

I finished my second drink feeling smug. It had been so easy. I was tired, but I managed to keep awake during the hundred-mile drive from Detroit to Battle Creek. Thoughts of new and better commercials around the ''Four Greatest Years'' theme kept my mind alert.

I woke up after four hours' sleep in a Howard Johnson Motel room that smelled of dead air and other people. I saw my notes on the bureau as I padded to the bathroom in my boxer shorts. I read them carefully. I read the commercial through twice. I picked the notes up, crumpled them into a messy ball, and threw them as hard as I could at the cheap tin wastebasket. The ball went clanging right into it.

I stepped into a hot shower, where I do my best thinking. That morning I vowed never again to put a piece of meaningless, vacuous shit down on a piece of paper. I would work with facts. I would give people facts.

It was a promise I wouldn't forget. But like all political promises. . . .

part two

The Planet Ford

7

"A CHANCE TO
TELL THE TRUTH"

When I had shown the last frame of the storyboard and read the punch line of the commercial, the president of Kellogg smiled. I knew my luck was holding.

It was a pretty far-out campaign, and I'd had no idea how he would react. Tea is tea. Our research had shown us that it would be impossible to convince people that Salada tea really tasted much better than any other tea. So our strategy was to develop a high-impact campaign that was so wacky that people would still be remembering the commercials when they walked by the Salada display at the supermarket. Instead of going after tea drinkers, we were going after people who drank both coffee and tea. Our research had shown that eighty percent of the tea drinkers drank coffee as well as tea.

We presented three commercials. One featured Tarzan and Jane. One featured Batman and Robin. The last featured d'Artagnan, "the greatest swordsman in all of France." In each commercial our hero admitted that he needed coffee to get him going. Tarzan was shown gulping a cup of coffee before swinging over a crocodile-infested river. Batman was shown drinking coffee before rescuing Robin, who was having the shit beat out of him in the background. D'Artagnan was shown drinking coffee while his enemy sliced the plume off his hat. After doing his thing, each hero was shown relaxing "with the bright taste of Salada tea . . . the perfect coffee break." At the close of each commercial, the hero delivered a punch line. Tarzan: "Jane—it's such a jungle out there." D'Artagnan: "Darling—I am ze lover—not ze fighter."

As soon as the president of Kellogg's left the conference room, his "Go produce 'em!" still ringing in my ears, Mary Moore, our associate creative director, threw herself in my arms and planted a kiss right on my lips. Derald Breneman, our Salada writer, let out a Tarzan yell. Jack Minor and Sam Sonnabend, our clients, who had lived with these commercials for six months, danced around the room in glee. It was the kind of scene that you see only in advertising—when the agency has finally sold something that they know is good. It's what keeps us going.

The real irony of that meeting didn't occur to me until Mary, Derald, and I were driving back to Detroit that afternoon.

Salada spends about a million dollars in advertising. By the time the commercials went on the air, a full year's work would be behind them. We had already spent eight months in research, in developing and testing concepts, in creating and testing alternate campaigns, and we had months of work to go before the job would be finished.

The President of the United States had known for two years that he had a national election coming up. He knew he had over twenty million dollars to spend. He knew that at least half of that would be going into advertising. Yet neither he, nor any of his people, had really started thinking about it yet. He'd only hired the agency yesterday!

Did the President of the United States know something that the president of Kellogg's didn't know?

Or did Kellogg's know something the President of the United States didn't know?

I was pretty sure I knew the answer, and it scared the hell out of me.

During the trip to Detroit I decided to tell Mary and Derald the news. I was particularly interested in hearing Derald's reaction. Mary's was predictable. She's a very professional advertising person. I knew she'd think of doing the Ford campaign as a great creative challenge. I knew she'd be excited about the idea, and she was.

But Derald Breneman is a very unusual kind of advertising man. When his door is closed, it's not because he's writing. It's because he's meditating. He's a good writer, but I'd often suspected that the only reason he was in advertising was that someone had sent him out to save us. How would he react to the inherent moral issues involved in selling a President to the people of the United States?

"Ford!" he screamed. He was driving the car, and he turned towards the back seat to shout it at me. We nearly careened into a truck at sixty miles an hour.

After he brought the car under control he stared ahead thoughtfully for a few moments.

"What year were you born?" he asked finally.

I was prepared for a morality argument, but it looked now as though he was so disturbed that we were going beyond mere morality and into some kind of mysticism.

"Nineteen twenty-eight," I said.

"I thought so," said Derald. "Year of the Dragon. It had to be."

"Oh," I said.

"And I suppose you were born in August, weren't you?" Derald went on.

"August 21."

"Leo. Had to be. A Leo in the year of the Dragon. You were born twice lucky."

"You don't think it's morally wrong to do a Presidential campaign?" I prodded.

"Why should it be?" said Derald. "Nobody knows anything about the guy. People think he bumps into things. You've got a chance to tell people the truth about the man. And I bet you'll do a pretty good job of it. You're lucky. You're shot with luck. A Leo Dragon."

Well, that took care of the moral arguments as far as I was concerned. And it confirmed my hunch. I *was* lucky.

8

THE PRESIDENT'S POLLSTER

Generally speaking, marketing research is fifty percent science and fifty percent bullshit. That's why I'm leery of research people. The worst researchers are half the time the best bullshitters.

When I arrived at Bob Teeter's office at Market Opinion Research, Inc. I feared that I had come upon the Prince of Bullshitters. A man from *Time* Magazine was hopping about the room, snapping his picture.

Now there are some researchers I know who would have staged this. They would have hired a friend with a Nikon and told people he was from *Time*. But as I watched Teeter pose, pretending to study voter registration charts, pretending to be engrossed in election statistics, pretending to be looking up some table in a huge volume of statistics, I began to feel better about him. The bullshitters I have known in the research business would have stopped the photographer when I entered the room. They would have tried to let me know that the little man from *Time* was one of the bothersome little penalties one had to suffer when one is famous.

But not Bob Teeter. He was clearly delighted to have his picture taken by *Time* Magazine, and he didn't give a damn if I knew it. He had me sit in a corner while the photographer got all the shots he could possibly want and kept assuring the photographer that he wasn't interrupting anything and could stay as long as he wanted.

I looked at the books on the shelves while the photographer

snapped away. You can usually tell a lot about a researcher by looking at his office. Some try to impress you with their success. Incredibly expensive sofas and chairs and glass-topped tables without a trace of their profession anywhere in sight. Others try to impress you with their sophistication. Little computers standing in a corner; video tape machines built into the wall; huge charts with twenty zigzagging lines in twenty different pastel colors propped casually against a blackboard; and on the blackboard, a scrawled equation no one could understand.

Teeter's office was a mess. Thousands of cardboard-bound books of statistics were stuffed haphazardly into the shelves. Other books were stacked on the conference table, which is what Teeter apparently used as a desk. There was no window in the place. No easy chairs. There was a video tape machine, but it was on a drab metal table and looked as if it had been rented for the day. The only chart in sight was the one Teeter pulled out of a closet so he'd have something to point at for the photographer. I looked for a picture of the President. I had heard that Bob Teeter was just about the closest person to the President these days. Surely there'd be a signed portrait of Jerry and Bob at Camp David. But the only pictures I saw were in the magazines that were lying open on various tables around the room.

When the photographer finally left, Bob Teeter greeted me warmly. He acted as though everything was official, everything had been cleared, and that we were now working together on the Ford campaign. It made me feel more comfortable. I just hoped he knew something I didn't know.

In about two minutes I knew for sure that Bob Teeter was no bullshitter. He gave me three thick books filled with Ford statistics and didn't try to tell me what they meant. He was the first researcher I'd ever met who didn't automatically assume that creative people couldn't interpret numbers.

The first book covered the issues that concerned Americans. I glanced at a few tables. If I had tried to guess how most people felt about things like busing, gun control, abortion, poverty, women's rights, religion, I would have guessed wrong on almost every count. I looked up from the second chart with an incredulous expression.

"I didn't believe those numbers either," said Bob. "I've run them through the computer hundreds of times." He looked sad. "I can't make 'em come out any other way. America seems to be considerably to the right of Barry Goldwater."

We talked about the campaign for a while, and we quickly went through several of the more pertinent charts. He was casual, obviously competent, and had an extraordinary gift for interpreting complicated statistics in a clear, precise way. He seemed to be the perfect kind of man to be at the elbow of a President who was not noted for his quickness of mind.

I had now met two of the people closest to the President, and I suddenly realized that I was beginning to like President Ford. I couldn't imagine Bob Teeter or Dick Cheney wearing little American flags in their buttonholes. I felt that if the President of the United States told them to get a crew cut, they'd tell the President what to do with his hat. They seemed like the kind of guys who, despite popular opinion, usually wind up at the head of the best-run American businesses—straightforward, competent, quick, humorous, pleasant people to be with. They were confident, but not imperious.

I noticed that there was no crease in Teeter's pants. And his white button-down shirt looked as if it had been made back in the *first* button-down shirt period. I guessed that he was in his mid-thirties; that he'd been one of the smartest guys in his class at a non-Ivy League college; that he'd been president of his fraternity; and that he'd reached the top of the research field the same way a surgeon gets to the top—by being better than the other people in the business.

I knew I could be proven dead wrong very soon, but first impressions run strong with me. I felt that Bob Teeter and Dick Cheney were a far cry from Bob Haldeman and John Ehrlichman. It was a gut feeling—the kind of feeling that was going to play a big part in the coming campaign.

We didn't spend much time reviewing the polling data because I knew that Bob planned to make a full presentation of his findings to John, Doug, and me later that night. The main purpose of our meeting that afternoon was to review all the previous Ford commercials. Bob had them racked up on the video tape machine (which *had* been rented for the day.)

There were about eight commercials on the reel. They all seemed to have been cut from the same footage. It was newsreel stuff. President Ford walking somberly through Congress and up to the podium to accept the Presidency of the United States. The footage was interspersed with stills of the President, the same technique Richard Nixon had used in his last campaign. It was cold, gloomy stuff, and I suspected that the editing had been done by some assistant at a local television station. The words matched the pictures: "America is on a steady course. . . . Goals that can be realized, expectations that can be fulfilled. . . . Truth is the glue that holds America together."

Christ! Elmer's glue wouldn't use that slogan! There were stills of the White House. Stills of the President staring moodily out the window, an obvious attempt to re-create the most famous picture ever taken of President Kennedy. The only trouble was that Ford's photographer had evidently used a Kodak Instamatic.

I thought I understood the strategy. Show Ford as our leader, our President. But to me, the result was a series of commercials that said Ford is the President—and pretty damned scared about the whole thing. There was no warmth. No life. Nothing was real, especially the uncomfortable smile on the President's face that closed every spot. No wonder he had so much trouble in the primaries.

The only commercial that wasn't cut from the same dull Presidential footage was a five-minute spot that had been used in Texas. It showed me one good reason why Reagan upset Ford in Texas.

The spot opened with Senator Tower saying nice things about Ford, and warning us about the war-mongering Reagan. It was filled with the old Nixon commercial techniques. Young American soldiers in foxholes, with an implicit warning that if you don't vote for Ford, they'll be right back in those foxholes. There was a call to patriotism, aerial footage of America and the words "Sea to shining sea." It was bad strategy. That had already been proven by hundreds of thousands of votes. But what made it worse, as far as I was concerned, it was bad advertising. It was, in fact, terrible advertising.

"Do you want me to run through them again?" Bob asked when the last commercial had been shown.

"Please." I said. "Spare me."

Bob understood. There was no point in our discussing the primary advertising campaign again. There was clearly not a single frame of footage that I would ever use again.

"Have you got the Jim Jordan spots?" I asked.

It was more than idle curiosity. I'd worked with Jim Jordan for fifteen years at B.B.D.O. He was now the president of the agency, and though he'd given up the title of creative director, I knew damn well he hadn't given up the job. Towards the end of the primary campaign, the advertising trade journals had devoted quite a bit of space to some controversial commercials that Jim had created for Ford. They were so controversial, in fact, that several of Ford's strategists had quit the campaign when they went on the air in California.

"I don't have them," said Teeter. "But you wouldn't want to see them."

"Why not?"

"They were awful. They were 'Ring around the collar' commercials."

"Well, Jordan did pretty damn well with 'Ring around the collar.' "

"And his commercials for Ford are a classic example of why you can't sell politicians like soap."

I found myself defending Jordan, not because he was an old friend, but because I knew that he didn't make "awful" commercials. He's one of the best in the business. He makes controversial commercials, but the controversy usually dies down when the sales curve starts to climb.

"Well, Jordan didn't make any friends in the White House," Teeter said.

That I could believe. Jordan is a table-pounder. He gets away with it when he's pounding his own table. But I suspected that he wouldn't get far by pounding Jerry Ford's table.

"He somehow managed to get an appointment with Ford," Bob said. "He convinced the President that it was important, and that the key campaign advisers should be present. He walked into the room smoking a big cigar. He started right out by telling the President that his commercials were, quote, 'the shittiest advertising I have ever seen in my life'—closed quote."

"Well, at least he was truthful," I said.

"But some of the guys in the room were responsible for that advertising."

"Jordan wasn't born to be a diplomat," I said.

"He made four commercials for us," Bob said. "He had them written out on some yellow sheets of paper."

"He probably wrote them on the plane coming down," I said.

"I'm sure of it. But we didn't have much choice. We decided to let him make the commercials."

"Did you run them?"

"Two or three times in California. We got so many complaints we had to yank them off the air. Awful. They were slice-of-life soap commercials. He got a bunch of actors to play your average voters talking about the two candidates. Housewives, hard hats—corny. Corny!"

I wanted to see those commercials. I didn't believe for a minute that they were as bad as Bob Teeter thought they were. And I knew that they couldn't possibly be worse than the commercials I'd just seen. Jordan hadn't had a chance. He'd presented his commercials badly. And he knew better. In our business, creating the greatest commercial in the world is less than half the battle. If you don't present it well to the client, you don't have a chance.

I made a mental note to present my stuff quietly during the coming campaign. To come across not as an advertising whiz but as someone who understands politics.

Bob and I left his office together about six that night and drove to the airport motel, where we were to meet John and Doug. I was tired, and I knew that I was heading towards a long session filled with facts and figures. I had no idea how long that session was going to be.

9

DISCOVERING AMERICA IN A SMOKE-FILLED ROOM

Deardourff had ordered a conference room. They gave us a small, stuffy single room with an unmade cot. The President's men didn't seem to cut much ice at Holiday Inns. We rearranged the furniture, called downstairs to have a table set up, and by seven o'clock we were ready to go. It was then that I realized I hadn't eaten all day. I felt a little better about it when John admitted that not only hadn't he eaten, he'd been up till four in the morning with a candidate in St. Louis; taken the seven o'clock flight to New York to review the convention footage; and just barely caught the plane to Detroit. That, it seemed, was a routine day for John.

The conversation started with the usual political speculation that always seems to precede campaign strategy meetings. When it comes to rumor, scandal, and gossip, political people are as bad as theater people.

The most serious rumor concerned Jesse Helms, the right of right-wing Republican who seemed to be doing everything in his power to throw the convention into utter chaos. He was supposedly working for Reagan. But it seemed to me that the son-of-a-bitch was trying to destroy the Republican Party. He was organizing a conservative walk-out at the convention, hoping to set up a third-party convention in Chicago. The third party's nominee was going to be Jim Buckley.

I asked Bob Teeter how a third-party candidate would affect our chances.

"In actual votes," Bob said, "it might not hurt us too badly. But it would tear the convention apart. And if we can't come out of that convention reasonably united, forget it."

"What about Reagan?" I asked. "The *Times* isn't conceding this thing to Ford. Neither are the networks."

Teeter paused. I had the feeling that I'd brought up a subject no one wanted to talk about. Bob pursed his lips. It was the first time I'd seen a look of real worry on anyone's face as far as the convention was concerned.

"John Sears may have made a brilliant political move. That's the only thing that worries me."

Bob then explained the Reagan strategy to me. It was painfully simple. There was to be a vote on rule 16-C on the convention floor Tuesday night. The rule would force a candidate to name his Vice-Presidential choice before the vote on his own nomination. Reagan, of course, had already named Senator Richard Schweiker. The rule wasn't really that important. The vote, however, was crucial. It was the acid test of the President's strength. If the delegates didn't stick with Ford on this issue—and Bob thought it was a pretty flaky issue—he was certain the President would lose the nomination. Rule 16-C was turning out to be a classic move in political chess.

While we were discussing the politics of 16-C, Doug Bailey, tight-lipped and narrow-eyed, burst into the room. I'd never seen Doug lose his temper, but he was close to it now.

"I just talked to my wife in Kansas City," he said to Teeter. Ford is *not* fighting for the E.R.A. plank. If he doesn't go to work, I go out."

"Don't worry," said Bob. "He's going to issue a statement."

"It'll be *over* by the time he issues a statement," Doug said.

"Wait a minute." Teeter went to the phone and punched out a long distance number.

"This is Bob Teeter," he said. "What about E.R.A.? . . . really? . . . good." He hung up.

"The President just issued a strong statement. It made the seven o'clock news. What did I tell you?"

Doug sat down for the first time, sighed deeply, and slapped his hands on the table. "Good!" he said firmly.

John laughed. "Well, that takes care of our wives for a while. We can go home now."

"What about Connally?" asked Doug. "The *Times* has him as the campaign chairman."

"Relax," said Bob. "Won't happen. Dick and I talked with the President this morning. The campaign is going to be run by a five-man steering committee. You two are on it. I'm on it. Dick Spencer. And Jim Baker."

I'd seen Jim Baker on television talking about the President's delegate count. He was apparently the President's floor manager in Kansas City. He seemed like a pretty nice guy—on television. The name Spencer meant nothing to me, and I didn't ask.

"Well, you know where I am on the Vice-Presidency," Doug said. "Ruckelshaus is the perfect running mate. He's the *only* running mate. We've got to get him on the ticket!"

"I handed the President the letter on Bill yesterday," Bob said. "It's the strongest statement he has on anybody."

"Who else is on the list?" Doug asked.

I noticed the smoke from my cigarette and Doug's cigarette curling towards the ceiling. By God, I thought. I finally made it. An honest-to-God smoke-filled room.

John pushed the ashtray, which was between us, back towards me. The conversation swung to other Vice-Presidential possibilities. Howard Baker. Bill Scranton.

I thought Doug would object to Scranton. Scranton sounded like a tired political name to me. Like a Volpe—okay for an ambassadorship, but Vice-President?

"Scranton." Doug rolled the name around thoughtfully. "You know that's not a half-bad move. Scranton's the goddamnedest stump speaker I ever saw."

Bob Teeter made notes on a pad of yellow, lined paper. He was interested.

John started batting at the air with his hands. He was bothered by something.

"Yep," Doug said firmly. "Scranton could do a job on the peanut farmer. Great stump speaker."

John finally spoke up. "Would you blow that damn smoke the other way," he said. "I can't stand it."

I scrunched out my cigarette. Deardourff was clearly not cut out to be a backroom politician.

"Scranton's not as good a choice as Ruckelshaus," John said once the smoke had been cleared.

"Nobody is," agreed Doug. "Bill is the perfect man for the job."

"The President knows how you feel," Bob said. "He knows how I feel. He likes Bill. I think he wants Bill. But he's being very close about this decision. I have a hunch he won't make up his mind until the last minute."

Other names were bandied about briefly, including Percy and Richardson, but no one mentioned Bob Dole.

Nobody mentioned Reagan as Vice-President, either. I assumed that he had never even been considered, and had been mentioned in press conferences only to get him mad.

Doug asked about the President's speech. We all knew that the campaign could well be won or lost on the strength of that acceptance speech. Doug had written two versions and they had been submitted to the President via Teeter and Cheney. Bob had bad news for Doug.

"We all feel as strongly as you do about the President's speeches," Bob said. "They are a disaster. But I'm afraid he's sticking with his speechwriters."

Doug looked disgusted.

"Cheney broke his pick on this one," Bob said. "He really fought the man hard. So hard that the President had to order him not to mention it again."

"Have you seen the speech?" asked Doug.

"Nobody has seen it," Bob said ominously. "Nobody. Except the President and that stand-up comedian."

"Do you suppose," said Doug, "that just this once they can have the speech written at least a day before it's delivered?"

"It's written. Hartmann and Penny are at Camp David right now. They have a full week to work on it with the President."

"That speech is so important," Doug said very seriously. "It's the only way we can pick up the points we need before Labor Day. If we're not within twelve or thirteen points of Carter by Labor Day, this whole thing is a waste of time."

Doug looked as though he was going to say something else. We waited to hear what it was.

"Debates," he said finally. "If he says nothing else in that speech, he's got to challenge Carter to debates."

"I agree with you," Teeter said. "It's risky. He could freeze. But I agree with you."

I agreed too. It meant that no matter how bad the speech was, Walter Cronkite could at least have some hard news to talk about when he analyzed the speech as soon as it was over. Doug's reasons were less theatrical.

"People will expect him to lose the debates," Doug said. "If he just holds his own he wins."

"I'll try," said Teeter. "There'll be some problems. But I think the President wants to debate him."

He put three large blue books on the table. The same books I'd seen in his office.

"You can look at these later," he said. "I just want to make some general observations."

He talked in general terms about his findings. They weren't too surprising at first. I'd glanced through those books earlier, after all.

The country was basically very conservative. The issues people cared most about were more social than political. People were concerned about honesty in government and moral leadership (Carter's issues). It was over twice as important as unemployment (Carter's issue) or reducing government spending (Ford's issue). The morality issue was ten times as important as protecting the environment, and five times as important as education. If there ever was a year when you could run on motherhood and Mom's apple pie, this was it.

The morality issue wasn't surprising to me. It's what created Jimmy Carter, after all. And I'd bumped into it some time ago. It was before anybody had ever heard of Watergate.

I was helping a friend of mine, Marty Linsky, run for Congress in Brookline. Marty was a brilliant, compassionate young guy with a spotless liberal voting record in the state legislature. He was the absolutely perfect candidate for a predominantly Jewish district. And his opponent was a Catholic priest whose only issue was the Vietnam War. The war was ending and Marty was on his side.

Our issue polling showed that Marty couldn't lose. But straw ballots showed he was losing—badly. One weekend I took all the questionnaires home to see if I could make some sense out of the situation. On the first page the questionnaire had a long list of things that could possibly concern people, and the respondents were asked to rank the most important issues. They dutifully marked off things like crime in the streets, the economy, education, etc. But on the last page of the questionnaire there was a blank space where people could write down their own feelings about government. I read fifteen hundred answers. And almost every one was the same. "Bunch of crooks . . . no moral leadership . . . they don't care about us." After reading them through, I understood why Marty Linsky, a liberal Jewish boy in a solid Jewish neighborhood, could not beat an opponent backed by the authoritarian morality of the Church.

So I wasn't at all surprised, two years after Watergate, when Teeter held up a chart labeled "Cynicism." The pollsters measured it deeply these days. And his chart showed that seventy-four percent of the people thought that government was run by a few big interests . . . that the government was wasting their money . . . that there wasn't enough morality in high places.

He had also analyzed the conservative mood of the country. He and his associates at Market Opinion Research had run the numbers through the computer several different ways to find out the relationship between people's feelings about the issues and people's feelings about the candidates. I thought Ford would look pretty good on this one. I considered Ford a conservative.

"Ford," said Teeter, "is to the left of the voters on every issue except one." That one issue was national health insurance, the only economic issue that the voters did not take the conservative position on. People were anti-busing, anti-abortion, pro-guns, anti-pornography, and anti-legal marijuana. A question about poor people particularly intrigued me. Forty-four percent of the people thought poverty was the fault of society. Forty-six percent thought it was because people were lazy.

Bob then went into some detail about regional and party differences. The border and mountain states were frighteningly conservative. The industrial states were an enigma.

Then Bob showed us a chart that he called "The Feelings Thermometer." He and his computer had taken careful temperature readings to gauge the voters' feelings about the two candidates. The results were shown on a large red thermometer. Towards the top of the thermometer was the name "Carter."

"Carter's temperature is sixty-five," Teeter said. "That's extremely high." He then pointed to Ford, who was well below Carter. "Ford has a temperature of forty-five degrees," he said. "Lukewarm."

"People feel good about Carter," Teeter went on. "We can't ever forget that. Of course we may surmise that he's a vindictive, vicious bastard. We know that the reporters who cover him every day will vote for Ford. We may fear that he's another Nixon—a cold, calculating son of a bitch without a non-political friend in the world." He pointed hard towards the thermometer chart. "But this is reality. *This* is the Carter we have to deal with."

"What about the religious thing?" I asked. "Don't people see him as a Jesus freak? Some kind of religious nut?"

Bob smiled at me and shook his head slowly.

"Let me tell you something interesting," Bob said. He leafed casually through one of the blue books. "Several years ago—long before anybody had ever heard of Jimmy Carter—I was at a research seminar with Pat Cadell. We both were speakers. He stood up and predicted that the next President of the United States would be a Baptist from Georgia."

The implication seeped gradually into my mind. Cadell. The kid from Harvard with a computer for a brain.

"That was even before Carter was born again!" added Teeter with a laugh.

Images of Machiavelli and Rasputin swam in my mind.

"What he'd spotted, of course, was the religious thing. The strongest movement in America. He saw the political implications."

"Did Cadell create Carter?" I asked naively.

"It's not that simple," Bob said. "And not that devious. Just a matter of the right man at the right place at the right time. Those two were destined for each other." He held the book open to a spread of charts.

"Here are the numbers. They don't lie."

He carefully took us through some of the most astounding statistics that I had ever heard.

Thirty-nine percent of the people had had an actual experience with Jesus Christ that they could identify according to time and place and that had changed their lives.

Fourteen percent of the people had actually seen or touched Jesus Christ.

Seventy-two percent of the people read the Bible regularly and found it the main source of comfort in their lives.

Seventy-one percent thought that their political leaders should pray to God before making decisions.

"Billy Graham," Doug muttered as Bob reeled off more statistics about the number of people in prayer groups. "We've got to have Billy Graham on the ticket."

"Or Oral Roberts," John suggested.

"What they want to do, of course, is turn the religious movement into a political movement." Teeter looked worried. "It could be the most powerful political force ever harnessed."

"It's kind of hard to fight Jesus Christ," I agreed.

"One of our own Republican state chairmen said he'd have trouble voting against Jimmy Carter. He'd been born again, too."

"Charles Colson was born again, for God's sake," said Doug. "We could do a commercial opening with Carter saying, 'I was born again,' after which Colson pops on and says, 'Me too!' "

"Let me give you an idea of just how strong this movement is," said Bob. He told us he had sent one of his researchers to the Midwest to conduct some focus group interviews among reborn Christians. He wanted to find out what made them tick politically, as well as religiously. The researcher conducted two sessions and flew back to Detroit. The next morning his phone rang early. It was an intense Jesus freak from the Detroit chapter of the religious group, hoping to convert the researcher to Christianity.

"They've got an underground communications network," added Teeter in his own voice. "And Jimmy Carter is plugged right into it."

Doug lit another cigarette. So did I.

"What about the Catholics?" I asked. "And the Jews. Doesn't this Baptist thing scare them?"

"We're still not sure," Bob said. "Maybe. Of course the Jews are Democrats. You've got to scare the hell out of them to get them to vote Republican. Carter's too smart to do that. But the Catholics are something else. They could be the key to the election. Carter knows it. We know it."

"Maybe we can arrange it so the President can perform a small miracle in Kansas City," John said. "Just a little one. Do we have any blind delegates who would be willing to see again? At a press conference?"

"I like it," said Doug. "It might be more practical though if he performed the miracle on a crippled Reagan delegate. We could kill two birds with one stone."

"Won't work," said Teeter. "Episcopalians don't perform miracles. People would never believe it."

"What interests me," said Doug seriously, "is that Ford *is* a very devout person. He and Melvin Laird led a Wednesday prayer group in Congress. The President *does* pray before making important decisions. His son is a divinity student. The President is a genuinely religious person. He doesn't wear his religion on his sleeve. I think we can use that."

"It's going to be very tricky," I said. "Very delicate." I was beginning to feel uneasy about the religious thing. When you run a commercial that says you don't wear your religion on your sleeve, you are, in fact, wearing your religion on your sleeve. People are smart enough to see that.

Teeter went to the back of the room and picked up what I had thought was a large cardboard chart facing the wall. He turned it around and placed it in front of him on the table. It wasn't a chart at all. It looked to me like a precisely drawn map of the solar system. There were several neat circles that resembled planets in a sky that had been divided into grids.

"This is something that's never been done before," Bob said proudly. "I call it a Perceptual Map. It places candidates in space exactly the way voters place them in space."

He explained the technique. He had interviewed many thousands of voters to dig out their perceptions of various candidates: Carter, Ford, Reagan, Rockefeller, Kennedy, Wallace, etc. The perceptions were based on issues, on feelings about the candidates, on the voters' own feelings and opinions about lots of things. Teeter and his associates at Market Opinion Research had spent a month tabulating their findings and running them through computers.

"We spent weeks staring into a cathode tube," Bob said. "We tried hundreds of variables. We tried to prove ourselves wrong. We tried to force the computer to come out with different answers. The result is the most internally consistent data I have ever seen. You know damn well it's right."

The computer, with Teeter at the dials, had projected the candidates into two-dimensional space. Hence the planets in the sky. It had then placed the voters' perceptions of the candidates into space. These voter perceptions were represented by little dots drawn on acetate sheets. There were about fifteen acetate sheets representing key issues and important feelings that people had towards the various candidates.

Teeter laid the acetate sheets against the solar candidate map one by one. A pattern quickly began to emerge.

The planet just above and to the left of the center of the map represented Jimmy Carter. As the voters' perceptions were laid one by one on top of the map, thousands of little dots began to cluster around Jimmy Carter. Blue-collar workers started clinging to the Carter circle. Intellectuals gathered around him. Catholics and Jews, a little more hesitantly, circled in orbit around him. Blacks and Chicanos smothered him with their dots. People who cared about busing dropped at his feet. People who were for gun control hung around him. People who were against gun control sided with him as well. Conservative women kissed his feet. Liberal women hugged his head. Environmentalists swarmed around him. The rich touched him. The poor clung to him.

About four squares below him and six squares to the right of him another pattern was emerging. This was the planet Ford. As the acetate sheets were laid on the grid we saw a small cluster of Republicans falling on Ford . . . a few farmers hanging around . . . some suburban third-generation Catholics looking in . . . and a nice little bevy of women eighteen to thirty-four standing discreetly at his side. The planet Ford looked like a pretty lonely place.

Directly above Ford, about eight squares away, there was a slightly bigger and busier group circling about the planet Reagan. The "anti"-satellites. The anti-gun controllers; the anti-abortioners; the anti-poor people, anti-black people group. There were a lot of them. Over half of that group stuck right by Reagan. The rest of them landed on a planet many squares above him. It was the planet Wallace.

"What a team that would have been," Teeter said, pointing to the Reagan and Wallace clusters. "That's a strong constituency. A Reagan-Wallace ticket would have siphoned off a ton of voters from here"—he swept his hand from the Carter planet to a space between Reagan and Wallace—"and put them here."

"They wouldn't have won," said Doug, "but they sure would have scared the hell out of a lot of people."

When all the acetates had been placed over the sky of candidates, one thing was very apparent. Carter had almost every issue. Almost every voter group was on his side. He was the king of the Perceptual Map.

I stared at the map in glum silence. If that had been troop strengths, and I'd been a general, I would have surrendered.

I looked at the cloud of little dots on Carter's side and saw an army of Democrats wanting a change from Republican scandal and misrule. I saw all the union bosses, their arms around one another's shoulders, leading the best organized union campaign since Roosevelt. I saw the slickest political organization in American history. I saw Pat Cadell whispering into the ear of a grinning Jimmy Carter: "Just don't blow it, Jimmy. Just do what I say. And don't blow it."

Bob Teeter, however, did not have the ring of defeat in his voice when he summed up his findings. He seemed more like a company commander, briefing his troops, who would hardly wait for the attack to begin.

"It's really very simple," Teeter said. "We don't move the dots. We move the circles. The majority of the voters are here." He drew an imaginary ring around the center of the sky. "At the moment Carter happens to be closer to this circle. But look closely. Ford isn't very far from that circle. Neither is Reagan. We have to do two things in the next two months. We have to move Ford up and into the circle. We have to push Carter farther away from the circle. We have to do both to win."

"Supposing Carter doesn't want to be pushed?" I asked.

"He'll continue to be all things to all people," Teeter said. "He'll try to seem liberal to liberals and conservative to conservatives. He will be a non-issue candidate. He has to be. But he'll be playing a dangerous game. Can that approach stand up to the test of a national election campaign? I don't know. It will be interesting."

"It will be very interesting," muttered John.

"Waffling on issues becomes an issue," Doug said in his best Fletcher School of Governmentese.

"If Carter were anything more than a celebrity," Teeter said. "If he were a prominent national figure who'd been on the scene for years, then this really would be a frightening map. But remember"—he pointed to the dots clustered about Carter—"these only represent perceptions. These are only the feelings people have today. Carter has a weakness." He lifted the map off the table, put it back against the wall, and turned towards the blue books again.

"All our polling tells us that the feelings about Carter are thinly held, the perceptions are weak perceptions. People like Carter. They think he thinks the way they do. But they don't know him. They're not sure of him. Carter's had it all his way for two years. But can his thin image stand up to a really tough Presidential campaign?"

"And we can offer them a damn strong alternative," said John. "The President *can* walk and chew gum at the same time. All we've got to do is prove it to people."

"Could be an interesting thirty-second spot," I said. "We show the President walking purposefully up the White House steps. When he gets to the top, he turns and blows a perfect bubble at the camera."

"I think it's getting late," said John.

"One more important thing," said Bob, picking up the three blue books. "When you go through these, don't get hung up on hard issues. There really aren't any hard issues."

"Social issues," John said.

"Not just that," said Teeter. "Values. Traditional American values. That's what people are really concerned about. Traditional American values. Love of family. Love of God. Love of country. Pride in yourself."

"And softball," Doug said.

It was so late when the meeting finally broke up that there was no place for us to eat. I went downstairs to my room hungry, tired to the bone, and, in spite of the cheerful optimism of Deardourff, Bailey, and Teeter, very discouraged about our chances of winning.

I knew Mimi would be asleep. And I'd talked with her earlier in the day. But I felt like waking her up and chatting about my first three days in the political arena.

I called our house in Gloucester. After about a dozen rings there was a clanging, crashing noise that indicated she had picked the phone up and dropped it on the floor. She finally murmured "hello" into the phone.

"Well, I've managed to survive my first three days in politics," I said.

"How do you feel?"

I came up with what I thought was an appropriate quotation. It was taken from the opening passage of an old Max Schulman book. I thought it summed up my first three days quite well:

" 'Bang . . . bang . . . bang. Three bullets tore through my groin . . . and I was off on the most exciting adventure of my life.' "

part three

The Kansas City Plan

10

SOME
HIGH-FLYING IDEAS

I was in Logan Airport early Tuesday morning, on my way to Kansas City, when I suddenly felt surrounded by Jimmy Carter.

I had managed to keep my mind off politics for the last four days. I'd cleared the decks at the agency. I relaxed with Mimi and the kids in Gloucester. I was well rested. Almost confident when I arrived at the airport.

My confidence seeped away as soon as I entered a Logan newsstand to buy cigarettes and a paper. Jimmy Carter's face was staring at me from dozens of magazines. The Republicans were supposed to be the big story this week, but somehow Carter had captured the newspaper headlines. Of course this had been going on for months. I wasn't surprised. But when I started browsing through the paperback books, the full power of the Jimmy Carter campaign hit me once again. The thing that hit me was the fact that the four most prominently displayed paperback books had his picture on the covers too. Four books on Jimmy Carter. Four best-selling paperbacks. His life, his religion, his hopes for America. I leafed through them. All four, including his autobiography, were so obviously ghost-written by campaign staffers. I looked around the store. I saw a stack of T-shirts with peanuts on the front, and the words, ''THE GRIN WILL WIN.'' This wasn't a clothing store; it was a newsstand. I saw someone buy one of the shirts. I felt like tearing it out of his hands. The *Reader's Digest* had a special paper overlay on the

53

cover, "The Real Jimmy Carter Inside." A movie magazine headlined "Carter's Hollywood Pals." *New Times* Magazine had a picture of Jimmy surrounded by rock stars on the cover. It was headlined, "Jimmy's Friends in Rock."

This wasn't a good old American publicity hype. This was blatant
propaganda. I figured that sort of thing might work in Georgia. But
this was Boston, for God's sake! We were too smart for Jimmy
Carter.

Or were we?

I remembered my own feelings of just a few days ago. Lillian
talking about wrestling with Eddie Andelman. Barbara Howar on
the "Tonight" show. I admired the Carter machine then. But now I
had something at stake. Now I had to fight this thing. And I was
damned if I could figure out how.

I looked in vain for one book about President Ford. Nothing.
Finally, in the hardcover book section, I found one mention of his
name. It was a book called *Old Faces of 1976* by Richard Reeves.
The large caption on the cover explained the contents, "A few
thousand fairly well-chosen words on Jerry Ford, Nelson Rockefeller, Teddy Kennedy, George Wallace, Hubert Humphrey, Ronald
Reagan, Ed Muskie, Scoop Jackson, George McGovern, Hugh
Carey, Abe Beame, Jack Javits, Jerry Brown, and some other men
you probably wouldn't want your daughter to marry."

At least Ford topped the list. That offered some solace until I read
Reeves's opening lines on Ford. "I have seen the future," Reeves
wrote, "and it scares the hell out of me." I bought the book.

As I left the store I felt that I had seen the future. And it scared the
shit out of me.

On the flight to Kansas City I wrote ads and headlines and slogans
for Ford. I knew that it was a waste of time, and that I was again
violating one of the basic rules of good advertising. You should never
write ads until you have written the plan. The purpose of the trip to
Kansas City was to write the Ford advertising plan with John and
Doug. We were supposed to present it to the President on Friday.
Then we were supposed to start writing ads.

"Performance, Not Promises" I scratched in Pentab green on my
yellow pad.

I decided that it had the tired ring of old political campaigns.

"You *Know* What Ford Has Done," I wrote.

Or do you? I asked quietly.

"There's Nothing Wrong with America That Four More Years
with Ford Won't Fix," I wrote.

It had a familiar ring to it. And then I remembered. *Advertising Age* had just done an article on the Carter ads. His first ad was headlined, "Nothing Wrong with America That Some Strong Compassionate Leadership Can't Fix."

Wasn't even a very good Carter ad, I decided.

"Ford Is Right for America!" I wrote.

Yeah, my mind said, foretelling the reaction of my liberal friends. Way right.

"A Lot of Things Are Right with America Today," I wrote. "One of Them is Jerry Ford."

Not much of a claim, when you think about it. I did.

My mind kept chasing around ideas, and kept coming back to the mood of America.

"He Put America in a Good Mood."

"Let's Keep the Spirit of '76—Let's Keep Jerry Ford."

"Four More Great Years."

"Ford Made America Strong Again."

"Ford Made America Smile Again."

I wrote several variations on that theme, each one sillier than the last. I spent the better part of an hour developing a special advertising campaign in which President Ford talked only about what was right with America. A series of uplifting talks to the American people. He shows how well the free enterprise system is working. He talks about people working harder than ever before . . . volunteering their services more than ever before . . . keeping in better shape than ever before . . . living better than ever before.

After a while I realized that I was creating the single most boring advertising campaign in American political history.

Out of frustration I picked up Richard Reeves's book about politicians you wouldn't want your daughter to marry. I knew it would make me mad as hell. But I liked the way he wrote. I opened it to the Ford section and read on. It was neither more nor less cynical than I expected. He actually had one or two nice things to say about the man.

Then I was stopped cold by one sentence. It was a phrase that had run through my mind while I was jotting down slogans. I'd dismissed it as too corny before my pen could put the words down. But in print the words looked real and almost believable. Reeves had written the words sarcastically. In the previous paragraph he had written about Ford as a mediator, a man who casts himself in a safe, narrow role.

"That, of course, is not the role Americans wanted him to play," Reeves had written. "They wanted him to be the man to make us proud again."

The man to make us proud again.

Reeves was derisive and had written it cynically. But I had seen the Teeter statistics. I had cried a little bit myself when I had seen the Fourth of July celebration on Boston's Esplanade. America was in a good mood again. America was proud again. And—dammit—Ford was the President.

Why not put the two together? The man who made us proud again. I wrote it down in big green letters.

"THE MAN WHO MADE US PROUD AGAIN."

I closed the notebook, and just before I fell asleep I heard a wee voice inside me ask one small question.

"Corny?"

11
ROOTING
FOR RUCKELSHAUS

The first political celebrity I saw in Kansas City was Elizabeth Ray. I had just arrived at the Crown Center Hotel.

The lobby was bedlam—but then you saw it all on TV. It was all staged. Everyone in the throng of people was really there in hopes of being seen by one of the three huge cameras, ABC, NBC, CBS, located in three corners of the lobby. Being there was like being trapped on a huge stage crowded with noisy extras wearing funny buttons and funny hats and carrying potentially lethal placards. Their cues were sudden bursts of bright lights. The TV lights that would send them surging forward or backwards in the direction of the camera that had snapped on the lights. I was standing just inside the lobby, holding a suitcase and an attaché case, looking for a house phone that would connect me with the Ford headquarters, when I got caught in the surge towards the camera that was filming Elizabeth Ray.

I was pushed twenty feet forward until I was nose to nose with a hard-looking blond who was smiling and waving at the crowd with one hand, trying to push people away with the other. I was bathed in light. It suddenly occurred to me that my children would probably see this on TV tonight. They'd be glued to the set, hoping to see their father with President Ford. Instead they'd see Washington's most notorious mistress pushing their father away like a common masher.

I finally fought my way to a telephone. John and Doug had come down two days before. I assumed that all the arrangements for my arrival had been made. When I got through to the Deardourff and Bailey headquarters I learned that John was out filming and would be gone all day. After another ten minutes I did manage to contact Doug. It wasn't reassuring.

"Stay there," he whispered into the phone. "I'll be down as soon as I can. Stand right next to the front desk. I have lots to tell you. And we may have a small credentials problem."

He hung up and I stood next to the front desk, just out of reach of the surges towards Jack Ford and Nelson Rockefeller and Barry Goldwater. It was relatively safe near the front desk, and my ears were almost becoming accustomed to the din when Doug arrived.

We finally found a corner of the lobby where the noise was a few decibels lower, and the crowd a few delegates thinner.

"I think we've got troubles," Doug said.

"The nomination?" I asked.

"No. The Vice-President. I think they're going with Howard Baker."

"What's wrong with that? He looked good on TV during the Watergate thing. What more do you need in a Vice-President?"

"Baker's got problems," Doug said knowingly.

"Anybody else being considered?"

"Well, if we lose 16-C it's probably Baker. But . . ." Doug straightened himself up and looked wistfully over the crowd. I got the feeling he was about to say something that was important to him. "If we win 16-C, and the President can make his own decision, he just might do a great thing."

"What's that?"

"Name Bill Ruckelshaus."

A small delegation pushed their way past us. They were wearing enormous blue buttons saying, "DOLE FOR VEEP."

"What about this Dole?" I asked.

Doug laughed.

That was the beginning of the nonstop speculation around Ford headquarters concerning the Vice-Presidency. For two days and three nights it went back and forth: Baker . . . Ruckelshaus . . . Baker . . . Ruckelshaus. And nary a mention of Dole. But to give the insiders credit, I guess the guy who had to make the decision wasn't mentioning Dole either.

The Ford headquarters was on the seventeenth floor and it was, of course, an armed camp. Tall men with hearing aids and obvious bulges under their neat brown suit jackets were everywhere. If you didn't have the proper badge on your chest you couldn't even get on the elevator that was labeled "seventeenth floor ONLY."

And my credentials were not in order. It was the politics of politics again. It still hadn't been officially announced that Deardourff and Bailey were taking over the management of Campaign '76. Therefore I was not the official creative director. Apparently some people didn't want it known, before the nomination, that the campaign was going to be run by a bunch of Liberal Republicans like Deardourff and Bailey. The Reaganites could use it as one more argument to put in the ear of conservative delegates who were still on the fence.

After another hour of back room finagling, I had my picture taken with a Polaroid camera—it was attached to a badge that said, "FORD STAFF"—and I became, unofficially, an official member of the team.

Even though our status was uncertain, I thought that our own headquarters inside the Ford headquarters was pretty impressive. It was a large room with a conference table, typewriters, and lots of telephones.

Phil Angell, John and Doug's assistant, was talking excitedly into two telephones at once. I gathered that one of the two film crews had run out of film. That the Secret Service wouldn't let them into a caucus. That they had to have more badges. That the only good chance to shoot Betty was at the reception and there weren't enough lights to do it. That Michael didn't want to be interviewed at all. That the sound man had lost one of the cars.

It set the tone for the next four days.

All I wanted to do was to sit down quietly with John and Doug and talk over the advertising plan we had to write. But John and Doug had disappeared. And it was obvious that no one could do anything quietly on the seventeenth floor of the Crown Center Hotel.

I walked down the corridor and found that everywhere you looked people were talking into two telephones at once. "Get somebody over to Tennessee and crack that bastard's knuckles . . . Doin' a good job, Jerry, just keep on holdin' em . . . It doesn't matter how he *feels* about 16-C, he's got to *vote* against it."

The doors to all the rooms stood open, and nobody seemed to mind if I wandered in and listened to their calls to the various delegations. What I heard, everywhere I went, was consistent and reassuring. These guys were unmistakably in charge. I didn't know what they were saying, but I felt that the person on the other end of the line was going to do what they said, whatever it was. I had no idea what it was like at Reagan headquarters, but I had a strong feeling that these were the guys I wanted on my side.

When I wandered back to our room, Angell was gone. The room was empty. I moved right to a typewriter. Maybe I could get some work done after all. But before I could slip the paper into the machine, a dozen people suddenly swarmed into the room.

I recognized the man who was leading them into my office. It was Howard Baker. He was much shorter than I had thought. And his face looked a lot less haggard on TV than it did in person. He paid no attention to me. I was part of the furniture. The group hurriedly settled themselves at the conference table with Baker at the head. I was at a table in a corner about four feet away.

Howard Baker didn't look like a man who was about to be named Vice-President of the United States. When I first saw him I thought his presence at Ford headquarters meant that he was definitely the choice for Vice-President. If that were announced just before the vote on 16-C, it would help Ford keep his conservative delegates in line. But as I looked at Baker, I felt that this couldn't be the case. He looked like a loser, not a winner. He looked tired and sad. It wasn't until later that evening that I found out why. A few minutes before entering the room, it had been announced that his wife had had a drinking problem.

I soon gathered the purpose of Baker's meeting. They were going over the delegate count one last time before the vote on 16-C. I could have stayed. No one seemed to mind my presence in the room. But I knew I didn't belong there. I wandered back out into the hall. They seemed cautiously confident. That's all I needed to hear.

My partners had disappeared. I'd been graciously evicted from what I thought was my office. There was no way to start writing the plan. I'd never felt such a strong sense of not belonging. I didn't know these people. I wasn't really part of all this. My badge may have said that I was inside a Presidential campaign, but as I wandered aimlessly through the corridors on the seventeenth floor, I had never felt more like an outsider.

I turned a corner and saw, half a corridor away, another man who looked as lost as I was. He was just wandering towards me, peering into open doors, sort of hanging around people who were earnestly talking in the hall. No one spoke to him. No one acknowledged his presence. He seemed as alone as I was. Tall. Balding. He smiled at me and said "Hi" as we passed in the hall.

The first friendly word I'd heard all day. I said "Hi" right back to the President.

As I passed him, I noticed the cordon of gray-suited men with hearing aids strolling casually behind him.

12

FIVE ROADS
TO VICTORY

Just after six o'clock Ford's delegate watchers left the seventeenth floor and headed for Kemper Arena. They were like a football team leaving the locker room before the big game.

"Now you hold that line in Pennsylvania," one staffer said, punching his friend in the arm.

"And you just sit on New York" came the reply.

When they were gone, the floor was empty except for a few secretaries, Phil Angell, and myself.

The film crews had managed to overcome their problems, and Phil's controlled panic had given way to a genial "What—me worry?" attitude.

Now it was my turn to panic. I asked Phil when John, Doug, and I would be going off to write the advertising plan. I had figured that it would take a good three days and nights of work to get the document ready for the President.

Phil pulled two typewritten sheets of paper out of his briefcase. Doug and John's itinerary for the next three days. Only four hours of each day were unaccounted for. Two A.M. to six A.M.

They were scheduled to be with the film crews, shooting the President and his family as they moved around Kansas City. They had to film the events in Kemper Arena, including the acceptance speech. And they had nine other political clients in Kansas City, potential and incumbent governors and senators who had hired the firm of Bailey and Deardourff and damn well expected to see them, in person, in Kansas City.

Now I had been around politics just enough to know that it is impossible to win a close election without a carefully thought-out plan. You don't have time to spin wheels in a political campaign. You can't afford to make mistakes in a political campaign. *All* advertising should start with a written plan. But especially *political* advertising. If Avis is only number two, they can try harder. But if Ford is number two, he has to play golf for the rest of his life.

I stared at John and Doug's schedule, feeling very alone. There was only one person in Kansas City who could possibly find the time to write the President's advertising plan. Me.

I was swearing at Phil Angell, because there was no one else to swear at, when John and Doug breezed into the room. It made me feel better to turn and start swearing at them.

The secret of John and Doug's success in politics is that nothing, absolutely nothing, worries them, excites them, amazes them, or upsets them. I have seen strong men go nearly berserk under the strain of one minor political campaign. They were handling ten major campaigns simultaneously, including a completely fucked-up Presidential campaign, and they acted as if it were all a stroll through the park. You can't get mad at people like that. Your anger just starts running down.

"We can give you one hour," Doug said cheerfully, when my anger had run down. "Right now."

That's all it took. The foundation for everything we did in the '76 election campaign was laid down during that one-hour conversation.

All three of us had arrived at the same basic conclusion about what had to be done. It was the same conclusion that almost everyone in America had reached. We had to sharpen Ford's image. We had to weaken Carter's image. I had an odd feeling as I sat down at the conference table with my big yellow pad and my purple Pentab. There was going to be an awful lot of second-guessing if I didn't do *this* job right.

We had a few minor strategy arguments at first. Doug wanted to stress Ford's vision, his plans for the next four years. John pointed out that he didn't *have* any plans. Doug came up with a few and said, "We can come up with the rest." John argued very strongly for a campaign that put heavy emphasis on the Ford family. He felt that the family was the best vehicle for showing the genuineness of Ford, proof that he believed in all the traditional American values. I wanted to emphasize Ford's leadership qualities, demonstrate his forcefulness. Doug felt that *forcefulness* was not the right choice of words.

"He's brought a new approach to the Presidency," Doug said. "He's not an imperial President, like Nixon and Johnson. He's open. Relaxed. Feet on the desk. We have to convey that."

John and Doug felt that we should try to portray Jimmy Carter as a contrived candidate.

"We should try to show Jimmy Carter as the natural successor to Nixon," Doug said. "Everything about him seems contrived. His humility seems contrived. His softball seems contrived. His peanut farm, his religion. It's the politics of deception all over again."

"That may be what he *is,* but it's not what people *think* he is," I argued.

But Doug was warming to his subject. "We could admit that Ford bumps into things. He bumps his head sometimes because he's natural. Every movement isn't contrived. Would Carter bump his head? Would Nixon bump his head? Of course not. Neither of them ever did *anything* that wasn't carefully planned out ahead—that wasn't contrived."

"Carter will do that job for us," John said. "People will start to see through his act."

"Carter will not make mistakes," Doug said.

"Nobody falls apart so fast," John said, "as a man who doesn't make mistakes."

We talked issues for a while. We agreed that there were no issues strong enough to decide the election. And it was clear to us that the debates—if Carter accepted the challenge to debate—would go a long way towards clarifying where the candidates stood on the issues.

"I think our biggest issue, if we can use it," said Doug carefully, "is Carter's waffling on the issues. He is on both sides of every issue. He's very clever about it. He uses double negatives to state his opposition—and double positives to say he favors something. He's developed a very ingenious use of the English language. I think we may be able to catch him on that."

I talked about an approach to advertising that I believed in quite strongly. It was an approach that our agency uses for almost all our advertising problems. We call it "The Accepted Premise."

The idea is to get people nodding in agreement before you start to sell them. Start the sale by telling them something that they already believe to be true.

I felt that there were a lot of accepted premises about the President.

"I've read the verbatims from Teeter's research," I said. "People think of him as an honest guy. A guy who's trying damn hard. They feel that the country is coming around. They think the economy is getting better. They feel that America is in a better mood. If we start our advertising with some of these accepted premises, we can make our message more believable.''

''I agree with you in principle,'' John said. ''But I'm scared to death of advertising techniques. We've got to avoid them like the plague. If people sense the heavy hand of Madison Avenue they won't believe a word we say.''

''I think there are five strategies,'' said Doug. He held up the five fingers of his right hand. He ticked off each of the five strategies very deliberately, folding one finger down for each one.

''One. Ford the man.

''Two. Ford the leader.

''Three. Ford the unelected President.

''Four. Ford the man of compassion.

''Five. Carter the Southern Nixon.''

''That number three there—now that's interesting,'' said John. ''Do we say 'Vote for Ford—The Unelected President?''

''Precisely,'' said Doug.

John laughed. ''And I think it would be nice somewhere in there, if just one of our minor strategies at least hinted at his accomplishments in office. I think the President would like that.''

''The unelected President strategy is really our *accomplishments* strategy,'' Doug explained very deliberately. ''You know, his accomplishments since taking office *aren't* really *that* dramatic. He rescued the Mayaguez, but a lot of people were killed. He went to China, but nobody cared. The economy is better, but it ain't booming. He cut the rate of inflation, but the housewives out there don't want to know how *fast* prices are going up; they want prices to go down. He hasn't once put his hand in the till, but we don't have to advertise that.

''But.'' Doug paused for emphasis. ''*But.* Consider those accomplishments, meager though they may seem, in the light of how difficult it was for him to operate. An unelected President. A man without a mandate. Facing a suspicious electorate. A suspicious Congress. A world waiting to pounce on any real sign of weakness.

''Consider his accomplishments in the light of the difficult conditions he had to operate in; then you have something. People will start to believe you.''

I agreed. It was a good approach. I said that he should admit his mistakes, as well.

"No specific mistakes," Doug said. "Just a few little unspecified mistakes."

"We've got to be a little more positive than that, though," said John. "We've got to show how far the country has come under this unelected President. From one of the worst crises in our history to a calm. From near depression to prosperity."

"Prosperity? With nearly eight percent unemployed? They won't let us get away with that," said Doug.

"Recovery, then," said John. He looked at his watch. "Hey, we've got to go. We're late."

They got up from the table. I looked at my notes. I had five sentences written down. "Wait a minute," I said. "When are we getting together again?"

"We'll be here tomorrow night around six. For half an hour."

"Where am I staying?" I asked. "I assume you did get a room for me someplace."

"Oh," John said. "I forgot to tell you." He wrote an address on a piece of paper. "You're staying in a house in Mission Hill. Nice place. Twenty-minute cab ride. The film crew will be there too, but they leave in the morning. You'll have the whole place to yourself. To write the plan."

"What do you think we should have *in* the plan?"

"Everything. You've got the research. We should summarize that. The five strategies—we'll need to elaborate a little on those. And then you should outline some of the commercials. Thirty or forty commercials probably. We're buying five-minute spots, one-minute spots, thirty-second spots. Plus two half-hour shows. And a lot of radio. And a few newspaper ads. And the usual brochures. And the regional stuff."

They were backing out the door as John finished the list. The room was empty again.

I wanted to go to the typewriter and start working, but I didn't seem to have the energy. I looked around the room. It was a lousy place to work. Papers were strewn all over the conference table. There were coffee cups everywhere, most half-filled with cold coffee. There was a cart against a wall piled with uneaten tuna fish sandwiches and half-eaten salads. The room smelled of mayonnaise.

I needed to hear the sound of a sympathetic voice. I called Mimi in Boston. She wanted to know why I wasn't on the convention floor, watching the historic vote on 16-C. I told her that I had work to do. I didn't tell her the real reason I wasn't on the convention floor. I didn't tell her that nobody had asked me.

When I hung up I felt good enough to put a blank sheet of paper in the typewriter. I could hear distant cheering coming from the television set next door. I tried to shut the sound out. I had to think.

I began the advertising plan by typing out a very simple sentence. It wasn't very original. It simply stated an obvious fact. The sentence was this:

"America is in a good mood."

Not a startling thought. But as I wrote it, I thought of something a good friend of mine had said about the 1968 Hubert Humphrey campaign.

David Herzbrun, who now works for our agency, had helped bring Humphrey successfully to the Chicago convention. He was sitting in a hotel room with Humphrey when the student demonstrations erupted in the street below. Herzbrun had felt sick as he looked out the window and watched Mayor Daley's police clubbing the demonstrators.

He quit the campaign the next day because Hubert Humphrey had not once bothered to look out the window. He couldn't work for a Presidential candidate who didn't want to see what was going on in America.

I looked out my hotel window. The only demonstrators I could see were a tiny band of Gay Rights activists circling sedately on the hotel lawn. It seemed important that America had changed so dramatically from the conventions of '68 to the conventions of '76. We had survived Vietnam. We had survived Watergate. And now we were in a good mood again. We were feeling good about our country again. It seemed to me that our advertising should capitalize on this good mood.

I had written a few more sentences about the good mood of America, when I was suddenly interrupted by wild gales of laughter from the room next door. This, I thought, is carrying the good mood thing too far. It was a girl laughing. I've never been one to avoid laughing ladies, so I got up from the typewriter to investigate.

She was still laughing when I entered the room. A plumpish middle-aged man who reminded me of an Irish bartender was laughing with her. They pointed to the television set when they saw me. Nelson Rockefeller was on the screen, holding up a telephone with a broken cord dangling from it. Edwin Newman, the NBC announcer, seemed to be enjoying the scene almost as much as my fellow viewers.

"I think he's drunk," the laughing girl said.

"Naw, he's just raising hell," the Irish bartender said. "He's just here to have a good time."

They described the scene I'd missed. Nelson Rockefeller had suddenly reached back and yanked a Reagan sign out of a delegate's hand. He had then proceeded to break the sign across his knee and shove it under his seat. The ensuing pushing and shoving and shouting was typical of all party conventions through the years. But it was probably the first time that the Vice-President of the United States had started it. It had ended when the Reagan delegate yanked the Ford telephone out of the wall.

"I don't think this is going to help the Republican cause all that much," I said.

"Probably do us some good," the man said. "Livens up the show. Proves we're not a bunch of stuffed shirts."

They invited me to have a drink, and I soon discovered that a strong Scotch and water was exactly what I needed at the end of my first confusing day in Kansas City. I was glad that I hadn't been the only member of the Ford staff who'd been left back at the hotel while the big event of the convention took place.

"I'm Stu Spencer," the man said after I'd accepted his drink and settled in an easy chair to watch the show. "And this is Nancy Thompson."

Stu Spencer. I thought about the name as I introduced myself. It rang a dim bell. I'd heard the name in Detroit. Stu Spencer was one of the members of the Ford steering committee. I remembered an article I'd read a long time ago about a political consultant in California who had masterminded several big political upsets. Stu Spencer. He didn't look like a mastermind to me. A genial-looking gray-haired man in unpressed gray flannel pants and an open-collared Arrow shirt. He didn't look like a guy who gave orders. He looked as if he took orders.

It was to take me two months to get it through my head that Stu Spencer was more important to the success of the Ford campaign than Jerry Ford. As we watched the roll call on the 16-C vote I got a few hints that Stu Spencer did know a little more about politics than the average Irish bartender.

By the time they had announced the votes from the first four states, the NBC commentator was speculating that Ford might very well lose on 16-C—and thus lose the nomination tomorrow. Stu Spencer laughed and casually announced that we were going to win by fifty more votes than any television announcer had predicted. Three Scotches later the state of Wyoming proved him right.

NBC wouldn't quit. Reagan's defeat on 16-C, they announced, could simply have been an honest reflection of the delegates' feelings about naming a Vice-President in advance. It didn't mean that Reagan had lost the nomination. So tune in tomorrow, folks.

Why let the truth louse up your ratings, I thought. It was to be a recurring thought.

When I left Stu Spencer's room, the hallways of the seventeenth floor were beginning to come alive again. Four or five young girls, campaign workers, were hanging up a giant handwritten sign over the entrance to the hallway. It said "HAIL TO THE HEROES OF 16-C." They were draping toilet paper along the ceiling from one end of the hallway to the other. Bunting.The Ford delegate hunters had finally won the long tactical battle for the Republican nomination. They were on their way back from the scene of the battle. I didn't want to hang around for the victory party. I needed some sleep. There was another long tactical battle ahead.

13
WRITING THE PLAN

The next morning, when I sat down to write the plan to elect President Ford, I thought of my all-time favorite advertisement.

"They laughed when I sat down at the piano."

This situation was far more laughable than the scene in John Caples's famous ad. I hadn't been secretly taking a course in how to elect a President.

Even the setting was ludicrous. A man wearing a flowered bathing suit and Converse All Stars, sitting beside a swimming pool, with his portable typewriter perched on an expensive glass patio table. I could *hear* them laughing. If this is how Jerry Ford is planning his campaign (laughter), Jerry Ford is in deep trouble.

The typewriter told me something even worse. I hadn't the vaguest idea how President Ford could move up thirty-four points in the short time between the convention and the election. I had no old political strategies to fall back on. To my knowledge, only Barry Goldwater had ever been this far behind in a Presidential campaign.

Laughable. That's what this situation was. Our commercials should have been in the can by now. We should have been out on the street, testing them. We didn't even have a plan, for Christ's sake. One sentence. That's all we had.

I remembered the sentence I'd written the night before. It still seemed like a good way to start. I took out a clean sheet of white paper, rolled it into my typewriter, and typed it out again.

"America is in a good mood."

I decided I wasn't going to put down any statistics. Just conclusions. I wanted to describe the mood of the country, and it seemed so much easier to do it with words instead of numbers. The President would be reading this. He was too busy to wade through a lot of statistics.

The sun was hot, and I could feel the sweat gathering on my back as I wrote and rewrote the first part of the plan. I wanted to make it as short and to the point as possible. I promised myself a swim as soon as I finished. I got my swim as soon as I had finished typing this:

The Mood of the Country

America is in a good mood. Most people feel that things are pretty good—and getting better.

Politically, the mood is conservative. The people take a conservative position on every issue except national health insurance.

There is a high level of cynicism in the country. The great majority of the people feel that the government is wasting their money and is run by and for a few "big interests."

Although inflation and unemployment run high on people's list of concerns, people will not be voting their pocketbook. In the present climate, social issues appear to be more important than economic issues. Busing, gun control, abortion, and a strong national defense are the kinds of issues voters will respond to.

The issues that people feel most deeply about concern traditional American values. These are emotional issues. Love of family and love of God. Pride in their country and pride in themselves. Morality, freedom, independence, individual achievement are among the things that are most important to people today.

People want a more honest government, and a far higher morality in every walk of life. In their leaders, they look for moral leadership, strength of character, religious conviction, love of family, and great personal integrity above all else. They also look for compassion in their leaders. They want a conservative government, but one tempered with compassion for all the people.

It is particularly important to note that the people are far more influenced by their own feelings about the candidates' personal traits than by the candidates' positions on issues.

After I had toweled myself dry and stolen a ginger ale from the refrigerator of my borrowed house, I thought about the next part of the plan. Bob Teeter had spent hours in Detroit trying to show us the perceived differences between Jimmy Carter and President Ford. I thought it was important to summarize those differences.

I opened my briefcase and pulled out a report on the verbatim comments that Teeter's research had elicited. I was particularly interested in the comments about Ford. What were the "accepted premises" about Ford?

I had ten pages of comments by men and women of various ages taken from a cross section of the country. I had been told that the comments typified the feelings of the country as a whole. They were divided between positive and negative statements. I noticed that there were three pages of positive statements, seven pages of negative statements. Not a good sign.

I felt worse when I read the comments in the "positive" category.

"I think he's a nice man," one woman over sixty-five said, "but I hate Betty and what she said about girls living with a man."

"He's honest," a woman between forty and forty-five said, "but clumsy."

"He's an honest man, but he doesn't have the capability to be President," said a man in the fifty to fifty-four age group.

"He's honest compared to Nixon," a woman between twenty and twenty-five said, "but I don't think he's favorable to women or equality and I don't think he's for labor."

And these, remember, were the *positive* comments. Over half the people repeated the same basic comment: "He's honest, but not too smart"; "He's sincere, but not very competent"; "He's a good man, but he hasn't done much."

The negative comments were as bad as I had feared. Half a dozen people found it necessary to say that Ford couldn't walk and chew gum at the same time. An equal number of wise guys allowed as how their President had played football without a helmet. I found myself getting mad. Why was I getting mad?

The majority of people seemed to think that he was a "boob" . . . that he was "inept" . . . that he was a "rotten President" . . . that he was "a big Zero" . . . that he was "befuddled" . . . that he was "in over his head" . . . that he was "dopey" . . . or, as one man between thirty and thirty-five succinctly put it, "He's an oatmeal man." Most of them also volunteered that he "bumps into things."

The comments that worried me most concerned the Nixon pardon. As I went over the list, a couple of violent statements about "the Nixon deal" had jumped out at me. I went over the comments again, reading every word carefully. I was surprised to discover that there actually were only two comments on the Nixon pardon. Both by women.

Maybe that wasn't bad, I thought. Dozens and dozens of people giving their harshest judgments of President Ford, and only two of them brought up the problem that concerned us the most.

I felt a little bit like the boy who waded right into the pile of manure, shouting, "There's got to be a pony around here someplace."

I had gone over the comments on Jimmy Carter previously. The positives had outnumbered the negatives two to one. The negatives weren't very negative. "Don't know anything about him." . . . "A little wishy-washy." . . . "Takes both sides of every issue." And the positives weren't very positive. "Not part of the old establishment." . . . "Heard he was a good Governor." . . . "Cares for the people," etc.

Using all these comments and the statistics Bob Teeter had shown me, I could easily have painted a very bleak picture in the second part of the plan. The real difference between the two candidates seemed to be that people liked Jimmy Carter a helluva lot better than they liked President Ford.

But like the king's messenger, I thought it would be prudent to salt the truth. Not because I feared for my head. I simply thought it would be more useful to look for some light, rather than comment on how dark it was.

I figured I'd earned another swim after I concocted this assessment of the differences between Ford and Carter:

Ford and Carter

At the present time, Jimmy Carter closely reflects the mood of America.

People feel that he represents the traditional American values that mean so much to them.

They feel that he can probably provide the moral leadership they are looking for. And they feel that Carter thinks the way they do on most of the important social issues.

However, these are not strong feelings. People relate to Carter now, but they are by no means sure about Carter. His support is wide but thin.

People do not relate to President Ford quite as well as they do to Carter. But they do have positive feelings about the President's personal characteristics.

They see him as an honest man who is doing a good job. They see him as a good family man. In fact they see in President Ford many of the things that they want most in a leader today. But these things are perceived only dimly.

To win the election, we have to strengthen the positive feelings that people already have towards President Ford.

And at the same time, we must weaken the positive feelings that they have towards Carter.

We must bring President Ford closer to the people.

We must move Jimmy Carter farther away from the people.

We believe that the right advertising, based on this single-minded objective, can do the job.

It took only a few minutes to write that. It was one of those things that's so easy to say.

After a swim and a sandwich, I tackled the hard part of the plan. The advertising strategy. I took out the notes that I'd scribbled down with John and Doug. Five bare sentences.

When you write an advertising strategy for a soap or a tea or a soft drink, you usually try to zero in on one sales message. Longer-lasting deodorant protection. The tea with enough flavor to satisfy even a coffee drinker. A & W root beer has that frosty mug taste.

People need only one good reason to choose one product over another.

But when you're trying to sell a President, one strategy just won't do. We couldn't elect Ford just by convincing Americans he was a nice guy. Or just by proving he was a strong leader (so was Nixon). Or just by showing what he had accomplished in two years. We had to convince Americans that he was a lot of things: good guy, strong leader, compassionate, someone who had done a lot and had a good program for the next four years. At the same time we had to try to convince Americans that Jimmy Carter wasn't what he said he was. That's why we needed five strategies. And if we executed each strategy flawlessly, I thought—with exciting, believable commercials that people remembered all the way to the voting booth—maybe, if nothing went wrong in the next two and a half months, if Ford clearly won the debates, then maybe, just maybe. . . .

It took me the rest of the afternoon to write the advertising strategy. It was built entirely around the five points we had discussed the night before. All the time I was writing it, I had a feeling that something was missing. Something important.

Advertising Strategy

To meet that objective, our advertising should accomplish five basic things:

1. Strengthen the human dimension of President Ford.
2. Strengthen the leadership dimension of President Ford.
3. More clearly portray President Ford's compassion for less fortunate Americans.
4. Portray his accomplishments in office in a believable way.
5. Cut Jimmy Carter down to size.

Obviously we can't accomplish all these things with a single ad or commercial. But all of the advertising we do will be designed to meet one or more of these strategic points.

We feel that it is important to unify this five-part strategy under one basic theme. The theme should end every commercial and be part of all campaign communications.

The theme we recommend is "President Ford. The man who made us proud again."

Although we will target our advertising to different sections of the country and to different voting groups, we will make the same strategic points to everyone. The strategy will be tailored to fit a wide variety of issues, and a wide variety of voter groups.

Here are some of the areas we will explore in creating ads to meet the five strategic points.

1. *The human dimension.* We will show the various members of the President's family not just as campaigners, but as warm, interesting individuals. We will show how they relate to one another and how they relate to their father. We will place heavy emphasis on Betty Ford. She will talk directly about traditional American values, about the feelings she has about her children and her husband. These talks should be uplifting to the American people—should help to give more purpose to their own lives.

We also think it is important to introduce the real Jerry Ford to America. We want Americans to meet his friends and hear what they have to say about him. We think Americans should know of his accomplishments throughout his life, not just his accomplishments as President.

Finally, we think the American people should hear how the President himself feels about the things that are important to him: his religion, his hometown, his youth, his feelings as he tries his best to solve the problems a President must face.

2. *The leadership dimension.* Americans should learn what Ford's

philosophy of government really is. A new, more decent kind of leadership. He does not arrogantly assume that one man has all the answers. His purpose is to inspire confidence in people themselves. An open Presidency. A Presidency people know they can trust. He does not claim that the President is always right. He admits mistakes. For he knows that government needs more to be restrained by humility than to be fed by ambition. He offers a higher standard of public service.

In addition to his leadership philosophy, we must *demonstrate* how those leadership qualities have resulted in workable programs that have benefited all the people.

3. *His compassion.* The most serious problem a Republican candidate has is the perception of Republicans in general as hard-nosed, big-business types—against the working people, against the poor people, against minorities. President Ford has to throw off the Republican yoke.

One way to show compassion is in his treatment of the issues. When he talks about economic issues, he must do so from the viewpoint of those who suffer most. And it is important that he express strong feelings, and take a leadership position, on such matters as the Equal Rights Amendment, black opportunity, the plight of the Indians, and the hardships of older people.

4. *His accomplishments.* It would be politically dangerous to overdramatize the President's accomplishments in the past two years. However, it is essential that we emphasize the things he has done in the light of the difficult conditions he faced. He had the handicap of Watergate. He had the handicap of being an unelected President. He inherited economic and governmental crises. Yet he got us back on the right track again. He may have made some mistakes along the way, but he got the job done. And it was as tough a job as any President has ever faced. People will accept the fact that times are good, that they have a new pride in their country. They will accept the fact that President Ford contributed to our present good fortune. But they will not accept the fact that he did it all by himself.

5. *Cutting down the Carter myth.* This, of course, is the most politically sensitive area that we will face in the campaign. This is the first year in history that political advertising has been paid for by the people. The very worst thing we could do would be to use that money for advertising that was misleading, or designed solely to undercut the opponent.

We feel, however, that Carter is vulnerable to an honest,

straightforward challenge on his positions. He takes both sides of too many issues. He uses different words to talk about the same issue to different people. In matters of defense spending, abortion, the B-1 bomber, Humphrey-Hawkins,* he has taken ambivalent positions that can be documented. If used forthrightly, by President Ford himself, these matters can be made genuine campaign issues that are of concern to the voters. We will run an honest campaign. But that does not mean we won't run a *tough* campaign. The politics of deception is a real and serious matter, and we think it should be explored in this campaign.

By the time I had finished writing the strategy, I could see the sun, low on the horizon, just over the roofs of the expensive Mission Hill homes. I had planned to meet John and Doug back at Ford headquarters at six-thirty. I took one last quick swim, put the plan in my briefcase, and headed back into the house.

While I was showering, while I was shaving, while I was dressing, while I was taxiing back to Kansas City, I kept thinking that I had left something important out of the strategy statement. But I just couldn't think what it might be. I finally decided it didn't matter much anyway. This was just a preliminary draft. John and Doug were bound to have additions. And I still had two more days to make my own additions to the plan, outline the ads, finish the job. I felt that I'd made a pretty good start.

I remembered that tonight was the night Jerry Ford was going to win his party's nomination for the Presidency.

Either that, or tonight was the night I headed back to Boston.

---

* The bill, still in legislation, calls for more systematic control of domestic economic policy. It proposes a yearly reassessment of national programs by both President and Congress. Two primary objectives are the reduction of unemployment through legislation to a maximum of 3% of the adult population, to be accomplished within a four-year period; and limiting the rate of inflation to the figure as it stands on the date of the bill's enactment.

14

BUT WHAT ABOUT THE NEXT FOUR YEARS?

Things seemed normal in our suite on the seventeenth floor of the Crown Center Hotel. Phil Angell was talking into two telephones, yelling at a Secret Service official through one phone, and yelling at a cameraman who was having trouble buying film through another. Lee Kenower, the head cameraman, was complaining to John Deardourff about the problems he'd encountered trying to film Betty Ford that day. Another cameraman was complaining that he couldn't shoot a reception for Steve Ford because the lights never showed up. An assistant was complaining about the lousy camera position the crew had been assigned for tonight's filming in Kemper Arena. John was smiling sympathetically and listening attentively with one ear, while talking on another phone to one of the Deardourff-Bailey workers.

"I need farmers," John was saying. "Real farmers. Earth people. Typical Iowa, Nebraska. I *don't* want them to look like delegates. We're going to be shooting man-on-the-street stuff. I want articulate farmers. Get six or seven of them there by ten o'clock tomorrow. Thanks."

I was skeptical about most of the filming that had been going on in Kansas City. John had hired two film crews, people he had worked with in previous campaigns. They were getting documentary footage of just about everything that happened in and around the convention. I knew time was short, and we would need miles of film to make the commercials for the campaign, but I just couldn't see the value of all this political footage. Rallies, receptions, speeches, demonstrations. And in the midst of the hoopla, they were taking delegates out into the street and filming them talking about Ford. We needed warm, honest, relaxed footage to make warm, honest, believable commercials. Here in Kansas City, everything was cold, staged, and feverish.

I told John my feelings when I finally got a minute alone with him.

"You may be right," he said with a smile. "But this may be the last time we get the whole Ford family together. And out of all this craziness here we *should* get *something* we can use."

"Well," I said, "it's only money."

"And that," said John, "is one of the only problems we don't have."

Doug finally appeared on the scene. We were supposed to have another hour to review the work I'd done on the plan and discuss commercial ideas.

"I've only got five minutes," said Doug. "They've asked me to write a nominating speech and an acceptance speech for the Vice-President."

"Who's it going to be?" I asked. At last I was going to get some inside information.

Doug laughed. "I don't know," he said. "Nobody seems to know. But they want the speech."

I laughed with him. "And I give you that Great American," I said, in my best oratorical style, "our next Vice-President, *Name Goes Here!*"

"But I know how to write it," Doug said proudly. "I'll write it for Bill Ruckelshaus. It is going to be one of the most eloquent speeches I've ever written."

"I've only got five minutes myself," John said, looking at his watch. "I have to be on the convention floor with the crew."

I shrugged, sat down, and pulled the draft of the plan out of my briefcase. It seemed that hours were very short in Kansas City.

Both John and Doug seemed to like the draft. But after they had read it, there was an expression on Doug's face that I'd seen many times. It's an expression that seems to say, "I am about to say something, but you may have to wait a long time before I say it."

When that expression comes over him, all conversation stops. Everyone in the room just watches him and waits. It's a trifle annoying, having to sit there quietly, watching his mind work, for up to two or three minutes. But no one has ever complained about it. Because everyone knows that what he says is worth waiting to hear.

Finally a slow smile began to creep across his face.

"The only trouble with this plan," Doug said finally, "is that we won't win if this is all we do."

There was another long pause. John and I waited.

"Even if we manage to convince Americans that he is competent," Doug said. "Even if we convince people that he is compassionate. That he has great integrity. That he is the right kind of leader for these times. Even if we do all of those things and at the same time manage to pop the Carter balloon, we still haven't done enough."

Doug paused again. I suddenly knew what he was going to say. How could I have spent all day, working over this plan, and not once seen the gaping hole in it?

"What is he going to do for us in the next four years?" Doug asked matter-of-factly. He paused again.

"Certainly one part of our strategy," Doug continued, "has got to be to express a sense of vision. We've got to convey the idea that he knows where he will be leading America."

A program for the future. Certainly some of our advertising had to provide some kind of program for the next four years. I wondered idly if the President did have a program.

John thought we should come up with a summary phrase for the program. He talked about some political labels that had worked, New Deal, Fair Deal, New Frontier, Great Society.

"I think the phrase should reflect the Bicentennial spirit," Doug said. "So far no leadership in America, political or otherwise, has turned the Bicentennial year into a launching pad for future programs. We have been *ending* our first two centuries rather than *starting* our third."

"That's terrific," I said. "The President should use that in tomorrow night's speech."

"Tomorrow night's speech is etched in concrete," Doug said. "Right now he is practicing the speech in front of a TV camera. They won't let me change a word."

John and Doug had to leave. I agreed to spend the next day outlining the commercials. Doug and I decided to spend tomorrow night working on "the program for the future."

Things seemed to be moving quickly. Tonight we get a Presidential candidate. Tomorrow morning a Vice-Presidential candidate. Tomorrow night the campaign begins with the acceptance speech. Friday morning we present the campaign plan. A busy two days.

I felt that I couldn't leave Kansas City without going to the convention at least once, and clearly tonight was my only chance. I called a friend of mine, Len Zelick, a veteran of innumerable politi-

cal wars. He was in town with the Massachusetts delegation. He and
I agreed to meet in the Press Bar just outside Kemper Arena.

The Press Bar was run by the American Railroad Association. It
was an enormous tent, with pictures of railroad trains hanging on the
canvas. It was packed with reporters. I found Lenny at the bar,
chatting with a publicity man from the Railroad Association.

The publicity man laughed when Lenny told him I was in
advertising.

"Advertising!" he sneered. "Who needs advertising?" He waved
his arm across the room full of beer-drinking reporters. "I get better
than a million bucks' worth of advertising just by giving these guys
free beers."

I wasn't going to argue with him. After a couple of free beers I felt
that the American Railroad Association was one helluva fine organization.

The convention, to me, was a piercing blast of plastic horns. I
entered Kemper Arena just as Ronald Reagan's name was being
placed in nomination. I left half an hour later. The Reagan delegates
were still dancing and shouting on the convention floor. The horns
were still blowing in my ear when I arrived back at the Crown Center
Hotel to watch the vote on television.

I felt sorry for the Reagan people. They cared so much. Their
demonstration was an expression of frustration as much as exuber-
ance. No, it wasn't spontaneous. It was staged, timed, orchestrated.
As they screamed and yelled for Reagan, I could see their eyes
constantly darting towards the television cameras trained on them
from above. But their enthusiasm for a lost cause was real. You
couldn't see it through a television camera. But you could clearly see
it in the arena by the way their fat cheeks puffed out, and their faces
turned crimson, when they blew those awful plastic horns. By the
anger in their eyes when they chanted "We Want Reagan!" This was
no long, loud cheer for Ronald Reagan. This was a long, loud scream
of dismay over the defeat of the conservative movement for at least
another four years.

I didn't like any of these yelling, banner-waving people. There
wasn't one of them that I'd ever want to sit down and have a beer
with. Especially the old woman with fat arms who was wearing a
giant "AGNEW" button on her pendulous breast. And the Texas
delegation, in their ten-gallon hats, trying to lead a snake dance
around the floor. I didn't like one of them. But I had to admire their
spirit. I would have stayed to the bitter end of their demonstration if
it hadn't been for those damn horns.

15

THE PRESIDENT'S
SPEECH

I have been involved in just enough political campaigns to know that, in politics, nothing should come as a surprise.

But when I heard that Robert Dole was going to be the Vice-Presidential nominee, I was surprised.

I also felt rather foolish. When I went back to the hotel after my brief visit to the arena, I got what I thought was a play-by-play description of the Vice-Presidential battle. The President was meeting in his suite with seven people: Bob Teeter, Stu Spencer, Nelson Rockefeller, Melvin Laird, Jack Marsh (a member of the White House staff), Bryce Harlow, an old friend of the President's, and a vice-president of Procter and Gamble.

In the early hours, Ronald Reagan seemed to be in the lead. This amazed me. And though I could clearly see the political advantages, it apalled me, too. Around midnight, the President apparently met with Reagan. After that, the Reagan rumors stopped abruptly. Baker, Scranton, and Ruckelshaus became the names that popped up most often. Then it seemed to boil down to Baker and Ruckelshaus. The only question seemed to be whether or not Baker's personal problems were serious enough to force a decision that would have Doug Bailey dancing in the street with joy. Dole? Hardly a word.

I called Mimi that night and gave her a hot inside tip. It was either Baker or Ruckelshaus, but bet the family fortune on Ruckelshaus. She, of course, told *her* friends. That's how political rumors get started. That's how reliable those "reliable sources close to the President" are.

Doug called me in the morning with the news that Robert Dole had been picked at nine A.M. after an all-night session. Apparently some Southern conservatives made heavy threats during the early hours of the morning. It must have become increasingly apparent that to hold the party together, the President should pick someone who was popular with both liberals and conservatives. Senators Griffin and Towers joined the decision-making group, and as the sun began to rise it apparently dawned on everyone that there was one man on the list whom everybody liked. Robert Dole. He had been the National Chairman. There were no great negatives. He was popular in the farm states. Both liberals and conservatives liked him. And he was very popular with the Southern wing of the party.

"Christ!" Doug said despondently. "I thought Ruckelshaus was in. I thought he had it." Doug paused. "He might help us in the West," he admitted. "And his new wife is attractive. And she's a lawyer. She could help. But I'm sick about it. We were so close."

The President announced the Dole decision on a televised news conference at noon. I didn't watch. The phone rang at twelve-thirty. It was Mimi. She wanted me to know that her friends didn't think I was too smart.

"Ought to teach you a lesson," I said. "Never listen to rumors."

I spent the rest of the day by the swimming pool, filling out the advertising plan and outlining some of the commercials I thought we'd need to execute the plan.

It still wasn't time to start writing commercials, but I couldn't resist. I had an idea. The perfect spokesman for the Ford campaign. Jimmy Stewart. Just the kind of man to tell America about the kind of man President Ford is. I knew that Jimmy Stewart was a Republican. Hell, he couldn't afford not to be a Republican.

I wanted to use him as a voice-over only. Never show his face. Never say who was doing the narration. People would know. They couldn't miss that soft, folksy, convincing voice.

I wrote a one-minute commercial that opened with a film of President Ford greeting his Cabinet on his first day in the White House and ended with scenes of Americans celebrating our two-hundredth birthday. The copy was short—Jimmy Stewart talks slowly.

"You know, it wasn't a good time for this country when Jerry Ford first walked into the White House. After Vietnam, Watergate, we were pretty much torn apart. The recession. And you remember how bad inflation was two years ago.

"But when Jerry Ford walked into the White House that day, he brought something with him. A kind of . . . *genuineness* . . . something most of us had never seen before in a President of the United States.

"Well . . . we had a birthday party a few weeks ago. And we suddenly woke up to something. We were together again. We were in a good mood again. We suddenly found ourselves singing the national anthem louder . . . and prouder . . . than ever before.

"Maybe Jerry Ford didn't perform any miracles. But he helped make us proud again. And a lot of us think that's a pretty good thing."

I was well aware that my Jimmy Stewart commercial was aimed directly at people's emotions. I felt that was the right target for this election. People would be voting more with their hearts than with their minds. As I put it in my briefcase, I thought it was a good commercial.

But when I took it out of my briefcase later that evening, I suddenly realized that it was a poor commercial. I had written it as an advertising copywriter. My instinct to use Jimmy Stewart as the narrator was a copywriter's instinct. I had approached it as I might approach a commercial for Kodak or Polaroid. I heard swelling music. I saw slow dissolves and soft-focus film.

I was about to show it to John and Doug when I put it back in my briefcase. I was learning. The heavy hand of Madison Avenue had to be kept out of this campaign. No tricks. They'd spot our tricks a mile away. I'd use the *hand* of Madison Avenue, maybe. The *deft* hand. But not the heavy hand.

Once again I had only a few minutes to show the plan to John. He was hurrying off to Kemper Arena. We had both crews ready to film the President's acceptance speech. He glanced quickly through my outlines of the various commercials.

"Basically it's good," he said. "But the slogan still bothers me a little."

"You don't think people will buy the fact that he's made us proud again?"

"How about 'He *helped* make us proud again,' " suggested John.

"I think we should make it active," I said. "He's helping to make us proud again."

"It sounds awkward. Why don't you and Doug work on it." He paused in the doorway. "One other thing. You have President Ford talking directly into the camera. I don't think we can pull that off. He's just not relaxed looking at a camera. I think we should film him with groups of people, farmers, workers, old people. He's terrific with people. He's warm with people. He freezes in front of a camera."

That's one of the things I'd been afraid of. A lousy actor for a candidate. One more cross to bear.

"And another thing we should put into the plan," John said, sticking his head back around the door. "Momentum. We should be prepared to take full advantage of our momentum during the final week of the campaign. We'll need a special five-minute commercial for the last week. Sheer momentum. That's when we'll be catching him. The last week."

He was gone again. I admired his optimism. I made a note to put momentum into the plan.

Doug arrived in our Crown Center headquarters about ten minutes later. We decided to watch President Ford's acceptance speech on Stu Spencer's television set, while we wrote President Ford's program for the next four years.

Doug was still deeply depressed over the Vice-Presidential choice, and he didn't try to hide his feelings.

"Every time I think about it, I feel like crying," he said. "Bill was so close. He could have won it for us."

We had dinner sent up. It occurred to me that I hadn't had a normal meal in a long time. It also occurred to me that I probably wouldn't be having any normal meals for the next two and a half months.

We watched the convention while we were eating. More Rockefeller hi-jinks came on the screen.

"He's stoned," I said.

"No," said Doug, "just relieved."

We listened to several uninspired speeches as Dole's name was placed in nomination.

"That's not my speech," Doug said. "But then mine wouldn't fit the nominee."

When the vote finally began, we turned off the set and got down to work.

"I have a name for the program," Doug said. "How do you like 'A New Generation of Freedom'?"

I thought about it. I ran it around my mind a few times. "I don't know," I admitted finally. "If someone had said 'Great Society' to me, I'd probably have said it sounded like sheer bullshit. But it worked for Johnson."

"I think the word 'Freedom' is essential," Doug said. "A new statement on what the Fourth of July was really all about."

"How about a new *Dimension* of freedom?" I suggested.

"Dimension," Doug said thoughtfully. "I'm not sure which I like better. Dimension. Or Generation."

"I'm not sure it makes any difference," I said.

"Not now it doesn't," Doug said. "But what if Kennedy's people had decided to use *Threshold* instead of *Frontier*? How would 'New Threshold' look in the history books?"

I thought about it. "Generation," I said finally. "It will be easier for schoolchildren to remember."

"Now," said Doug, "all we have to do is figure out what it is."

"It's our man-of-vision strategy. To make sure that President Ford doesn't go down in history as the man who vetoed the school lunch program."

"What do you want?" said Doug, pounding the table. "Vision or compassion? You can't have both."

"One small question," I said, opening my Pentab and getting ready to go to work. "Does he actually *have* any programs for the future?"

"As a matter of fact, he does," said Doug. "Scattered programs—without any real direction. A fine national parks concept. A plan to expand home ownership. A program to cut government departments in half. There's plenty of existing stuff we can use. Lots of stuff we can recommend. If we have the umbrella, the organizing concept, we have a whole government full of experts who can come up with the programs to put under it."

"I liked what you said yesterday," I said. "We've been ending our first two centuries rather than starting our third. I think that should be in our preamble."

"Right," Doug said. "Capture the mood of the Bicentennial. Turn that mood into a modest call for a commitment to the future. A New Generation of Freedom."

"It's beginning to sound good," I said.

"Freedom is a process that must be continually renewed," Doug said. He is a speech writer. At times like these he sometimes talks like one of his speeches. "The revolutionaries of 1776 won independence. But it took another one hundred years to end slavery. Still another one hundred years to give blacks any real opportunity. Jefferson, Lincoln, Roosevelt. They all talked about this constant process of freedom's renewal. If there ever was a time to talk about it, it's right now, in our Bicentennial year. And if Ford talks about a New Generation of Freedom, while Carter is still reminding us of the New Deal, we'll win the election."

I'd been jotting down Doug's remarks, knowing I could use them in the plan. I wanted to get him back on his imaginary platform again, delivering his speech.

"What will we call on America to do?" I asked.

Doug began to pace the floor very slowly, very thoughtfully . . . three steps . . . turn . . . three steps . . . turn.

"The New Generation of Freedom" . . . turn . . . "will call on America to" . . . turn . . . "free our women from unequal laws" . . . turn . . . "free our unemployed from dependence" . . . turn . . . "free our aging from inflation" . . . turn. He stopped. Evidently the ideas had stopped as well.

"Free the people from crime?" I suggested.

He started pacing again. "Free our law-abiding from crime" . . . turn . . . "free our farmers from restrictions" . . . turn . . . "free our taxpayers from bureaucracy" . . . turn . . . "free our families from war." He stopped again.

"We're not *at* war," I reminded him.

"Maybe that is stretching the umbrella a bit," he admitted. "But," he continued, starting to pace again, "we can use this on political issues as well. We can free Congress from reflex spenders. We can free the voters from deception."

"We can free our children from forced busing," I added. "We can free our sportsmen from gun controls."

"We can free the White House from peanut farmers," Doug announced triumphantly.

"We may be missing the speech," I said. I flipped on the television set.

"*This* should be the speech," Doug said.

"I'll write it up and put it in the plan," I said. "It can be his *next* speech."

There was a Reagan delegate on the screen, shouting angrily. He was demanding that his delegation be polled. It was such a meaningless gesture that I immediately suspected the worst.

"Christ!" I said to Doug. "The bastards are sabotaging the President's speech. They're going to delay until we've lost prime time. I thought we paid their ransom when the President picked Dole."

"I think the man just wants to get on television," Doug said calmly.

There were more delays, and to me they seemed highly suspicious. It was eleven-thirty before the film was introduced.

Up until now, all I knew about the convention film was that it was a production miracle. Someone had decided, shortly before John,

Doug, and I had been contacted, that there ought to be a film of the President shown at the convention. Jimmy Carter had had a film. It had been a powerful film. Therefore, we should have one, too. There was only one trouble with the idea. There hadn't been any time to make the film. That hadn't stopped the President's men, however. Two weeks before the convention they called Ed Spiegel, a documentary filmmaker. He told them that it was an impossible job, but he finally agreed to fly in from the coast, assemble a crew, and do his best.

He had spent two days taping the President and his family at Camp David. He had spent another two days taping various Cabinet officers in the White House. He spent another day taping the President at work. He accumulated miles and miles of tape, some of it usable.

Editing tape, someone once said, is like giving birth to a Franklin stove. Ed Spiegel had worked around the clock for a solid week giving birth to a twenty-minute Franklin stove. The effort had cost the President Ford committee its last $120,000. The finished product arrived at the three networks by courier a couple of hours before air time. A cassette of the unfinished version had arrived in Kansas City, for the President to see, in the afternoon. John Deardourff had seen it in New York three days earlier, and had been able to make a few minor changes based on political considerations.

Now seventy million Americans were going to see it. It was the real kick-off of our campaign. As the film started, I was one of the most interested spectators in the country.

When it was over, I breathed an immense sigh of relief. Okay. It hadn't been colossal. There were jump cuts. Some scenes were too long. Some scenes were too corny. But it was a warm, enlightening twenty minutes. We met the President. We met his family. We had a better understanding of the problems he had faced as President. We learned about his accomplishments. We saw what kind of leader he was. Ed Spiegel had done one helluva job. The campaign was off to a good start.

The delegates apparently liked the film too. They cheered for three or four minutes when it was over.

As the cheering subsided, I became aware of the time again. It was nearly midnight. Kansas City time. That meant it was nearly one o'clock in the East. Our most important market would be sleeping through our most important speech.

Finally the band struck up "Hail to the Chief." There was the President, walking down the aisle, waving to the cheering delegates. The band swung into "The Michigan Fight Song." The delegates cheered louder. The President waved with both arms.

The demonstration looked sincere on television. A united party. There were some wonderful cut-away shots of the Ford children, cheering happily, and of Betty Ford smiling proudly. There was a shot of Reagan, pretending to applaud. His palms weren't quite touching. His wife was looking brave. And there was an interesting shot of John Connally scratching his nose.

When the President finally quieted the crowd, he waded right into his speech. His voice sounded strong. He looked tanned and healthy. Right from the start, he was clearly in command of himself and the audience. Best of all, the camera angles were perfect, especially the tight close-up of his profile that revealed tiny beads of perspiration glistening in the Klieg lights.

He talked about his family, and his voice broke almost imperceptibly when he mentioned Betty. It was real. He couldn't have possibly rehearsed that honest little catch in his voice. America wouldn't miss that, I thought.

Doug had been slouched in his chair, obviously fearing the worst. Before the President had started he had turned to me and said quietly, "This is either the end of the campaign or the beginning. One or the other." Now I saw him straighten up in his chair.

"This evening I am proud to stand before this convention as the first incumbent President since Dwight D. Eisenhower who can tell the American people: America is at peace!" He said it proudly. The convention erupted.

Then the President looked up meaningfully from his text and stared at the camera as though he were staring directly into Jimmy Carter's eyes. He challenged Carter to debate him. The convention erupted again, at twice the previous volume. Doug and I found ourselves cheering. The announcer was telling us that this hadn't been in the text that had been released to the press.

No sooner had the President restored order in the arena, than he had them back on their feet again.

"This nation is on the march to full economic recovery and a better quality of life for *all* Americans!"

Doug was sitting straight up, almost on the edge of his chair. "My God," he whispered. "He sounds *good.*" Doug sounded amazed.

The President made a few necessary party-unifying remarks, then hit his stride again.

"You at home, listening tonight—you are the people who pay the taxes and obey the laws. You are the people who make our system work. You are the people who make America what it is. It is from your ranks that I come, and on your side that I stand.''

He said it with such ringing conviction that my only wish was that so many of those Americans weren't asleep.

Then he swung into the preamble to our ''Generation of Freedom.'' At least that's how it sounded to my startled ears.

''Something wonderful happened to this country of ours these past two years. We all came to realize it on the Fourth of July.

''Together, out of years of turmoil and tragedy, of wars and riots, assassinations and wrongdoing in high places, Americans recaptured the spirit of 1776. We saw again the pioneer vision of our revolutionary founders and of our immigrant ancestors. Their vision was of free men and free women enjoying limited government and unlimited opportunity.

''The mandate I want in 1976 is to make that vision a reality.''

Doug and I looked at each other. What an opening. What a moment to announce new programs for a New Generation of Freedom. But it was too much to ask. The President was talking now about needing more than Republican votes to make his mission possible. The moment was lost.

The President had them on their feet again a minute later.

''So tonight it is not the power and glamor of the Presidency that leads me to ask for another four years. It is something every hardworking American will understand. The challenge of a job well begun, but far from finished.''

Doug and I, of course, were looking for segments of the speech that we could lift and use in future commercials. There had already been some good ones. But we needed something that would come right out of our strategy—something that would succinctly describe his accomplishments and demonstrate his capacity as a leader.

We soon got it.

''I faced many tough problems,'' the President said, in a magnificent close-up. ''I probably made some mistakes, but on balance America and Americans have made an incredible comeback since August 1974.

''And the plain truth is that the great progress we have made at home and abroad was in spite of the majority who run the Congress.

''For two years I have stood for all the people against the vote-hungry, free-spending congressional majority!

''Fifty-five times I vetoed extravagant and unwise legislation. Forty-four times I made those vetoes stick! Those vetoes have saved American taxpayers billions and billions of dollars!''

This was music to my ears. He was coming out fighting. The

delegates went wild. We had another Harry Truman. And hell . . . Harry Truman hadn't even been a football player. Ford continued his slashing attack on Congress. The delegates loved it. I loved it. With every well-constructed phrase he was sharpening the image I'd have to work with for the next two and a half months. Even the clichés sounded strong.

"As Governor Al Smith used to say: Let's look at the record.

"We are in the full surge of a sound recovery to steady prosperity.

"My record is one of progress, not platitudes; specifics, not smiles; performance, not promises."

"We will build an America where people feel rich in spirit as well as in worldly goods. We will build an America where people will feel proud about themselves and about their country."

It didn't even sound like a cliché when he slid into the most over-worked oratorical gambit of them all. The "I see an America" speech.

"As I try, in my imagination, to look into all the homes where families are watching," he said softly, "I can't tell which faces are Republicans, which are Democrats and which are Independents. "I cannot see their color or their creed. I see only Americans. . . . "

He went on to see just about the same America Nixon had seen in his last acceptance speech, and that Carter had seen in his acceptance speech just a month earlier.

"My fellow Americans," Ford concluded, "I like what I see; I have no fear for the future of this great country."

The crowd erupted. Horns bleated. Placards were waved. And now, thanks to the magic of overnight printing, all the placards said FORD AND DOLE. After ten minutes of jubilant demonstration, the balloons were released. Hundreds, thousands of red, white, and blue balloons went soaring towards the ceiling of the immense arena. I was delighted.

"My God, balloons!" I said to Doug. "Somehow they found the money for the balloons!"

"Yes," said Doug very seriously. "But something even more important has happened tonight. We may have lost a Vice-President. But we have gained a President."

part four

Instant Madison Avenue

16

TWO
FOUR-LETTER WORDS

In Kansas City I had naively thought of the coming campaign as a marketing problem. A very difficult marketing problem. In my mind I saw the Gallup poll, the Harris poll, the Yankelovich poll, and the Teeter polls as sales figures. I saw a long chart stretching from September to November. I pictured a red line labeled Carter and a blue line labeled Ford. There was a wide gap between the two lines in the beginning. In fact Carter's red line was thirty-three little squares above Ford's blue line. The problem, as I saw it, was simply to move our blue line steadily upwards until it crossed the red line at the point marked November second.

That's how little I knew of Presidential elections. If my mind had conjured up an accurate picture, it would have been of two roller coasters standing side by side. And I would have seen two little cars straining upwards and whooshing downwards for two long and giddy months. There would be nothing steady. There would be nothing predictable. And all along the way you would feel that you had very little control over this particular ride.

My ride started at a high point, with all the delegates still stomping their feet, waving their banners, and yelling for Ford on TV. It took an immediate little dip just as I turned the set off.

I had fully expected to stay up the rest of the night finishing the plan. I wanted to include several pages on the "New Generation of Freedom" program. I wanted to outline some more commercials.

And Doug and I had already decided that we should include ways to get more mileage out of the great speech the President had made. The finished document would surely run over thirty-five pages, and I would have to spend the rest of the night making it presentable. Our meeting with the President had been scheduled for ten o'clock in the morning, the last order of business before he flew off to Vail.

Bob Teeter walked into our room as soon as I switched off the set.

"I have some good news and some bad news," he said to Doug and me. "The good news is that you can get some sleep tonight. The plan won't have to be ready until Monday. The President just won't have time to see it here in Kansas City. You'll have to show it to him in Vail."

For me that was particularly bad news. I had intended to fly to Washington to start hiring the people and setting up the facilities that were essential if we were going to carry through the plan. And long ago I had scheduled a vital meeting with the president of Dutch Boy Paint for that Monday. Had I thought my presence in Colorado was important to anything but my own ego, I probably would have stood up the president of Dutch Boy for the President of the United States. But I knew that John and Doug wouldn't really need me in Vail. I chose business over pleasure.

Disappointing, but it turned out to be a wise choice. John and Doug spent the entire week in Vail. The plan was finally approved, almost as written. But while they were working in Vail, I was pretty busy. I was creating an instant advertising agency.

John had told me that Campaign '76 consisted of an empty floor in Washington, D.C. That was not accurate. It wasn't a floor, and it wasn't empty.

Campaign '76 had been assigned about a quarter of the tenth floor of a very ordinary-looking modern office building in downtown Washington that housed the President Ford Committee. Many of the people who had been doing the advertising through the primary were still there, and they had just learned that Campaign '76 was now under new management.

There were about fifteen people sitting in various offices, trying to look busy, when I walked in with Phil Angell, who was supposed to look after things for John and Doug while they were in Vail. We introduced ourselves. Everybody was very friendly. One of them had just read in *Advertising Age* that I was the new creative director, but he obviously wasn't ready to believe it until he heard something official. As far as they knew, Rogers Morton was still the chairman, and nobody could find Rogers Morton.

Phil and I did the best we could. All the large offices were taken, so we settled into two tiny offices without doors. And then we started to interview the existing employees of Campaign '76. We had no official capacity. But somehow we managed to get through all the interviews without being thrown out on our ears. By the end of the day, we decided that we had an exceptional media department, headed by Dawn Sibley, who was on leave of absence from Bates Advertising. We found that we had another essential member of the team, a skilled and competent treasurer named Barry Lafer. When you're handling twelve million dollars in two months and know that your books are going to be scrutinized down to the last decimal point by congressional committees, the Federal Election Commission, the Democratic Party, Jimmy Carter, and the press, you need a good treasurer.

I had made two decisions about the creative department before I went to Washington. I didn't want any of the people who had worked in the primary to work in the final campaign. I figured they would be stale and opinionated. More importantly, I hated the commercials they had created. I had also decided to put together the smallest possible creative team. The fewer people, I figured, the fewer problems.

I never broke my second rule. But I broke my first rule when I met Jack Frost.

Jack Frost had been an art director on the Campaign '76 staff throughout the primary. He had even worse credentials than that. He had worked in the last Nixon campaign. I had sworn to myself that under no conditions would any of the Nixon people be on my staff. I didn't care if they *had* won, and they had been professionals, and they had never met the man. They were all guilty by association as far as I was concerned.

But Jack Frost quickly changed my mind. You just can't think of Nixon when you're looking at a man who reminds you of an out-of-season Santa Claus. He had a nice white moustache, a roundish belly, and a jovial expression. He had been with J. Walter Thompson, and I suspected that he'd been reluctantly let out to pasture when a young new head art director decided he didn't "fit into his plans." He seemed younger than his years, and he was calm—that was important. Clearly he was a man who would not get hysterical when I asked him to do impossible things. I decided to keep him. And I decided I was going to have to ask him to start doing impossible things that very day.

One of the first things I had learned at Campaign '76 headquarters was that little creative thinking had been done since the primaries ended. As a result, the President of the United States was the only candidate running for public office in 1976 who had not yet begun work on his posters, brochures, buttons, and bumper stickers.

I didn't know whether all those things actually got any votes, but I did know that a Presidential campaign just wouldn't be a Presidential campaign without them. I also knew that state chairmen all over the country were screaming for their buttons, bumper stickers, etc.

Designing the "look" of a Presidential campaign, and all the campaign paraphernalia, is not a small job. It took the firm of Lippincott and Margulies one year to design the new logo for NBC. The logo cost almost a million dollars.

I asked Jack Frost to design the Ford campaign in one night. The cost was five dollars—for paper and glue.

Bob Dole may not have been the best thing that ever happened to President Ford, but he was the best thing that could have happened to Jack Frost. If Bill Ruckelshaus had been named the Vice-Presidential candidate, he might still be working on the bumper design.

My advice to Jack on the Ford-Dole design was very simple. "Just give me a dignified treatment of two four-letter words."

Within half an hour he was back in my office with his first design. He had placed Ford against a blue background, Dole against a red background. It was a simple, uncluttered design. Dignified. Presidential. He had put the candidates' names in an italic face. He said he thought the slant of the letters gave the feeling of a team that was moving America forward.

I told him that I didn't think people wanted to move forward this year. They wanted to stand still. I asked him to try putting the letters straight up and down. He did. And that's all there was to it. We had the Ford-Dole campaign look.

Jack sat hunched over his drawing board most of that night, and through most of the next day. Before my second day in Washington was over, I had complete mechanicals for all the basic campaign materials that we would need. Letterheads. Press release forms. Three full-color posters in two different sizes. One showing the President alone. One with the President and Betty. One with Ford and Dole. Banners. Bumper stickers. Two buttons in three different sizes. One with both names, one with just "FORD." And a basic brochure headlined, "He's making us proud again." Jack had designed everything around the same, simple, bold, red-white-and-blue Ford-Dole look. It was good design. It was good communication. A job that would have taken a large design firm a month to do, a job that would have taken an advertising agency about two months to do, was complete, ready for the printer, in fewer than twenty-four hours. In fact the only part of the package that wasn't ready was my part. The words.

I turned to the typewriter and within an hour I had the copy that would soon be stamped out of a giant press twenty million times. I wanted to squeeze as much of our strategy as I could into a very small space. I wrote short sentences about his accomplishments, about his leadership quality, about his plans for the future. I wanted it set in large, readable type. I put the theme line on the cover, then repeated it inside the brochure.

He's making us proud again.

A bitter, depressed, vulnerable America has become a confident, strong, proud America.

Inflation has been cut in half.

Prosperity has returned.

Our jobs are secure.

We are at peace.

The world respects us again.

We trust our own government again.

President Ford has started something great.

Now he needs your support to finish a job well begun.

He wants to beat inflation.

He wants to balance the budget.

He wants to return control of our children's education to parents and local school authorities.

He wants to insure jobs for every worker.

He wants to keep prosperity surging.

He wants to keep America strong—and at peace.

He wants to continue to stand for the people against a free-spending Congress.

He wants to build a fairer tax structure.

He wants to build a new dimension of freedom that will allow all Americans to share equally in all the advantages of a free society.

He took on the toughest job in the world—at one of the toughest times in our history.

He proved that he's tough enough to get the job done.

He asked for your prayers in one of our darkest hours.

He asks for your support in one of our brightest hours.

17

A NEW LOW FOR NIELSON

The roller coaster was already beginning to pick up speed. Between September second and September ninth we surged upwards in the polls at a rate none of us had anticipated, and that I could hardly believe. There didn't seem to be any reason for it. Had the President's speech been *that* good? Before I could savor the joy of it, the little car tipped, and my emotions started screaming down again. They hit the low point the night I threw my shoe at the evening news.

All through the ride, I was having my own little ups and downs in Campaign '76. Things were looking up when I rounded out the creative team with three writers. Bob Gardner quit a high-paying creative spot with J. Walter Thompson in San Francisco because he couldn't resist the campaign. Dennis Altmann got a leave of absence from Marshalk in New York. And Gene Russo was just the man I needed to write tons of special material—the ads and brochures for farm groups, Jewish groups, Catholic groups, veteran groups, etc.

They arrived just in time. Our first commercials had to be ready in three weeks. And I received a call from John in Vail informing me that the Ford Committee had bought a prime-time half hour on CBS the night of September seventh. They wanted to show a slightly shortened version of the President's speech for those who had fallen asleep the first time. It looked like another impossible job. Three working days to edit the tape, add the disclaimers, prepare an introduction, and write and place the tune-in ads that would tell people the show was going on. The impossible became possible when just the right man again wandered on to the scene. Tom Angell (no relation to Phil Angell) had been executive producer of countless tape documentaries. He had lived with the medium. He had worked with John and Doug in previous campaigns. He was hired as our executive producer, and we went immediately to work on the half-hour show.

But there was bad news for us that week, too. As I look back on it, it loomed as a piece of very bad news indeed.

Doug arrived back from Vail pleased that the overall plan had been accepted, but a little disappointed that one phase of our strategy still needed to be sold. Everyone, including the President, had seemed interested in the "New Generation of Freedom." But they weren't sure of the phrase and were uncertain about the programs they could produce to support it. Doug had made an impassioned plea for the inclusion of at least some strong program for the future in speeches and in the advertising. He could report at the time only that the idea was not enthusiastically received. He said he was not discouraged. But he didn't say it in a very encouraging way.

I found that I was having my own personal ups and downs during this early phase of the campaign. President Ford, still vacationing and plotting strategy in Vail, made an important speech about the National Parks System. Okay, I thought. Maybe the speech was designed to shore up his lousy image among conservationists. But, political or not, it committed the country to spending millions of new dollars for wilderness protection. I liked that. I liked President Ford for doing it. I also knew that he did care, personally, about protecting wilderness land. This was not a grandstand play. President Ford was going up in my eyes.

But then two days later, Bob Dole went before the American Legion. And I began to feel the faint stirrings of a moral dilemma. Dole had been following Carter around the country. Whenever Carter made a speech, Dole would appear on the same platform one day later and refute just about everything Carter had said. It was shrewd political strategy. And it was that strategy that brought Dole to the American Legion convention one day after Jimmy Carter.

Jimmy Carter had said that he would pardon all Vietnam draft resisters. He had, of course, couched his statement in his usual semantic fog bank. He said he did not believe in amnesty for the Vietnam deserters and draft resisters. But he would pardon them. The fact that there is no semantic difference between "amnesty" and "pardon" made no difference to either Carter or the Legionnaires. The word "pardon" popped out of the fog bank, and the Legionnaires booed lustily.

Dole sharpened his hatchet and struck the next day.

"No blanket pardon! No blanket amnesty! No blanket clemency!"

He shouted each sentence and the Legionnaires shouted back their approval. It made good theater, good headlines, good TV shots. The most amazing part of it all is that Carter had been right. He had figured that no one—not Dole, not any of the Legionnaires, not a single member of the press—would bother to open his dictionary and look up the difference between "amnesty" and "pardon." How he must have smiled that morning. It was the best little joke of the campaign.

My personal problem was that amnesty or pardon or any other name smelled a helluva lot sweeter to me than the Ford-Dole position. On this one issue I was solidly behind Carter, solidly against the President.

I closed the door to my office that morning (I had finally commandeered a good-sized office) and tried to rationalize my feelings. I'm not a one-issue person. I rarely agree with anyone wholeheartedly, or disagree wholeheartedly. I can think of no candidate, for any office, that I suspected of being perfect. I liked Ford's economic policies far better than Carter's. I'm scared of big government. An experience I once had at the Bureau of Motor Vehicles left me emotionally scarred for life. I liked Ford better as a person. He seemed more human to me. I decided that I could forgive him his stand on the pardon issue. I wouldn't put it in any of the ads—but I wouldn't quit the campaign in a huff either.

One of my duties, during the early days of the campaign, was to review all the ideas that had been sent to the President from well-meaning people from all over the country. We looked at every idea, and every letter was answered. At least one secretary was busy full time writing polite thank-you notes to the people who had found the secret to victory in November, and wanted to share it with us—sometimes for a fee, sometimes for a modest percentage, but usually free of charge.

When I arrived in Washington, there were two file drawers bulging with suggestions. New ideas arrived in bunches every day of the campaign.

My particular favorite—and I still wish we could have used it—was "Whistling for Ford." It was an idea submitted by a group of senior citizens from Florida. They suggested that President Ford should be seen whistling wherever he went. Before he made speeches, he should whistle a few patriotic songs. The audience would, of course, start to whistle along with him. The idea would catch fire immediately, the senior citizens assured us. Wherever Ford went, everyone would be whistling with him . . . and for him. Whistling for Ford! I loved the idea. They sent along a little tape cassette so we could hear their social group whistling patriotic songs together. It sounded terrific. I wondered if I could get them into a television commercial, standing behind the President, harmonizing with him as he whistled "God Bless America." The audience at home, of course, would be urged to whistle along. Once you've whistled for a man, you're going to vote for the man. What a campaign it would have been. On election eve we could have shown the Seven Dwarfs skipping to the voting booth, singing "Whistle While You Vote."

Most of the ideas involved music, usually patriotic music.

A few typical titles, taken at random from the files:

"Let's Put New Glory into Old Glory."
"America Forever."
"This Great Land of Ours."
"Bicentennial Marching Song" or "We The People."
"Wondrous Land."
"Miss Liberty's Prosperity Parade."
"It's the Ford Victory Plane—Everybody Aboard."
"Make the Traitors Bite the Dust."
"Forward with E-cology, Justice, and E-Quality."

All had original lyrics, and many had copyright numbers at the bottom of the page. The following is a typical lyric, variations of which could be plucked, at random, from any section of the files:

> *Forever may old glory wave*
> *O'er our valleys, hills and streams*
> *Remember Ford is steering us*
> *Down the road to all our dreams.*

I did come across one song that I thought should be used. It was submitted by Frank Sorkin, a Hollywood agent. It was called "First Mama Reggae," and he had recorded it with an orchestra and singing group.

He had apparently heard that Betty Ford sometimes used her CB radio to talk with truckers and other motorists. Betty Ford did, in fact, own a CB—and she'd generated quite a bit of good publicity with it. "First Mama Reggae" was a funny song with a great beat. I wanted to use it on California radio, and if it caught on, I was ready to put it on youth stations across the country. I was overruled. Apparently the President didn't think it was quite dignified enough. Here's the lyric:

FIRST MAMA REGGAE

I heard de First Mama
She got a new CB
Dat is really something
It's marvelous to me.

Now I got to go get me one
And won't it be just grand
If I can talk to the first Mama
It's like talking to the man.

I got to tell that woman
To tell to her old man
I think he's doin a real hard job
The hardes job in the land.

I'm a United States American
I'm really proud to be
I don't care who the President is
He's gonna get support from me.

I got to tell the First Mama
I dig it very much
I like de way dat de First Family
They really keep in touch.

I'm a United States American
I'm really proud to be
I don't care who the President is
He's gonna get support from me.

(THREE TIMES . . .)

I don't care who the President is
He's gonna get support from me.

Bob Gardner and I played the song most of one day in our Washington headquarters. We had the entire staff singing along. But I never could get it on the air. I still don't know whether it was killed because it lacked dignity or because the White House people just weren't quite comfortable with that line in the chorus, "I don't care who the President is. . . ."

While I was setting up the agency in Washington, I was also trying to work on the half-hour show in New York and set up production facilities in New York. This involved a different sort of ups and downs. The Eastern shuttle. On one memorable day I flew to New York in the morning. Flew back to Washington for a noon meeting. Flew back to New York for more editing. Flew back to Washington again that night for a dinner meeting with John and Doug, who had just returned from Vail.

Compared with the schedule of John and Doug, who were involved in nine other campaigns, that was a relatively calm day.

I spent three days with Tom Angell, working on the show that nobody watched: the half-hour rerun of the President's speech. The show managed to achieve the lowest ratings of any network half-hour show that was aired in 1976. Quite an achievement. A tribute to America's interest in old campaign speeches. The effort cost the Ford Committee a little more than $100,000 for time and production. You could have doubled that if you figured in the cost of the nervous energy expended by Tom Angell.

When Tom edits tape he resembles a nervous bullfighter. He dances around the editing room, waving his arms. He shouts. He points. He throws himself into chairs despondently. He suddenly leaps up from chairs ecstatically. It's not showmanship. It's tape editing. Man against machine. A thinking human being who knows what he wants versus an unthinking electronic device that doesn't want to give him what he wants.

Our problem wasn't just to squeeze a fifty-minute speech into a half-hour show. Our problem was that half of the speech was on film and half on tape. We had to make the live, liquid look of tape match the objective, documentary look of film. We had to change the "cut-away" shots. The networks liked to cut away to people picking their noses while the President was speaking. We had to substitute shots of serious Americans listening in rapture to the President's words. We had to decide which parts of the speech were expendable, knowing we'd offend someone important no matter what parts we cut. And because we were working with film and tape from four different cameras, we had to decide which angle was the best angle for every scene in the show.

The final editing was done in a room that looked like the Apollo Command Center. There were eight TV monitors on the wall, a battery of oscilloscopes flashing their squiggly green lines, three consoles crowded with buttons to push and numbers to watch. Tom and I spent the entire night behind two engineers, ordering this scene changed, that scene cut, cutting frames, goosing the sound. All night long our ears rang to the screech of the fast forward, the cheers of the crowd, the screech of the fast reverse, the President's voice, the screech of the fast forward again.

The tone for the night was set the minute I walked into the editing room. Tom was on the telephone, talking excitedly to someone about some film that a network wouldn't release. While he was talking, he spotted a scene on one of the monitors. He leaped up from his chair to get the engineer's attention. His foot hit the edge of the table. He hurtled to the floor, yanking the telephone out of the wall.

"Are you all right?" I asked. It had been a nasty fall.

"Yes," Tom said, still trying to talk into the phone. "But some idiot cut me off!"

Eight hours later our first Ford commercial was completed. As I made my way to the hotel, by dawn's early light, I prayed fervently that they would not all be like this one.

18

TRIPPED AT
THE STARTING GATE

I was standing in an open phone booth near the Eastern shuttle, talking to Phil Angell.

"When are we going to shoot the President? . . . Thursday? . . . Good . . . Are we going to be able to shoot him in the Rose Garden?"

As I was talking I began to feel eyes on my back. I looked behind me. Several businessmen seemed to have stopped whatever it was they were doing. They were looking at me strangely. It finally dawned on me. The language of filmmaking had been overtaken by events.

Unfortunately filmmaking was about all I talked about during the early phase of the campaign. We had to make just as many commercials as we possibly could just as fast as we possibly could. That meant a division of effort between John, Doug, and me.

Doug went with one film crew to Grand Rapids to get footage for our commercial on the life of the President. He filmed just about everyone who had ever known Ford. His scoutmaster. His high school football coach. His coach at the University of Michigan. His classmates at Yale Law School. His friends. His brothers. His minister. And the man who owned the carnival where President Ford had worked one summer. According to Doug, the man clearly couldn't remember young Jerry Ford. But that didn't stop him from talking for half an hour about what "a fine lad" he had been.

Meanwhile John was with a second film crew, filming Betty Ford and the children. I had to be in New York, setting up editing facilities and turning the miles of film into commercials.

Before going to New York I spent half a day prowling the White House, looking for the best locations for filming several different informal chats with the President. After visiting the first few rooms, I understood why Betty Ford had described the place as "kind of a scary house."

I couldn't have conjured up a more fitting description. I found the White House to be the coldest place I'd ever visited. Before I had seen only the offices. Now I was in the main living quarters. They seemed far less lived-in than the offices. There wasn't a touch of humanity anywhere to be seen. Even the picture of Betty, behind the President's desk in the Oval Office, looked like a prop.

We finally decided to do the filming in a small corner on the West Portico, next to the Rose Garden, and against a bookcase in the Oval Office. We would have to rearrange the furniture to make the President look comfortable in that shot.

John and I then discussed the President's wardrobe. He remembered how comfortable the President had looked in Vail. We decided to film him in pretty much the same outfit, open-neck sports shirt, cashmere sweater, comfortable slacks.

We were looking for one last place to put the sofa when two large Secret Service men entered the Oval Office. They wanted to know what the hell we were doing there. Fortunately Terry O'Donnell, the appointments secretary, arrived in time to straighten the matter out. He escorted us out one door as the President and Henry Kissinger entered another.

I felt thwarted again. I'd still seen my client only in corridors. John said he would have stayed and introduced me (he and the President had gotten along well in Vail), but the President looked preoccupied.

I understood why when I saw the news that night. Kissinger was off on his African shuttle. He'd had his final briefing with the President that afternoon. I wondered if he had noticed that one of the couches was askew.

The next day I flew to New York to start turning film into commercials. We needed editors. We needed a nice warm place to edit. And we needed a genius who could handle the incredible logistics of shipping thousands of tapes to thousands of different television stations almost every night from September twenty-third (our first air date) to the end of the campaign.

John and Doug already had the editor they wanted to work with, a man named Ed Deitch. They recommended him highly, but said if I didn't think he could handle the work load of the Ford campaign, I was to get my own chief editor.

Ed Deitch's offices were located in an apartment building on Eighth Avenue, surrounded by porn movie houses and massage parlors. The mugging capital of the world. As I rode the elevator up to his office I thought about going home from here late at night after a long editing session. I wondered how many of us would still be alive on November second.

He was editing some footage from Kansas City when I entered his office. After introducing myself, I stood behind him and watched him work. It's the only way to judge an editor. He was hunched over a Steenbeck with a cigarette stuck firmly between his lips. A Steenbeck is an editing table the size of a single bed. It is the best way to edit 16-millimeter film. You thread the film roll through one series of rollers and sprockets and attach it to a reel at the other end of the table. You do the same thing to the sound roll, attaching it to another reel. Synchronize the sound, and the film rolls; flip a switch, and the picture appears in a screen the size of a small TV set, while the sound is played through a loudspeaker. You splice and cut right on the table.

It took me only a few minutes to realize that Eddie Deitch was a master of the Steenbeck. He was the fastest editor I had ever seen. And I was soon to learn something more important: he had as much taste and judgment as I had ever seen in a film editor.

We had our editor. And he assured me that he had four excellent assistants who were ready to start work immediately.

Now all we needed was the logistics genius. And that was easy. He was already on board. He had worked on Ford's primary campaign. His name was Bob Winkler. He owned Winkler Video, New York's largest post-production house. He knew more about post-production logistics than anyone in the city. Once we had finished making our commercials, we could forget them. He would make sure they got to the stations on time—somehow.

Winkler is a short, dapper man with a neat white moustache. He just looks as though he can get just about anything you need. What we needed most was a better place to work than Ed Deitch's place.

"I'm glad you happened to ask," said Winkler. "I have a large, empty office in a penthouse on Forty-second Street and Second Avenue. I can give you five separate editing rooms, complete video tape editing facilities, and four comfortable offices where you can work. I have a receptionist there too."

The next day we were in business. Six Steenbecks were moved, reassembled, and ready to go. A smiling Eddie Deitch was surveying his new domain, and issuing orders to his four assistants. Bob Gardner, Dennis Altmann, and I were pounding away at our brand-new rented typewriters. Tom Angell was playing with the videotape editing equipment. A receptionist was taking our calls. Couriers were beginning to arrive with cans of film from around the country.

We still had thirteen days before our first real commercial was scheduled to hit the airwaves. Plenty of time. We had closed to within eight points of Carter. We were rolling.

Mimi and I had settled into a nice room at the Gramercy Park Hotel. Quaint—but nice. All was well with the world. Until I turned on the seven o'clock news. That was the night I threw my shoe at Robert Dole. He was denying any knowledge of an illegal campaign gift from Gulf Oil.

I had no idea whether or not he was guilty of the charge. I have been in enough political campaigns to feel that a charge like that is likely to be leveled against anyone who has ever run for office, Republican or Democrat. Guilty or innocent, damage has been done when the charge is made. And I could feel the damage that this had done. We were just getting our momentum up. For the first time, I was beginning to see a shot at victory in November. And then this. I threw my shoe so hard it's a wonder the television set didn't break.

part five

Feelin' Good

19

DISCOVERING THE REAL GERALD FORD

I had received two good pieces of advice about making commercials for President Ford.

The first came from my mother. She called me from Vermont when she read in a Boston paper that I was going to be made creative director of Ford's advertising.

"Don't try to make him into something he isn't," Mother advised. "What he is is plenty good enough for most people."

The second piece of advice came from Crocker Snow, Jr., chief editorial writer for the *Boston Globe* and a neighbor of mine in Gloucester.

"Don't try to make him into something he isn't," he advised. "Nobody will believe you."

I tried hard to keep that advice. And it wasn't the easiest thing in the world to convey the real President Ford.

I had never even met the man when I began editing his commercials. I had been in the same room with him on three or four occasions. But I had never talked with him face to face. The only clues to what he was like came from John and Doug, who had spent a week with him in Vail. "Considerate." "Friendly." "Outgoing." "Warm." "Great guy."

Then I spent four days with him in an editing room. For about nine hours a day I watched him through the little screen on the Steenbeck. I listened to him talk about his boyhood. I watched his eyes as he talked about each member of his family. I watched and listened as he retold stories I'd heard before—about his days as a football hero, about his years in the Navy, about working his way through Yale Law School, about his early years in Congress, about what it felt like to get a call from the President and suddenly realize that you are the Vice-President and next in line. I watched and listened and replayed it over and over again as he talked about the kind of President he thought he was, the kind of leadership he thought he could offer America, the concerns he had for the future, the accomplishments that he was most proud of since he had taken office.

After a while I stopped seeing him as an image on a screen and started seeing him as a man.

Of course he had known that the cameras were there. He was talking for the benefit of the cameras. And many of the things he said he had undoubtedly said before in countless interviews. But the most interesting thing was not the smoothness of his dialogue but the uncertainty, the awkwardness of his dialogue.

It was the uncertainty, the awkwardness, the embarrassing pauses, the "errs" and the "ummms" and the "er-ahs" that made him seem more sincere than any political candidate that I had ever seen.

As I watched him speak, I began to wish that there was some way we could put him on television just as he was, with all the "errs" and all the "umms" and all the "er-ahs." I wished that I could show him dropping his pipe in midsentence as he did in one scene. I wished I could show him fumbling for words and fumbling for matches. Because it was *so damn genuine*. There was not a trace of glibness, not a touch of rehearsed sophistication, no suggestion of deception.

But I knew, of course, that it was impossible. The electorate would point and laugh at an unedited Ford commercial. The press would hoot and howl right on the front page. Chevy Chase would do a one-hour special on the Ford commercials.

That's the trouble with us. We say we want an honest President. But do we really want an honest President? Or do we want a terrific actor who can *play* an honest President?

And so we began editing. By the time the campaign was over, Ed Deitch had an entire reel of Presidential "umms," Presidential "errs," Presidential "erumms," and long Presidential pauses that he had clipped and cut in our month of filmmaking.

When you think about it, it's an interesting souvenir of an American Presidential election.

20

SOMETIMES A MAN'S FAMILY SAYS A LOT ABOUT THE MAN

A normal advertiser, with a ten-million-dollar budget, makes anywhere from three to five commercials that will run throughout the year. Many advertisers will run their commercials two or three years.

But there was nothing normal about us. We made fifty different TV commercials. And they all ran during one five-week period.

Our production costs were about three-quarters of a million dollars, very low by industry standards, and incredibly low when you consider the fact that we had to pay overtime rates for studios, labs and taping facilities. It costs about twenty-five thousand dollars to make an average thirty-second product commercial. We made sixty-second commercials and five-minute commercials for less than ten-thousand dollars apiece.

Why did we make so many? Because we had so many different things to say.

We had proposed six different packages of commercials in the plan that had been approved by the President. And we followed the plan pretty much to the letter.

We made five five-minute commercials. The Ford Family . . . A Biography of Ford . . . Ford's Accomplishments . . . Ford the Leader . . . and "Feelin' Good," a special five-minute commercial designed to run at the end of the campaign, boosting momentum in our drive to the wire.

We made another package of sixty- and thirty-second spots featuring the President talking to different groups of people: old people, farmers, factory workers, and children.

The third package consisted of man-on-the-street interviews conducted in five different states. Out of the interviews we made nine sixty-second spots and nine thirty-second spots and dozens of radio spots.

Our fourth package consisted of regional spots. Some were on issues that affected people in key states. Others were directed to special voting groups: Mexican-Americans, Cuban-Americans, Puerto-Rican-Americans.

Our fifth package was a grab bag of sixty- and thirty-second spots, some pro-Ford, some anti-Carter.

In normal commercial production, you begin with a storyboard: frame-by-frame drawings of every major scene that will appear in the final film. You simply bring the storyboard drawings to life.

But again, there was nothing normal about our operation. We made only three storyboards in the entire campaign. Those were for thirty-second anti-Carter spots, and we needed storyboards so we could show something to our lawyers.

Our commercials were put together from existing footage, mostly with film that was made with only the broadest idea of what the finished commercial would be. We hardly ever shot from a script. In fact we hardly told people what we wanted them to say.

When the President talked about his children, he just said what he felt like saying about his children. When the people of Grand Rapids talked about their old friend and neighbor, they said whatever was on their minds. When Commander Cadwalleder talked about Ensign Ford shooting down two Jap torpedo bombers, hell, that was his story, not ours.

We wanted our commercials to have a documentary look, not a Madison Avenue look. The product was the President, after all, not a bar of soap. If the commercials weren't simple, direct, honest, believable, they would do him more harm than good.

And we didn't *need* Madison Avenue techniques. Soaps and cereals *have* to stand on their head and make funny faces. It's the only way to get your attention. But when a Presidential candidate comes on the tube, people want to watch. We had one of the best attention-getting devices an advertiser could ever have, the President of the United States.

And when we made our first five-minute commercial, we not only had the President as our star, we had his wife, his four handsome children, and his dog all playing supporting roles. How can you top that? Especially when you're creating a commercial to follow the final, tear-jerking scene of "As the World Turns."

The only problem with our "Family" commercial is that it seemed too good to be true. Bob Teeter had told us that the people out there wanted "traditional American values," and, boy, did we have them!

We had a loving father proud of his children. We had loving children proud of their father. We had a loving husband proud of his wife. We had a loving wife proud of her husband. We had your traditional golden retriever, your traditional birthday party, your traditional fatherly hug, and your traditional husbandly peck on the cheek. We even had your deep, traditional religious feelings.

We had five minutes of love, pride, respect, patriotism, and family unity set to music.

The structure was simple. We would show the President talking about one of his children, then cut to that child talking about the President as a father.

I had to write only one sentence of copy for the entire film: the opening line and the closing line. We opened with Susan hugging her father at her birthday party, and the narrator said, "Sometimes a man's family can say a lot about the man." We closed with the President kissing his wife on the cheek as the narrator repeated, "Sometimes a man's family can say a lot about the man."

Corny? No, because it wasn't contrived. And that's my answer to those who snicker at what they assume is "corny" political advertising.

In corny advertising you try to *invent* wholesome American families. You spend weeks casting for each member of the family. But no one invented the Ford family. They *are* real, they *are* wholesome.

In advertising, we pay copywriters enormous salaries to put carefully researched words in people's mouths. We pay directors exorbitant fees to make sure that the people speak those words with conviction.

No scripts were ever written for the Fords. Each member of the family said whatever he or she felt was important to be said—without direction, without cue cards, without prompting, without rehearsal.

I freely admit that the last scene of the commercial, showing the President kissing his wife on the cheek, was something of a tear-jerker. It had that extra little emotional impact that wins gold Clio awards for advertising creative people. But the fact is that there was nothing creative about it. The Fords didn't even know the camera was there. Mrs. Ford was saying a few words to a small gathering of people. In the middle of her talk, she happened to turn, pat her husband on the cheek, and say, "Thank you, Mr. President." There was nothing contrived or staged. The President just did what was natural to him. He leaned down, kissed her on the cheek, and then smiled that boyish smile. That was a real, honest-to-God moment.

We did, of course, edit most of the film in that commercial, but editing is hardly a Madison Avenue exclusive. Every picture that moves has to be edited. Eddie Deitch had to eliminate quite a few Presidential pauses. The President seemed to be particularly hesitant when he talked about his children, as if he were searching for the most appropriate words to describe each child. But Eddie Deitch was an old hand at editing politicians. "Hell," he said after smoothing out one particular rough passage, "if you think he's bad you should have seen Eisenhower. He couldn't talk at all."

Two of his children, Michael and Susan, seemed to have inherited their father's deliberate, hard-to-edit, manner of speech. Especially Michael, the divinity student. He clearly loved his father and wanted to talk about him, but it pained him to do it in front of a camera. He said some deep and touching things, but he said them in long, tortured sentences. One of the things we wanted to include was something he said about his father's religious beliefs. It was a simple enough sentence: "Mom and Dad are very religious and they believe deeply in their Lord." It took Eddie Deitch the better part of a Sunday afternoon to give that sentence a smooth reading, and bring it in within the allotted time.

Steve and Jack Ford were very articulate. We had an embarrassment of riches for Jack and several good takes of Steve. After a short battle between Doug and me, we decided to use part of a speech that Steve had given to a farm group. It looked wonderful. But it made no sense whatsoever. Steve was shown urging the farmers to vote for President Ford.

"You'll get to keep a heck of a President," he said. "And I'll get to keep a heck of a father."

"What do you suppose he means by that?" I asked Doug. "If the President loses, is he going to get another father?"

"Well," Doug said thoughtfully, "it looks so darn good and it *sounds* so darn good that nobody will stop to think about that."

I agreed.

Shortly after the "Family" film was finished, we showed it to a couple of reporters who were doing stories on Ford's advertising. I was nervous. These were two cynical members of a cynical profession. I was sure they would think that the emotional scenes were contrived. I was equally sure that they would feel that a family commercial was inappropriate in a Presidential campaign. They had no way of knowing, after all, that portraying Ford the *man* was a key part of our advertising strategy.

But when we showed the commercial, I heard no laughter. They just sat there, seemingly fascinated. When it was over, they agreed that it was beyond corn. They said it was one of the best political commercials they had ever seen. They wrote nice things, too.

21
MAKING US PROUD AGAIN

I had a lot of good reasons for feeling good during this phase of the campaign. The roller coaster was going steadily up again, the Dole dip safely behind us. Carter was hurtling down with an advance copy of *Playboy* clutched in his hand. The campaign was in its silly season, with the President holed up in the Rose Garden and Carter taunting him to come out and fight. The polls were improving; Ford was just eight points behind. Kissinger was making peace in Africa. The President's kick-off speech at Michigan University was a rouser—though all they showed on TV were the firecracker and the boos. We had the momentum, we were moving up, the first debate was just around the corner. And Bob Gardner had written a song.

"There is absolutely nothing worse in a political campaign," Doug had said, with a long authoritative pause, "than a bad song." Then Bob Gardner played the "demo" that he had secretly recorded. When it was over, Doug got up from his chair, strode back and forth across the room a couple of times, and made another authoritative pronouncement. "There is absolutely nothing better in a political campaign," he said firmly, "than a *good* song."

Bob Gardner had written a *good* song. A good-mood song. The instant I heard it, I thought of the first sentence in our campaign plan. "America is in a good mood."

The song captured the spirit we wanted the campaign to have. "Feelin' Good About America." A happy, simple, singable song.

Bob had recorded it in a march tempo with a mixed chorus. It could easily be arranged for a rock beat, a Latin beat, a Western—no matter what tempo it was played in, it would be upbeat and uplifting. And Bob's lyrics, I thought, were perfect:

> *"There's a change that's come over America*
> *A change that's great to see*
> *We're livin' here in peace again*
> *We're going back to work again*
> *It's better than it used to be.*
>
> *I'm feelin' good about America*
> *I feel it everywhere I go*
> *I'm feelin' good about America*
> *I thought you ought to know*
> *That I'm feelin' good about America*
> *It's something great to see*
> *I'm feelin' good about America*
> *I'm feelin' good about me!"*

It was a sing-along song if I ever heard one. A Mitch Miller song. I looked at Bob Gardner, smiling proudly in his neat, pointed beard. He *looked* like Mitch Miller.

And John Deardourff came up with the ultimate sing-along idea.

We had been accumulating lists of celebrities who wanted to do something for Ford. Some of the biggest names in the sports and entertainment worlds were on our side in this campaign.

"We'll bring all our celebrities to Washington," John said enthusiastically. "They'll gather at the foot of the Lincoln Memorial. With the Ford family. And thousands of campaign workers. We'll film them singing 'Feelin' Good About America.' We'll use three cameras. Four cameras."

I loved the idea. I wanted to take it still further. "That could be our final half hour. We do the whole show, live, from the Lincoln Memorial. The President makes a terrific speech. The celebrities all say great things about him. Then we close the campaign—everybody singing together."

The idea just fizzled two days later. The logistics problem would be a nightmare. There were so many other things to do. I still think it was a good idea. That's the most frustrating thing about political campaigns. If you don't do it *now,* you can't do it *ever.*

But we did make good use of "Feelin' Good About America."

The next day we sent Bob Gardner off on a junket around the country, recording different versions of the song with different musical groups for use on radio and TV. We made a country-Western version, a hard-rock version, a soft-rock version, a California-Sound version, a Latin version with Spanish lyrics, and a couple of versions with full marching bands and big choruses.

And we featured the song in our first two network sixty-second TV commercials.

It was easy to put pictures to those lyrics. All we had to do was show a lot of people feelin' good. Our first commercial was chock full of people feelin' good. We managed to include almost every voting group in America. We called the commercial "Peace" because its main purpose was to remind America that we were at peace. We brought the song down about halfway through the commercial and brought up the President's voice, a short passage from his acceptance speech:

"Today America has the most precious gift of all. We are at peace."

Then, over shots of the President in the White House, we brought in an announcer's voice:

"America is smiling again. We are at peace with the world, and at peace with ourselves. Peace. When you think about it, is there anything more important than that?"

I didn't think there was anything more important than that, so I felt pretty confident when a courier flew off with a cassette of the commercial. It had to be shown to the President before it could be released to the TV networks. We had just twelve hours to air date when word came back from the White House:

"Change the ending. The President wants to say 'Peace with *freedom*.' Instead of just 'peace.' "

We had to open a studio and a lab to work that night, and we had to bring an announcer in from out of town, but we made the change and made the air date. Conservative Republicans were not going to be able to nudge each other, point to the commercial, and say, "See, that man wants peace at all costs!"

When I saw the finished spot, I had to admit to myself that we *had* let the heavy hand of Madison Avenue into our campaign. But, I decided, it had a nice touch.

Our second sixty-second commercial was called "Accomplishments." We wanted to show the changes that had come over America, before Ford and after Ford, in the starkest possible contrast. We used black-and-white headlines to show Vietnam, Watergate, recession, and runaway inflation. We cut away from each problem to show people today—celebrating the Fourth of July, back at their jobs, housewives at the supermarket, a little child looking happy. To heighten the contrast, we used the drone of newsroom teletype machines over the headlines and played our "Feelin' Good" song over the quick cuts of happy Americans.

As in the first spot, we ended with a dramatic picture of the President and our slogan, "He's Making Us Proud Again."

Meanwhile more footage kept streaming into our New York headquarters. There were so many films to put together we decided we needed help. Ed Spiegel, who had produced the convention film, agreed to fly back and work on our final half-hour film and one or two of our five-minute commercials. And I hired another free-lance producer, Pat Barnes, who took some more of the production load off Tom Angell's sturdy but sagging shoulders.

By now we had a team of about fifteen people, in New York and Washington, creating and producing the Ford campaign. The hours were long, and the food was lousy. Ham and cheese sandwiches for lunch and dinner. Lukewarm coffee with powdered cream. The editing rooms were beginning to smell of pickles.

We stared at the little screen on the Steenbeck until our eyes were blurred and our heads hurt. Fast forward, fast reverse. Searching for the cutaway to the black kid . . . for the cheering crowd . . . for the take where the President looked just a little bit more forceful. It was tedious, teeth-grating work. But almost every day another commercial emerged from the assembly line and was sped to the laboratory.

The commercials featuring the President with old people, with kids, with farmers, and with factory workers were relatively easy. The President had been relaxed. He spoke fluently. You could tell he enjoyed being with people. And because he talked issues, rather than philosophy, he was clearly at ease with his subject matter. These commercials weren't setups. We didn't just find a bunch of Republicans, put them in work clothes, and tell them to fire easy questions at the President.

But when you film the President of the United States, it's not a casual affair. When the commercials featuring factory workers were filmed, for instance, the Secret Service sent dogs through the plant sniffing for explosives. The room where the film was made was heavily guarded by large men with hearing aids. And though it may not have been known whether the workers preferred Ford or Carter, there was very little else the Secret Service didn't know about them.

The kids were another problem. They were a little ill at ease in the

Oval Office and so was the President. One kid asked him how he was going to solve the unemployment problem. The President thought about it a moment, and said he had to "get people jobs." Even the young boy didn't seem to think that answer would make too good a TV commercial. But once the kids and the President started to relax together, we were able to get some nice footage.

One of our most important commercials was the five-minute biography of President Ford. And at one point we thought we would have to leave out the most heroic part of his life: his role in the Pacific war.

We'd heard rumors that President Ford's aircraft carrier had been under Jap torpedo attack. Somewhere, we were told, there was a Commander Cadwalleder, Ensign Ford's commanding officer, who had seen Ford's gun crew shoot down two planes. It sounded like a great story, perhaps another "P.T. 109," but we couldn't find Cadwalleder.

Ed Spiegel had tried to get the story from Betty Ford, while he was filming her, but this is how it came out:

QUESTION: There was an incident on shipboard, your husband was rather conspicuously brave, capable. How did you first find out about it?

MRS. BETTY FORD: Well, of course I didn't find out about it until after we were married because we were married in '48 after he had come back from service.

QUESTION: Would you tell me what it is I am talking about so I can cut my own questions out.

MRS. BETTY FORD: Well, that was when he was aboard the *Monterey* in the Navy, and that was during the war. And at that time, of course, we were not married, and consequently I didn't know about it until after we were married.

They were still in the water. They had stopped to load for fuel and they couldn't even load for fuel. They were very high in the water, and being an aircraft carrier, the tilt of it was terrific. And, of course, they had general quarters alarm because this typhoon hit.

He dashed up and tried to get to his position. When he went across the flight deck, which was very wet, he slipped and slid. Right at that point, the *Monterey* shifted and he slid right down. Fortunately, he went spread-eagle, and his feet just caught on a very small edge. And he was just knocked right into the catwalk on the edge of the deck. Otherwise, he would have been in the ocean and he probably wouldn't have survived.

That was not exactly the war story we had in mind.

We finally found Commander Cadwalleder. We filmed him in Philadelphia. He remembered Ford's heroism well. He had seen him shoot down two Jap torpedo bombers. In the final commercial, his voice told of the incident while we showed actual war footage of an aircraft carrier shooting down two Jap torpedo bombers. It was the best scene in a very strong commercial.

President Ford's innate modesty caused us some trouble on another commercial. We wanted to do a spot about the basic differences between Jimmy Carter and President Ford. We thought it would be interesting to have President Ford talking about the differences between himself and Carter. Most politicians, given a chance like this, would describe a Dr. Jekyll and a Mr. Hyde. Here is what President Ford said:

PRESIDENT FORD: I don't know Jimmy Carter personally, so I'm not really qualified to pass judgment on his personal characteristics or traits. I can say that there is a difference in experience. He's had experience in the state legislature, and as governor, and that's a different experience than I had. I had many, many years in the Congress of the United States dealing with national problems, while his principal focus was on state and local problems. We did have one similarity. I was in the Navy for four years during World War II. He was in the Navy for a longer time, but in a different branch of the Navy. So our careers, to some extent, were comparable there, but likewise a little different. I've had an experience or two that I think is different from his. I taught. I was in the legal profession. He went to the Naval Academy, and never really had any experience working with people problems like a lawyer has. I think that is really the fundamental difference. The experience on my part of dealing with national and international problems. His experience was primarily in dealing with local and state problems.

I had mixed emotions when I saw that film. I felt good about having such a decent, modest man in the White House. But I wished, for the sake of our commercials, that we could have had a tough son-of-a-bitch for a candidate.

I realized that if Jimmy Carter was going to be "cut down to size," it wasn't going to be done by the President. I had to write my own anti-Carter material. And not only did I have plenty of material to work from, but our opponent was beginning to do a pretty good job of cutting *himself* down to size.

22
PLAYBOY
AND THE FIRST DEBATE

The *Playboy* interview was a gift from heaven. It seemed like God's way of slapping Jimmy Carter's wrist for wearing his religion on his sleeve. In one strange, rambling monologue, the answer to the last question in an otherwise positive interview, he managed to worry or offend four distinctly different voting groups.

He worried the *Playboy* readers, the very people he was trying to impress, when he said that he had "committed adultery in my heart many times." Hell, the *Playboy* readers had tried every position and they knew damn well you couldn't commit adultery with your heart.

He deeply offended many of his fellow Southern Baptists. They didn't agree that "Christ set some almost impossible standards." They didn't like it at all when he admitted that "I've looked at a lot of women with lust." Maybe God forgave him, as Carter claimed, but a lot of Southern Baptists wouldn't. Carter admitted that he would condemn someone who "leaves his wife and shacks up with somebody out of wedlock." Many of his parishioners were ready to condemn anyone who even used words like "shack up" and "screw," as he did in the very next sentence.

One other little item in his monologue should have cost him twenty-six electoral votes. When he said Lyndon Johnson was a "liar and a cheat," the whole state of Texas was in the palm of our hands. By not capitalizing on this, by waiting weeks before we even mentioned his remark in Texas, we lost our chance. He was able to repair the damage. Early in the campaign, Doug Bailey had made a prophetic remark.

"He's an elusive target. It's important that whenever he shows his ass, we kick it!"

Doug does not use three- and four-letter words lightly. We should have taken his advice and kicked Carter's ass from one end of Texas to the other.

Of course the biggest mistake Carter made was granting the interview in the first place. His strategy was to shore up his "kind of weird" image among young voters. Apparently either he or Jody Powell had overlooked one obvious fact. *Playboy* is not one of our traditional American values. In most parts of the country, it's a dirty magazine. No matter what he said, the very fact that he allowed himself to be interviewed by "those people" shook the very foundation of his support in rural America.

I think *Playboy* could have killed Jimmy Carter. But we weren't mean enough or shrewd enough to make a mountain out of the molehill. We thought the media would do the job for us.

Before we knew what was happening, the media found something else to laugh about. Us. By the time we got around to using *Playboy* in our advertising, it was in an almost desperate attempt to focus attention away from our own troubles.

But it was fun while it lasted. And for the first time, a lot of very smart Democrats began to say that, yes, it was possible: Jimmy Carter was capable of blowing the biggest lead in political history.

Shortly after the *Playboy* interview I had lunch with a brilliant political strategist who works primarily for Democrats. He is not known for giving free advice, certainly not to Republicans. But in that friendly setting, in the heart of a big campaign, it was impossible for him to conceal everything he knew.

"The trouble with Carter," he said, casually sipping a martini in the Oak Room of the Plaza Hotel, "is that he has a very short fuse. The trouble is, nobody is taking the fight to him. You've got to hit him. He's not going to be able to handle it if you attack." He looked up from his martini thoughtfully. "The flip-flops. You've got to hit him with the flip-flops."

I told him about my idea for a commercial on Carter's flip-flops. He liked it.

"Know how to beat him in the debates?" He asked rhetorically. "Wait until he talks about the job he did as governor of Georgia. When he's through, Ford should look him right in the eye and say, 'Tell me, Governor Carter. If you're so good at finding economies in government, why did you leave Georgia with more employees, more debt, and a bigger budget?' He'll wilt.

"You're letting him get away with murder," he said. "So is the goddamn media. Know what he did last week? He came here to New York and accept'ed the endorsement of the Liberal Party. Within twenty-four hours he was in Alabama, having his picture taken with George Wallace! There's not another politician in the country who could get away with that. The papers would crucify anybody else who tried that. Within twenty-four hours! You guys should have hit him with that."

I agreed. We should hit Carter harder. We should kick his ass every time he gave us a target.

But it wasn't easy. Right after that lunch I learned that my hardest kick had just been blocked by our own people. Phil Angell called to tell me the lawyers had killed my "Flip-Flop" commercial. I was crushed. I was ready to be a hatchet man, but they wouldn't give me a hatchet.

The "Flip-Flop" commercial was a sixty-second review of all the issues that Jimmy Carter had taken both sides on. It was nasty in its simplicity. Working with "The Truth Squad," two dedicated young men who worked night and day trying to document Carter's position on every issue, I developed what I thought were eleven clear-cut Carter flip-flops. Everyone had suspected that for years he had been saying one thing to one audience, another thing to the next audience. Most people also suspected that he shaded words and sentences to make his position seem more compatible with whatever audience he was talking to. Being against "amnesty" but for a "pardon" was a classic example—and it was the only time he got caught.

Our research showed that he had taken two distinct positions on right-to-work laws, revenue sharing, energy policy, the Panama Canal, busing, capital punishment, aid to New York City, amnesty, defense spending, government-created jobs, and the integration of neighborhoods.

I wanted to do an ad, a booklet, and a TV commercial showing his flip-flops.

The trouble was that newspaper reports of what Carter said—even newspaper quotes of what Carter said—were not considered strong enough evidence by our lawyers. And that's really all we had to go on. Newspaper reports. In retrospect, I have to agree with the lawyers. Newspaper stories make pretty thin evidence.

My disappointment was short-lived. The first debate was about to take place. I had a funny hunch that our guy was going to win, maybe even win big. We probably wouldn't even need the flip-flop commercial.

I think I was more nervous than the President on the night of the debate. There was a moment, just before the first question, when I thought I just might have to throw up.

But as soon as Carter started to answer the first question, I knew I'd be all right. I was watching with Mimi and a friend. I decided that they needed a running commentary on the real meaning of what was happening on the screen.

"He's scared to death!" I said ecstatically. "Look at him! He doesn't have the answer! He doesn't remember the question! It's a disaster for Carter! This will cost him the election!"

Then Ford began his two-minute rebuttal.

"Brilliant!" I shouted. "Absolutely brilliant! He's nailed him to the wall!"

That's the way it went throughout the long first debate. I found myself standing up and cheering when Ford nailed Carter on the number of government employees he'd added in Georgia and on the fifty-two percent increase in the Georgia budget. I was even convinced that Ford was far superior during the half-hour sound failure, when both candidates just stared at the cameras in frozen silence.

And I was absolutely furious when the commentators, at the end of the show, thought it had been a draw.

When we went to bed that night, Mimi asked, quietly, if I didn't think that, perhaps, I just might be losing my objectivity.

"Of course not," I replied quite rationally. "This is a job. I've been hired as a professional. I'm completely objective. Any idiot could see that Ford won every point in that debate—every point!"

I slept well, blissfully unaware that our little car was dipping its nose over the scariest part of the roller coaster.

part six

From
Earl to
Pearl

23
KEY STATE STRATEGY

For the past three weeks I had pretty much lost track of what time it was, even what day it was. Such things didn't seem important. The only time of day that seemed important was the seven o'clock news. Every night at seven o'clock sharp we would gather around the TV set in a small office and switch from Cronkite to Reasoner to Chancellor–Brinkley, clicking constantly back and forth, holding the image on the screen only when the subject was Carter or Ford. For the past few days Ford had steadily, surely been winning the election on the seven o'clock news. *Playboy*. The debate. Ford's triumphant swing through the South. Every night we had left the TV set and gone back to work feeling a little bit more confident.

But on the evening news of September twenty-eighth the strong Ford tide seemed to be ebbing steadily out again. Ford's golf outings with lobbyists had been a nagging problem for days. So had reports of a mysterious investigation into Ford's past campaign finances. But on September twenty-eighth the two came together and led the evening news on all three networks.

Carter was having a wonderful time with the golf outings: proof that you can't trust the tired, old Washington establishment, proof that big business really runs the country.

And the investigation into Ford's finances was now more than a rumor. Charles Ruff, the Watergate prosecutor, was definitely looking into some "serious matters." Woodward and Bernstein were

back at their typewriters, interviewing "certain highly-placed offi-
cials," reporting in the *Washington Post* and being re-reported on the
evening news.

It was Watergate all over again. It was devastating to our campaign. The momentum we so desperately needed had been stopped
cold. Overnight the focus of the campaign had gone from Carter's
troubles to Ford's troubles.

The next morning I had to fly to Washington for a meeting with the
campaign steering committee. I watched the "Today" show and
took three Gelusil tablets while I was packing. The first news report
said people were still wondering why President Ford remained silent
on the matter of his frequent golf outings with lobbyists. The second
news report said people were still wondering why there was still no
comment from the White House on President Ford's campaign
finances.

Mimi watched with me. "I'm beginning to wonder too," she said,
looking worried and a little confused.

"So am I," I admitted.

I was convinced that most of America was wondering with us.

Reading the *New York Times* on the propeller-driven, second-
section Washington shuttle was no help. Reston, Safire, and Shan-
non were all wondering.

Phillip Angell, who was now the Washington Office manager, appeared to be in a state of near panic. When I walked into his office,
he was snuffing out a cigarette with one hand, trying to light a fresh
cigarette with the other hand. The phone was cradled against his ear
and he was shouting angrily at someone. His large desk was covered
with pink message slips. His head was visibly twitching with tension.
I decided to leave and go into my own office. I didn't think Angell
would make it through the morning, much less another five weeks of
campaigning.

I ran into John Deardourff on the way out. I was somewhat relieved that he was his usual calm, smiling, unruffled self. But even
Deardourff seemed uncertain.

I went to my own office and was greeted by piles and piles of giant
four-color Ford posters. Apparently someone on the Washington
staff had decided I was never coming back, and so they were using
my office as a storage room for campaign material. I stepped gingerly
over the piles of posters and boxes of bumper stickers, just barely
managing to reach my desk without stepping on the President's face.

I wanted to make one phone call before my meeting with Baker,
Spencer, and Teeter. Arnold Palmer wanted to do a commercial for

Ford. He was leaving for Europe in a few days, and I was supposed to call him this morning.

I had been given his home phone number, and I felt quite pleased with myself as I started punching out the call to Ligonier, Pennsylvania. Here I was calling my hero—direct. Should I call him "Arnie"?

I stopped just as I came to the last digit. I slowly replaced the receiver. It had suddenly dawned on me. Arnold Palmer. That's all we needed now. A smiling Arnold Palmer reminded America what a nice guy Jerry Ford was on the golf course.

Phil Angell pushed his face into my office. He was clutching the doorjamb with both hands.

"We have to kill both sixties," he said.

"Why?" I asked as calmly as I could.

"Because we used some footage that hadn't been released."

"I thought you owned that footage."

"Well—they're raising hell."

"They're scheduled to go on tonight," I said, still calm.

"They can't."

"We don't have anything to replace them with."

"I know."

He was gone again. He had apparently just wanted to add a little something to brighten my day.

I thought about the problem for just a moment. There was clearly nothing I could do to change the TV spots with the borrowed footage. New commercials had to be at the station for legal clearance at least forty-eight hours before the air date. We would just have to run the forbidden spots again and pray.

I got up from my desk and headed for the meeting in Stu Spencer's office.

Stu Spencer and Jim Baker were already in the room, talking earnestly, when Angell, Deardourff, and I walked into the room. Bob Teeter joined us while we were still giving our coffee orders to Stu's secretary.

It made me feel better, being here. These men had been through the ups and downs of so many political campaigns that they had clearly learned how to hide their feelings. To see Teeter, Spencer, and Baker chatting about little campaign sidelights, you could have guessed that we were ahead by five points and pulling away. Even Phil Angell seemed to calm down immediately and get into the easygoing spirit of things.

The purpose of the meeting was to discuss the five million dollars' worth of advertising that still hadn't been allocated. Based primarily on Teeter's polling data and Spencer's political savvy, eighteen key states had been isolated. The election would be won or lost in those states. In this room no one spoke of popular votes. The only thing that mattered were electoral votes.

We sat at a large round table facing a simple map of the United States. The number of electoral votes was printed in large red numerals on each state. And on each state was a priority designation. Priorities went from one to four. The fours were the states we could forget. We had either already won them or already lost them. Massachusetts was a four. So was Georgia.

Priority One states were California (45 votes), Illinois (26), Michigan (21), New Jersey (17), Ohio (25), Pennsylvania (27), and New York (41).

Priority Two states were Texas (26), Missouri (12), Maryland (10), Washington (9), Wisconsin (11), Connecticut (8), Virginia (12), Iowa (8), Florida (17), Kentucky (9), and Tennessee (10).

Those eighteen states represented four hundred electoral votes. We needed only two hundred seventy to win. We had decided to concentrate all of our remaining five million dollars' worth of advertising in those states. Obviously some of it would be wasted. We would have preferred to have an even shorter list of target states. But at least we weren't in the position of the president of Macy's, who declared, many years ago, that he knew half of his advertising dollars were wasted but he was damned if he knew which half. I felt that we'd be pinpointing our dollars about as effectively as we possibly could.

The other states would have to get along with our three-million-dollar network penetration, which of course hit all states equally, and whatever small advertising budgets each state committee was allowed under the new campaign spending laws.

After some general talk about which combination of states would most likely give us our two hundred seventy votes, Stu Spencer got down to business by pointing his finger at the big state of Texas with its twenty-six votes.

"I think we ought to move Texas into Number One priority right now," he said. "Carter could have his ass whipped over that *Playboy* thing. They love Lyndon and Lady Bird down there, and we're not going to let them forget that."

"I think you're right," Jim Baker drawled. His accent seemed to deepen whenever the talk turned to Texas or Oklahoma. "When the President made those remarks about gun control in Mississippi last Saturday, I think they perked up their ears in Texas."

Deardourff agreed. "I think Texas definitely can be ours," he said quietly. "And I think gun control could be the big issue down there."

"Except in Houston," warned Teeter, who seemed to be aware of some polling statistics that we hadn't seen yet.

Stu laughed. "He's right. In Houston they get shot up all the time. They don't like guns in Houston."

"But it's a big rural issue," Baker said. "I think we can use gun control in every Texas market except Houston. And maybe Dallas."

"I was surprised the President came out so *strongly* on gun control last weekend," John said.

"I happened to show him some statistics just before he got to Mississippi," Teeter said.

"Connally's people are outside waiting to see me right now," Baker said. "They want to do something for us in Texas."

"What about Reagan?" John asked.

"Reagan is still fantastic in Texas," said Teeter. "He's by far our best bet. Put him on the tube."

"He's making four commercials for us tomorrow," Phil Angell said. "I sent you the scripts."

I'd seen the Reagan scripts, and I'd already objected. He constantly referred to the Republican party, which was hardly one of our assets.

I asked Baker if we couldn't rewrite the scripts a little. Everyone seemed to agree with me about the Republican thing, but no one thought he could talk Reagan out of it. It was pretty clear to me that Reagan was either coming into this thing on his terms—and with his scripts—or not coming in at all.

"Why do we bother with politicians at all in Texas?" I said finally. "Nobody really gives a shit what politicians say. We've got Tom Landry of the Dallas Cowboys. He'll do a spot. We've got Bud Wilkinson. They love him in Texas. He-man stuff. Texans will love that."

"We've got Duke Wayne, too," Baker said.

I laughed. The idea of John Wayne talking about gun control in Texas was so obvious, so corny, that it might work.

"He's getting pretty old," Spencer said.

"But he's still the number-one box office attraction in central Texas," Baker said.

"I'll work on it," I said.

"I think we have to use Reagan, too," said John. "He'll be good on the serious issues. Big government. Texans hate big government. And taxes."

"Texans hate taxes," Spencer agreed.

"They don't pay any," Teeter said.

"But let's let Connally do the energy thing or something," Baker said.

"It's agreed then," said Stu, "that Texas is going to be a Priority One state."

"Might as well call it that," said John. "We're going to be spending damn near half-a-million dollars in Texas media during the last three weeks."

"What about Iowa?" Baker asked, his eyes riveted on the Midwestern states.

I was glad he had asked. It was about the only state I could talk intelligently about.

Teeter had called us a few days ago to say things were too close for comfort in Iowa, a normally Republican state in a Presidential election. He had discovered that the governor of Iowa had a fantastic eighty-two percent approval rating, and thought we should contact him. I had talked to Governor Bob Ray the night before, and I'd been lucky.

"Bob Ray is making a spot for us tomorrow," I reported. "It's a good thing we got him. He's going to Taiwan tomorrow night."

"What's he going to say?" asked Spencer.

I hesitated. I knew what he was going to say, but I didn't think it would sound too good in a meeting like this. But what the hell.

"He's going to talk about bonding the packers," I said.

Stu laughed. That gave me courage.

"Big thing in Iowa," I went on. "Ford was about to veto the legislation on bonding meat-packers. But Bob Ray called him up and talked him out of it."

"Another example of our President's strong leadership," John said. Fortunately, he chuckled as he said it.

"It sounds a little strange," I said, "but Bob Ray thinks it's a perfect example of how President Ford listens to the people of Iowa. He thinks it's going to win us a lot of votes."

"We'll take 'em anyway we can get 'em," said Spencer.

"The embargo's the issue in Iowa," Baker said flatly.

"True," said John. "But the President absolutely refuses to say that he won't use the embargo again if he feels it's necessary."

"He said it in his convention speech," said Baker.

"But he regrets saying it now," John said. "He's not going to say it again."

"Bob Ray is going to sort of mention the embargo thing, obliquely, at the end of his commercial," I said.

"Good," said Baker. "We should use Dole in Iowa, too."

"We're filming Dole next week," John said.

"We should use Dole in Iowa, South Dakota, and maybe North Dakota," Teeter said.

"What about Kansas?" I asked.

"If we haven't got Kansas we're just pissin' into the wind anyway," said Spencer.

"What about Oklahoma?" asked Baker. "Maybe we should use John Connally in Oklahoma."

"It's a Priority Three state," said Teeter.

"What the hell," said Spencer. "We could put Connally on radio in Oklahoma. It costs only thirty-five dollars a spot."

Then they started going across the country state by state, reeling off names of people I'd never heard of as possible surrogate spokesmen for our commercials.

"Dan Evans in Washington," Spencer said.

"Reagan in California, of course," said Teeter.

"He wants to do a half-hour special for us in California," Spencer said.

"Can't hurt," offered John. "No one will watch it."

"Tom McCall in Oregon," said Teeter.

"And Laxalt in Nevada," said Baker.

"Congressman Manny Luhan in New Mexico," said Spencer. "He's dynamite in northern Albuquerque."

"Is Goldwater okay in Arizona?" asked Baker speculatively.

"No," said Teeter. "Use Reagan."

"How about Wisconsin?" asked Baker.

"We're in deep shit in Wisconsin," Spencer said. "We're on the wrong end of every issue."

"Missouri?" asked Baker.

"We're not in good shape there either," said Spencer glumly. "It must be John's fault. He's the Missouri expert."

John was running two major political campaigns in Missouri.

"My people are doing great in Missouri," John admitted. "But they don't seem to have very strong coattails."

"What can you do for us in Illinois?" Spencer asked John. "Your man Thompson seems to be doing okay."

"I think he'll do something for Ford. I'll talk to him."

"Butz in Indiana," said Teeter. "And Milliken in Michigan."

"And Woody Hayes in Ohio," said Spencer. "Lots of Ford and lots of Woody Hayes. And Arnold Pinckney."

Baker laughed. "Who the fuck is Arnold Pinckney?"

"President of the Cleveland School Board. Good man."

"Let's use Howard Baker in Tennessee," Teeter said.

"Tennessee is just plain, bad fucking luck," Spencer said, shaking his head. "Bad news. Always has been. Don't know why. Bad news. So is Kentucky."

"We have John Sherman Cooper in Kentucky," Jim Baker said.

"He's ninety years old," Spencer said.

"He's deaf," John said.

"But they still love him," Baker said defiantly.

"Bear Bryant and Strom Thurmond in Alabama," Teeter said. "Maybe the whole South."

That gave me another chance to offer my two cents. I had talked to several political biggies in Alabama, and they had promised that Bear Bryant would do some commercials for us. Unfortunately, we had to wait until things had cooled off a little before I could talk to the Alabama coach. The newspapers had criticized him pretty strongly for riding in the motorcade with President Ford last Saturday. I told them I thought we could film Bear Bryant in a week or two.

Spencer was still musing about Tennessee. "I just don't understand Tennessee," he said. "Kentucky either. It's got to be the Baptists. Goddamned Baptists. They should be Republican, goddamn it. They *are* Republican. It's the goddamned born-again thing again."

"I thought you were doing something about that this week," Teeter said.

Spencer chuckled. "Might just work, too," he said. He turned to John, Phil, and me, the only ones in the room who hadn't heard of his latest political masterstroke.

"We're having two hundred evangelical communicators to the White House for dinner Friday night," he said proudly.

"What's an evangelical communicator?" John asked with a laugh.

"They communicate to eight-million Baptists and others who have found the Lord," Spencer explained. "For ten bucks I can get you on one of their mailing lists."

"How did you get them?" I asked. "They're Carter people."

"Not anymore they're not," Stu said, with a delighted grin. "They're mad as hell at their boy for the dirty things he said in that dirty magazine. We don't even have to sell them. I'm just going to hand each one of them the actual copy of the AP wire report on the *Playboy* interview. The AP report starts with a warning that "You may find the material in this story offensive to the readers of family newspapers.' "

My spirits were beginning to lift. I had forgotten all about the golf outings and the Watergate investigator. Things were looking up.

"We're going to suggest," added Stu, "that they communicate very strongly to their parishioners about that *Playboy* article. We'll let them use any part of the Bible they want to justify their stand."

"I think Lowell Weicker will help us in Connecticut," Baker said.

"How's he doing against the girl?" Spencer asked.

"He's going to kill the girl," Teeter said.

"I hear Telly Savalas wants to come in," said John. "He would be damned good in New York."

"How about Rockefeller for New York?" asked Baker.

Spencer held his middle finger up in salute to the picture of Rockefeller that had appeared on the front page of the *New York Post*. "His traditional American values aren't looking too good these days," he said.

"New York could be the one place we could use Kissinger," Teeter said.

"Hold your breath," said Spencer. "The legs are beginning to fall off the African deal."

"I just got a call on that," said Baker. "It's getting messy."

"He should have gotten it in writing," said Spencer.

"We really have to go all out during the President's swing through New York. He's got to do it all there."

"When's he go to New York?" Phil Angell asked casually.

"October thirteenth."

Phil consulted some papers. "Super," he said. "His biorhythms will be almost perfect October thirteenth."

I laughed. It was the first time biorhythms had been a factor in the campaign.

Spencer seemed pleased. "How will they be on the sixteenth?" he asked.

Phil consulted his papers again. "Perfect. He's at his absolute peak on the sixteenth."

"Well, that does it, Bob," Spencer said, turning to Teeter. "We'll go ahead with the Wabash Cannonball."

Three of us repeated "Wabash Cannonball" with a question mark and a chuckle. Spencer explained that tentative plans had been made to have the President swing through Iowa, Missouri, and Illinois aboard the Wabash Cannonball starting October sixteenth. He would be traveling with Johnny Cash, Eddie Arnold, Roger Miller, and the usual political straphangers.

"It'll be great TV," John said, always thinking of camera angles.

"And if nothing else, it'll clinch the railroad-nut vote."

"That's going to be the best day of the year for the President," Phil said, consulting his charts again. "Carter's biorhythms will be at their lowest point. Ford will be at his peak."

Spencer turned the conversation to the Mexican-American vote. He was clearly an expert on Mexican-American politics. He reeled off half a dozen Spanish names, important political leaders who were going to deliver votes for Ford. It seemed to my untutored ear that he pronounced the names fluently. Stu thought the unemployment situation would be a problem, but Carter's born-again Baptist thing was a very big plus. He explained some of the subtle differences between the Texas Spanish community and the California community. He thought we could gear the same basic message to both if we used an entertainer as our spokesperson instead of a Spanish politician.

I suggested Cesar Romero. Spencer thought he was too old. John suggested Chi Chi Rodriquez. I reminded him of our golf handicap. Ricardo Montalban was vetoed. Too slick. Carmen Miranda was dropped. Too silly. Finally someone suggested Vicki Carr. For years few people had known of her Mexican-American ancestry. But now that she was a big star she was capitalizing on it. They asked me to try to line her up for a commercial.

Jim Baker talked about a Catholic mailer and a farm mailer that were about to go out on White House stationery. I thought the letters financed by Campaign '76 were too long, but Spencer pointed out that a personal letter on White House stationery was hardly junk mail.

"How're we doing on the anti-Carter stuff?" Bob Teeter asked casually.

I had been afraid that question would come up. My three anti-Carter commercials still hadn't gotten beyond the storyboard stage. The strongest spot, the flip-flop commercial, had been killed by the lawyers. I still hadn't come up with any hard evidence that Carter had actually changed his position on busing, right-to-work laws, abortion, and gun control. I had newspaper articles that said he'd changed positions. But after three weeks of research, I still couldn't pin Carter down with specific, recorded quotes. Carter had been just too slick. He changed his position on the issues from audience to audience, but his use of the double negative to say he favored something, his use of the double positive to say he was against something, had drawn a semantic curtain across every stand he had taken.

I described my problem. Then I told them about the Carter record spot. It opened on the last lines of a Carter commercial. The announcer says " . . . and what he did as governor, he will do as President." Our commercial would then cut to a map of Georgia. As the announcer talked about what had happened in Georgia during Jimmy Carter's one term as governor, the words "More Spending" . . . "More Government Employees" . . . "More Debt" . . . would be superimposed over the state. The camera would then pull back to show the entire country and the words would be left on the screen.

Baker, Spencer, and Teeter seemed generally to be in favor of completing the spot, but John Deardourff wasn't sure.

I knew that John was basically against negative advertising. So was I. It could so easily backfire. He felt that it should be used only as a last resort, and we hadn't quite reached that stage yet.

"Well, I think we'd better tell them about the pardon spot," Teeter said.

He told us. And the little flicker of optimism that I had been feeling since I walked into the room was quickly snuffed out.

They had been told the details of a commercial that the Carter people had just completed. It opened on Nixon telling the American people, "I am not a crook." Then it cut to Ford saying, "I know that Nixon is innocent." Then it cut to Nixon leaving the White House by helicopter. Then it showed Ford saying, "I hereby grant an unconditional pardon to Richard Nixon." Devastating.

"I'm surprised," I admitted. "They're ahead. I didn't think they'd stoop to that kind of thing."

Spencer laughed.

"They're Southerners," he said. "That's the bottom line. Southern politicians."

"Southern politicians. Jimmy Carter. Jody Powell. Jerry Rafshoon. Hamilton Jordan. Southern politicians get nasty in the last weeks. They always do. It's in their blood. Doesn't matter whether they smell victory or defeat. They're Southerners."

I got the message. I was ready to jump in the mud and wrestle. But I wished that I had a punch as strong as that pardon spot to deliver.

I was beginning to feel gloomy again, so I decided that I might as well ask about the problems no one seemed to want to talk about.

"When are we going to resolve the goddamned golf thing and the campaign finances thing?"

"Dunno," said Spencer slowly. "But that will quiet down soon."

"Good," I said.

"Oh, no, it isn't," Spencer said, shaking his head. "It's going to quiet down because something much worse is coming up."

"Don't ruin their day," Teeter said.

"This can't go beyond this room," Spencer said. "Just possibly, with the help of a miracle, we can still keep it from being a disaster." He paused, looking as though he didn't really believe what he was about to say.

"Earl Butz got on an airplane after the convention. He sat with John Dean and Pat Boone. John, you know, is now a writer for *Rolling Stone*. Our distinguished Secretary of Agriculture decided to make a point about what he called 'the coloreds.' He said that all the coloreds want, quote, is a tight pussy, a loose pair of shoes, and a warm place to shit, closed quote."

Neither John nor Phil nor I could speak.

"It is, of course, going to appear in the next issue of *Rolling Stone*," said Teeter. "Tight pussy. Warm place to shit."

"Why doesn't the President fire him now, before it appears?" John asked finally.

John, of course, has a brilliant political mind. But even my non-political mind told me that firing Butz right now was clearly the only possible strategy. The major thrust of our campaign was based on Ford's strong leadership . . . Ford's compassion . . . the good people Ford had around him. If Ford didn't fire Butz the instant he knew about the racial slur, people would laugh when our ads appeared.

"He's going to give Butz a very strong reprimand," Teeter said. "It will probably come out by Saturday."

"He won't fire him?" John asked.

"Earl Butz is a good friend," Spencer said. "The President likes Earl Butz. The President thinks he is doing a good job. The farmers like Earl Butz. Hell, the farmers will like Earl Butz even more when this comes out."

I argued that point briefly. I had met with the Farmers for Ford group on two occasions to get material for some ads and a brochure. Representatives of almost every farm state had asked me not to mention Earl Butz in the advertising. Earl Butz, they felt, was a liability.

Well, he was a lot more than that right now.

I folded my notes, put them in my pocket, and left with John and Phil. We didn't talk as we went back to our separate offices.

24

EXIT EARL BUTZ

The Butz storm broke four days later, with a report that the President had reprimanded his Agriculture Secretary for a racial slur. The storm began as all hurricanes do—strong gusts turning to gale force winds and steadily increasing in ferocity until you start to fear for the old elm tree, then for the house, then for your life.

The President had decided to ride it out. That's fine when you're aboard an aircraft carrier. But we were in a canoe. Four days later, while we were being washed ashore with the debris, the Butz resignation was accepted.

I was in the Farmers for Ford office on the Saturday morning the story broke. Officially, I was there to check some copy on our farm brochure. Unofficially, I was there to see how our head farmer felt about the Butz mess. Like me, he had known that the storm was coming. He looked depressed when I walked into his office.

"It's terrible," he said.

I tried briefly to cheer him up. "At least the *Times* and the *Washington Post* didn't report what he said. According to them he alluded to women's sexual organs and said blacks wanted a warm place to defecate."

"The *Star* got it right," he said. "Even the *Boston Globe* had it word for word."

"How long have you known?" I asked.

"A couple of days. I had Earl in here the day before yesterday. I introduced him to the people at our black desk.''

"What was their reaction?''

"They liked him. They didn't know, of course. But they liked him. And he liked them. That's the tragedy. He really isn't any more bigoted than any of us.''

I shook my head. What difference did that make?

"What do you think they would do if Butz walked in here right now?'' I asked.

"I don't know,'' he said.

He looked at me seriously. "What do you think Butz should do now?'' he asked. He seemed to be looking more for a sounding board than for real advice.

"I'm not sure,'' I said honestly. "I think the President should have fired him five days ago. But now I don't know.''

"The farmers like him,'' he said.

I reminded him that the Farmers for Ford group had been arguing among themselves for weeks now about whether or not to use Earl Butz's name in the farm brochure.

"He's controversial. We all know that. But he's a good, decent man.''

"He's *hurt* a good, decent man,'' I said.

"It's a mess,'' he said. "But I think we can weather the storm.''

The telephone rang. He seemed to know who would be calling him. I watched him pick up the phone and say "hello.'' He listened, and the sad, sympathetic look on his face told me who was speaking.

"I don't think you should do anything rash,'' he said, very quietly, into the phone. I could tell that he wasn't just giving advice—he was trying to make a friend who was in trouble feel a little better.

"I think you should wait awhile,'' he said. "We still don't know what the repercussions will be.'' He said it as though his heart really wasn't in it.

Earl Butz dashed any hopes we had of capturing the thirty percent of the black vote that Republicans normally can expect. It raised new questions about the President's leadership qualities—questions that had started to subside since our commercials began.

But the Earl Butz story wasn't all bad. For a few days it forced the newspapers and TV stations to give only second billing to the investigation of Ford's campaign finances.

25
WAITING FOR WAYNE

It's hard to pick the absolute lowest point of the whole campaign. But I think my choice for the absolute rock bottom moment will have to be the day after the second debate, at precisely two o'clock on Thursday afternoon, October seventh, as I was standing with Doug Bailey and a film crew on a scruffy ranch in Coldine, Texas, waiting for John Wayne.

A ranch hand walked up to me at that moment and told me John Wayne wasn't coming.

I wasn't surprised. I had known that was what he was going to say when I saw him coming. The only thing that had surprised me on that particular day was the fact that the plane hadn't crashed between Washington and Houston.

I had flown to Houston with a four-man film crew headed by Lee Kenower. Doug flew in from St. Louis and met us at the Houston airport.

We hadn't talked very much that morning. If we had talked, someone would have brought up the debate that had taken place the night before. Someone would have speculated about the ramifications of Ford's remarks concerning Eastern Europe. Someone might have wondered out loud why we were going to all this trouble to make films in Texas—after the Butz disaster, the Watergate prosecutor disaster, after the Eastern Europe disaster.

We were hungry when we landed in Houston. But I convinced

everyone that we should drive to the ranch first, pick a location, set up the cameras, then have lunch. I hinted that some rich Texas ranchers might invite us to join them in a real Texas barbecue.

I didn't know that it took an hour-and-a-half to drive from Houston to Coldine. And I certainly didn't know that Coldine consisted entirely of twenty miles of weeds and one small, ancient building with a corrugated tin roof, a thick tangle of cobwebs in the eaves, and two faded block letter signs reading "POST OFFICE" and "BEER."

We couldn't find the ranch, so we went to the post office to scrounge for food.

The lady inside looked terrified when we entered. I learned later that the radio had just announced that some convicts had escaped from a nearby prison. The look of hunger in our eyes could easily have been mistaken. We found some old hamburger rolls and some even older salami. That was lunch.

We sat on the steps of the old building, in the hot sun, eating our salami. Doug stood on the top step, hands on his hips, surveying the scene.

"Oh, how the mighty have fallen," he said.

Doug was more depressed about the debate than any of the rest of us—and he had good reason to be. He had spent days in Washington briefing the President on the strategy for the foreign policy debate.

He settled himself on the top step and began talking about it in a slow, head-shaking way.

"We had it won," he said. "If he had just stuck to two things. 'We are at peace,' and 'Carter has no experience.' Peace and experience. Just two things. He could have answered every conceivable question with just those two things. We are at peace. Carter has no experience. Peace and experience. Peace and experience."

Doug paused for a long time, and then looked up, his hands spread in a helpless gesture.

"I guess he froze."

Doug paused again.

"He didn't use the word *peace* until fifty-eight minutes into the debate. He didn't use *experience* until the close."

"He could have won it in the first question," I said. "Carter didn't answer that first question at all. He didn't come close to answering the question. Why didn't the President point that out? Why didn't he pin Carter down on that?"

Doug thought about it a moment. "He's a guy without strategic spontaneity. Of course we knew that. The debates were set up so he wouldn't need to have strategic spontaneity. He only had to say two things. Peace and experience. He froze."

Doug paused again.

"We never should have agreed to have the debate in California," Doug said. "He nearly got assassinated in California—twice. He went there during the primary and it was a disaster. California is bad luck for him."

A little later we finally found the ranch. I had envisioned the King Ranch, or something a little smaller. What I found was lots more weeds, some scruffy trees, and a shack. I never did see any cattle, though the rancher claimed that they were around someplace. John Wayne's excuse was that he'd gotten sick in Houston.

But we had nothing better to do for the rest of the day, so we decided to drive to his hotel in Houston and see whether we could talk him into doing the spot.

John Wayne was part of the Texas strategy that I'd written the week before. We had wanted to do a series of commercials on specific hard issues that Texans cared about: energy, right-to-work laws, property rights, defense spending, and gun control.

The more I thought about using John Wayne to attack Carter's gun control position, the more I liked it. I knew that he was a strong Ford supporter, and I suspected that he was against any kind of gun control law.

I had called his office in Los Angeles to sound him out about doing a commercial. I got his secretary on the phone. She said that John Wayne was going to Houston and would probably be happy to do a commercial for the President.

"How does he feel about gun control?" I asked.

She laughed. "He has often said that 'if anybody tries to take my gun away, he'll have to pry it out of my cold, dead fingers.' "

He was our boy, all right. I had spoken to him personally the night before we flew to Houston, and everything was all set for filming at the ranch in Coldine at 2 P.M. He said he was a little nervous about sounding too conservative on the issue, so I had written three different scripts. He could say whatever he wanted to say. Texans would get the message.

We were so discouraged driving back to Houston in our two station wagons, that the film crew began looking for diversions. That's always potentially dangerous. They had portable two-way radios that they used in their filming. Their legal frequency covered a short radius around Washington, D.C. The sound man happened to tune into the frequency shortly after 4 P.M.

We listened casually as a man named Sam, who was apparently in a helicopter, chatted with a man named Phil, who was apparently at a radio station.

Suddenly our sound man burst into their conversation.

"Hello out there in radio land," he said. "Hello, hello. This is Ronald here, with a request that you play a little tune on your radio station for my dear grandmother."

At first Sam and Phil were startled. As Ronald continued to request tunes in a thick Western drawl, they became furious.

"Get off this frequency, boy. You hear, boy? This is a federal violation, boy."

When Texans start to get mad, they call people "boy." Sam and Phil pretended to be tracking us down by some method of triangulation. I began to get a trifle worried. But not Ronald. He became friendlier than ever. When they realized threats weren't working, they started to plead.

"We're closing in on you, boy. But if you get off this frequency right now, we won't prosecute you. You see, we're about to go on the air with our traffic report on this frequency. We don't want you messin' up our traffic report, boy. You'd get in real serious trouble if you did that."

Ronald was just as nice and friendly as he could be, and he just kept on talking. I had visions of a headline: "Ford Staffers Arrested on Federal Communications Violation." But this was getting to be fun. What harm would one more nasty headline do now? Ronald chatted away. We switched on the car radio. We finally heard Bart's voice, reading the news. We waited for the traffic report. They announced that they were having trouble with the helicopter, and would not be able to report traffic conditions that night.

While they spent the rest of the evening looking for Ronald, we spent the evening looking for John Wayne. Neither party was successful.

We had to leave for Dallas later that night in order to film the President and John Connally at the Texas State Fair Friday and Saturday.

I felt bad about wasting an entire day—Doug's time, my time, the film crew's time. I apologized to Doug.

"I'm really sorry about this mess," I said. "We accomplished absolutely nothing. We wasted an entire day."

"What are you sorry about?" Doug asked quietly. "That makes this the best day we've had in two weeks."

26
DIRTY TRICKS?

It was the weekend of the Texas-Oklahoma football game, and the cab driver felt that he should warn me about it.

"Oh boy," he said. "Oh boy! And ooo-eee!"

"Pretty wild?" I asked.

"Oh boy, oh boy!" he said. "If you got no business being out tonight, buddy—stay in, hear? Stay right in your room and double-lock the doors. Oh boy, oh boy, and oh boy again! It's the Fourth of July, Mardi Gras, and New Year's Eve all rolled into one. Yes sir, it's Oklahoma-Texas. Oh boy, and wow. Yes sir, and wow again. Call out the state troopers. Yes sir, it's quite wild. Quite wild. Oh boy!"

I did venture out that night very briefly. I thought it would be nice to have dinner in the bar-dining room at the Holiday Inn where I was staying. The bar was crowded, but there didn't seem to be any students. I'd been told to stay away from the students. These were just a bunch of happy businessmen and their wives. Most of them were wearing jackets. I sat at the bar, ordered a drink, and started to listen to the medley of Cole Porter songs that a pretty young pianist was playing. A big man at one of the tables suddenly started hollering for her to play "Boomer Sooner." She smiled and said she'd play it later. The man stood up and started to sing "Boomer Sooner" at the top of his voice. The lyrics were simple enough. They consisted entirely of two words—"Boomer Sooner." Within seconds almost everyone in the room was singing "Boomer Sooner." The young pianist and Cole Porter didn't have a chance. She soon gave up and retreated to a corner of the bar, a frightened look on her face. One of the singers slid onto the piano stool and started pounding out "Boomer Sooner." A very large middle-aged man was sitting at the bar next to me, singing along at the top of his voice. Suddenly he stopped and turned to me.

"Why aren't you singing?" he said in a menacing Texas drawl.

I couldn't very well say I didn't know the words.

"I'm from Boston," I said pleasantly.

He looked at me coldly. "Just so long as you aren't from Dallas," he said, shaking his head meaningfully.

He decided to start singing again. And I decided that it would be nice to have dinner in my room.

As I made my way down the corridor to my room, people seemed to be chasing one another in and out of suites. The carpet was already squishy from spilled beer. I could hear lots of voices, behind closed doors, singing "Boomer Sooner."

It's a sound I listened to all night. That and the sirens and the screams. There were lots of screams that night. I'll never know whether or not those women were in distress.

I probably wouldn't have had much sleep anyway. It had been another depressing day on the campaign trail. People seemed to want to talk about the second debate, the investigation by the Watergate prosecutor, Earl Butz, the new economic report showing that both inflation and unemployment had gone up again, and Wall Street.

I had had lunch with a Texas businessman who was particularly upset by the fact that the market had lost ninety points in nine days. Fortunately, he didn't blame it entirely on Ford.

"It's both of those clowns," he said. "The two of them. Whenever either one of them opens his mouth, Wall Street panics."

I had done a radio spot that day featuring Tom Landry, coach of the Dallas Cowboys. I had written a script for him that had some pretty strong anti-Carter material. I wanted him to say that "it wasn't right for Jimmy Carter to say what he did about Lyndon Johnson in *Playboy*." That would have been strong stuff in Texas, but Tom Landry gulped hard when he read it.

"I'd like to do everything I can for the President," he said in his pleasant Texas accent. "But if I said this, some of our fans would start throwing bottles at me."

He read my alternate script, praising the President but not mentioning Carter. When he was through, he swiveled in his chair and started staring at the huge Super Bowl trophy next to his desk.

"Tell me something," he said thoughtfully. "When is Ford going to start saying the right thing?"

"You mean the debate?" I asked.

":I mean everything. He was going great, and then—boom. It's like calling the wrong play on the goal line. You go backwards. And he keeps doing it. Calling the wrong play. Going backwards."

Most of the people I met in Texas, including the cab drivers, were disturbed by the direction the campaign seemed to be taking. Even though they weren't connected with the campaign, they seemed to sense as strongly as I did that we not only had lost the momentum, but were now sliding backwards. I felt that the President's visit the next day, to open the Texas State Fair and attend the Texas-Oklahoma game, was crucial to our chances here.

After I retreated to my room that night, I turned on the television set to find out how the local news people were treating the President's impending arrival.

What I saw didn't exactly cheer me up.

The station I watched mentioned the President's visit briefly after discussing the repercussions of his Eastern Europe remark, and the news that there still was no news concerning the Watergate prosecutor's investigation of Ford. They devoted the next fifteen minutes or so to one of the most extraordinary "special reports" I had ever seen on television.

Someone who described himself as part of the "Channel Eight Investigating Team" seemed to be trying to prove that either President Ford or Richard Nixon—I couldn't for the life of me figure out which one—had made some shady deal with Jimmy Hoffa.

It was fascinating reporting. They showed a group of people described as "wealthy Texans" at a Republican fund-raising dinner. The people were all wearing evening clothes and did look wealthy as hell. They kept cutting from the people in tuxedoes to posters of Ford and our slogan: "He's making us proud again."

Then they cut to someone who said he was a member of the Teamsters Union. He said that he'd been having a fight with the union over something. He said that Chuck Colson had told him personally that if he didn't drop the fight with the Teamsters, he would be investigated by the tax people.

The announcer then said, in a voice dripping with sinister implications, that "Nixon's people are still involved."

To prove it, they cut to a man in a tuxedo at the Republican dinner. A man who, according to the announcer, had received a $125,000 legal fee from Jimmy Hoffa's union.

The "investigator" then talked of President Ford's attempts to woo the Teamsters Union. He said that the President wasn't really interested in the rank and file Teamsters, but was "trying to influence, for mutual benefit, the union bosses."

I turned off the set and literally scratched my head. What in the world were they trying to prove? I decided to give them the benefit of the doubt. They *were* trying to prove *something*.

Okay. But what did Richard Nixon have to do with it—whatever it was? He had been in retirement for two-and-a-half years.

And what did Jimmy Hoffa have to do with it—whatever it was? Jimmy Hoffa had been dead or missing for a year, and hadn't been head of the Teamsters for many years.

And what did Chuck Colson have to do with whatever it was? He'd gone to jail and been born again and written his book.

And how had the President wooed the Teamsters? I figured I might check that angle. Might learn something. The President hadn't done too good a job of "wooing" those Teamster bosses. They were all working their tails off for Jimmy Carter.

There were so many questions running through my mind after I saw that "special report" on Channel Eight in Dallas, that I just had to ask myself one further question.

Was this a dirty trick?

An attempt by persons unknown, with the aid of the TV station, to smear President Ford?

Richard Nixon. Jimmy Hoffa. Chuck Colson. The Teamsters Union. Paunchy Republicans in evening clothes. Big legal fees. Threatening "the little guy" with a tax investigation. Put them all together in one juicy glob, then smear it all over President Ford.

Could that be possible?

I thought about that a great deal that night. Between the screams and the sirens and the choruses of "Boomer Sooner," my mind kept trying to figure out what the story was, what roles the various characters played, what the hell was being reported. I'm an old newspaper reporter. Who, What, When, Where. I know all about that. So who did what to whom, when and where?

Or was it all innuendo?

I hadn't really thought much about dirty tricks in this campaign. Too dangerous. I didn't think our people would try to pull any. And I thought Carter, who was ahead, was too smart for dirty tricks. When Howard K. Smith had said that watching the campaign was like being nibbled to death by ducks, I knew what he meant, but I never believed that they were Jimmy Carter's ducks.

I thought about "the politics of deception," as Doug liked to call it. The shading of the meaning of words, the changing of adjectives without really changing positions, the deliberate attempt to avoid hard issues. Carter's accepting the Liberal Party endorsement one day and hugging George Wallace the next. Running against the political establishment in the primary, and running *to* the establishment in this campaign. Trying to be all things to all people: liberal to liberals, conservative to conservatives. And getting *away* with it. Saying, ''I will never lie to you.'' And getting *away* with it.

And the manipulation of the press. The softball games on the evening news. The talk shows. Sunday church in Plains, Georgia. The garment bag slung over the shoulder. God, that garment bag! Wouldn't Nixon have *loved* that garment bag? The smooth, beautifully orchestrated campaign.

There had been nothing smooth or orchestrated about that *Playboy* interview. The attempt to say things to young swingers without being heard by Middle America—that might have been a Nixon approach.

But Richard Nixon would never have done it in *Playboy*. And Richard Nixon would never have used words that would come back to haunt him.

Another Nixon?

It was something to think about between the sirens and the screams and the ''Boomer Sooner.'' It was something I was going to think about again before the campaign was over.

27
NOBODY'S CHEERING

The next morning the President insisted on sticking his head and shoulders out of the top of his limousine as his motorcade wound slowly through the streets of Dallas, Texas. He wanted to wave to the crowd.

I was in the back seat of a van, two cars behind the President. I had the eerie feeling that I was playing a role in an old newsreel. There was the familiar white head of John Connally standing beside the President. There was the Texas Schoolbook Depository, a helicopter circling over its roof. The motorcycle policemen suddenly darting ahead, sirens whining. The Secret Service men, trotting beside the limousine, looking up, eyes piercing the darkness behind the endless rows of windows.

It was a tense, nervous ride all the way from Love Field on the outskirts of Dallas, where Air Force One had landed, to the Texas State Fair grounds. The ride took us about an hour and a half. The distance was less than ten miles. Doug and I sat together in the back. We hardly spoke. I'm certain he was thinking the same dark thoughts as I.

Ron Nessen, the President's news secretary, was riding in the van with us. He was nervous for other reasons.

"Nobody's cheering," he said, almost in desperation, as we drove through the heart of downtown Dallas.

I looked at the crowd. People were lined three deep on the sidewalk. All I saw were faces staring at me. Mostly black faces with wooden expressions. There were lots of children sitting on the curb in the front row. Some of them had FORD-DOLE signs, but they weren't waving them. They were just holding them. Just resting them on the cement.

"Nobody's cheering!" Ron Nesson said again. "Why aren't they cheering?"

I thought about all the reports I'd read in the papers about voter apathy. I hadn't believed the reports. I had figured that the columnists needed something to write about. Like sportswriters after a rained-out game. You had to write something. So they invented apathy. Better than writing about issues, or what the candidates might have said. But I looked at that crowd and began to believe those stories. Apathetic. That's what those people were.

But then it occurred to me that if they were really apathetic, they would have stayed in bed. They wouldn't have gone a long way to stand on a crowded street and wait for a glimpse of the President.

"The advance people blew it," Nessen was saying. "They should have had bands. Marching bands. That would have gotten them cheering."

I looked at the silent crowd. They didn't look unfriendly. They didn't look friendly, either. As we rounded a corner I could see the President standing up and waving to the crowd. The people in his direct line of vision would wave back. But as soon as they were out of his sight, they stopped waving. It was as though they were waving to be polite, but they hadn't come to wave at the President.

And then it occurred to me why most of them had come. They weren't waiting for the President. They were waiting for Oswald. Not all of them, of course. But some of them. And I knew that it was on the minds of every one of them. Because it was uppermost in my mind.

Suddenly we heard the first faint sound of cheering several cars ahead. The motorcade stopped. The crowds were thicker here. The cheering grew louder.

"Hey, listen," Ron Nessen said. "Cheering. They're cheering him!"

Our cameraman, Lee Kenower, stepped out of the van and peered up ahead. Suddenly he was running up the street towards the cheering, holding his camera over his head as he ran. Doug and I got out to look. I could see the President walking into the crowd on the sidewalk. He was wearing a white shirt. His hands were stretched out towards the crowd. That's where the cheering was the loudest, but now I could hear cheering from all around me. People behind me were cheering, even though they could have no idea what they were cheering about.

I wanted to tell them. His hands were outstretched, reaching to touch their outstretched hands.

He plunged on into the crowd. He was completely engulfed in people. All I could see was the top of his bald head. The Secret Service men were frantically trying to get between him and the people, but it was hopeless. People were smiling and cheering and waving like hell.

I saw Lee Kenower standing on top of a car, recording the scene with his camera. I remember thinking that this was a moment that you just can't capture on film. You had to see it live. You had to feel it. You had to understand it.

The people of Dallas understood it. Lee Oswald, after all these years, had finally been defeated.

The moment lasted only a few minutes. Somehow the Secret Service men got the President back into the limousine. The motorcade proceeded through the last little stretch of road to the Dallas fairgrounds. The people were cheering all along the way. The tension was gone. I felt so good that I leaned out the window and held my hand up in a "Hook 'em, Longhorns" salute. Almost everyone gave me the "Hook 'em, Longhorns" salute right back, and cheered even louder. I didn't give a damn whether Texas beat Oklahoma that afternoon. I was hooking Jimmy Carter. The campaign had begun again. Not with a well-rehearsed speech. Not with a brilliant ad. Not with a Carter gaffe. But with a little walk from a limousine to a crowd.

28
THE SOLID SILVER SURROGATE

I once shook the hand of Mayor Curley. It was part of a Harvard *Lampoon* stunt. We had just stolen a fifty-pound marble punch bowl from the Harvard *Crimson*. We thought it would be nice to present it to Mayor Curley, who was in his very last hurrah as mayor of Boston. We said that we were the Boston College for Curley Club, and wheeled the bowl into his office on a child's little red cart. He had invited some reporters to witness the presentation. After handing each of us an autographed copy of his book, *The Purple Shamrock,* he gave an impressive little speech about getting more aid for parochial schools. Just before he ended the speech, an aide hurried into the room and handed him a message. The mayor glanced at the note, and without missing a beat began talking about the spirit of youth and the pranks he used to pull as a youngster.

The headline in the paper the next day said, "College Prank Amuses Mayor." I realized how easily it could have read "College Prank Infuriates Mayor" or "College Prank Fools Mayor."

In Curley I thought I had met the ultimate politician—that was until I spent a morning with John Connally of Texas.

John Connally is as smooth as Texas oil. I had previously thought of him as something of a phony politician. How else could a man jump from the top of the Democratic Party to the top of the Republican Party? But when I saw him in action at the Texas State Fair, I realized that he wasn't a phony politician. He was a genuine Texas politician. Clearly he was proud of every inch of Texas. His first job

159

at the Texas State Fair was to take the President on a tour of the cattle barn, the sheep barn, and the swine barn. It was staged for the press, of course. As Connally led the President from stall to stall, he always seemed to be facing the right cameras at the right time. He talked knowledgeably about the animals while the President listened attentively and laughed appropriately. What struck me most was that Connally, whom I had always associated with oil and business and politics, really *knew* what he was talking about. He knew the names and weights of the prize cattle. He knew by name the ranchers who were handling them. And they didn't talk to him as they would to a politician. They talked to him as if he were a fellow rancher.

John Connally may have seemed like a phony politician to an outsider like me, but I could see that to a Texan, he was a purebred Texan. And for my particular political purposes that day, that was a good sign.

Connally was going to be our surrogate spokesman for Texas. We would have preferred Reagan, but Reagan would do no more than the very general spots that he had already taped. Now we were going to do spots on the specific issues that concerned Texans. Connally knew those issues and felt strongly about them; just maybe, I thought hopefully, he was the better man to speak out on those issues.

By the time we got through admiring the sheep, I looked at my watch and felt a sharp twinge of panic. We had exactly forty minutes to make four TV commercials and six radio commercials. We had no cue cards. Connally had not seen the scripts. And there was a marching band rehearsing on the location we had selected for the filming.

John Connally and the President were still chatting about sheep ranching when they emerged from the sheep barn. I had no choice. I had to interrupt them.

"Excuse me," I said nervously, not knowing where I got the gall. "We're filming some commercials for you here today."

He shook my hand firmly. "Sure," he said. "How's everything going? Did you get everything you needed in the barns?"

"Just terrific, Mr. President. Terrific. We were planning on filming Governor Connally now. I understand we have only forty minutes before the opening ceremonies."

"He can do it," the President said. "John's an old pro."

I thanked him and started to leave with John Connally.

"By the way," the President said. "I think the commercials look just great."

We made fourteen different commercials, unrehearsed, in forty minutes. The first eight were the hardest. Four sixty-second spots and four thirty-second spots for Texas television. We filmed them right on the Midway of the fairgrounds among crowds of people, some of whom insisted on making funny faces and giving "Hook 'Em Longhorns" salutes behind Connally's head. We made them in spite of a country music band—the worst you have ever heard—that was blaring at us over a loudspeaker. We made them in spite of a cordon of fifteen police motorcyclists who kept starting up their engines the instant we started up the camera. We made them because of John Connally, who is the most polished, the most articulate, the most confident actor that I have ever seen in front of a camera.

For technical reasons, a thirty-second TV commercial has to come in at twenty-eight seconds on film. My first commercial, one on gun control, had been written a trifle long. I timed the first take at thirty-two seconds. His reading was perfect, even though he had taken only a couple of minutes to study the copy.

"I'll cut the copy." I said.

"No," he said. "I'll just shorten my drawl."

He went through it again. Twenty-eight seconds on the button. The reading was even better. He looked genuinely outraged as he said, "Most of our farmers and ranchers resent the idea that Jimmy Carter supports gun control legislation." You felt that he was speaking for Texas when he closed with, "Ford is the best choice for Texas."

The next commercial he did in *one* take. I had asked him to take his jacket off, and I was holding his expensive blue jacket over my arm while he concentrated for about two minutes on my script. I remember thinking how good he looked—that tanned Texas face, the silver hair, the clean white shirt.

He handed me the script and said, "Okay, let's roll 'em." Lee Kenower pointed his camera for a tight close-up and Connally set his square jaw in anger.

"Most Texans feel the way I do about their property rights," he said, glaring into the lens. "They don't want strangers coming on their farms and ranches without permission. Well, the other day Jimmy Carter came out in favor of a proposal that will *allow* union organizers to come on a man's property without being asked.

"Now I know that President Ford feels that a man's property rights are sacred. I think most Texans feel that way, too. That's one more good reason to vote for President Ford on November second."

I gave him two more scripts. A sixty-second and a thirty-second commercial on a subject dear to John Connally's heart. Right-to-work laws.

"I'm really going to *feel* this one," he drawled as he gave me back the shorter script and set his face in an outraged expression. Lee and the sound man started their motors, and Connally started his:

"When Jimmy Carter was governor of Georgia he was for the right-to-work laws that protect the workers of Georgia—and Texas. But now that he is running for President, with the support of the big Northern labor unions, he is committed to signing the bill that would *do away* with our right-to-work laws. Many working people in Texas feel that this is not just another flip-flop, but a betrayal of Texas working people. That's another reason we're supporting President Ford."

I told him that we had a perfect take. We did. It took him three takes to do the longer right-to-work spot. Not because he wasn't perfect the first time, but because he wanted to put a little more anger into the part where he talked about the "price" Jimmy Carter had paid to win the support "of George Meany, Leonard Woodcock, and the big maritime unions."

He was just as quick and just as slick as he silver-tongued his way through two commercials on the energy issue ("There are some issues Jimmy Carter can be vague and fuzzy about, but here in Texas we have one issue on which we need a clear answer—energy.")

He then did two positive spots about the President's visit to the State Fair, and another on tax reform.

As we finished the tax reform spot, an aide appeared at his elbow and said we had five minutes left. Having seen him in action, I was convinced that five minutes was all the time we would need to complete the five sixty-second radio commercials. The only trouble was we couldn't do them in the street.

John Connally, the sound man, and I practically ran to the pavilion that had been reserved for the President's party. The quietest spot we could find was a small, bare room in the back. Three or four Secret Service men were there, and one of them was talking on the radio. At least it was better than country music and roaring motorcycles. I asked him to please talk quietly. We found a little stool for Connally. And I handed him five scripts. We had two minutes left. If it had been humanly possible for anyone to read five one-minute commercials in two minutes, I was sure John Connally was the man who could do it. Unfortunately, however, we kept the President waiting three minutes. I didn't think that was too bad. We'd completed fourteen commercials in forty-three minutes. It sometimes takes me six months to complete *one* thirty-second product commercial. But, of course, we don't have John Connally as a spokesman.

From a professional standpoint, we had accomplished a small

miracle. Despite all the physical problems, I knew the commercials would be technically perfect. Kenower is a superb cameraman, and he had filmed tight close-ups, the best way to wring all the conviction out of an angry man. Fourteen perfect commercials in forty-three minutes! I would have been pleased, if all that mattered was getting the job done.

But I felt something far removed from pleasure that night when I took off from Dallas. I felt that I had just completed the worst commercials I'd ever put on film.

I had made a strong commercial about gun control. The issue could win votes. But I knew two important things about that commercial. Carter had not advocated gun control, as the commercial implied. He had said he favored the registration of handguns. Hell, in most states handgun registration is already in effect. The other important thing I knew was that I, personally, was for gun control. I didn't want to take rifles away from ranchers and farmers. But I did, and still do, favor stricter control over who gets guns.

I had made another commercial on property rights. No, I don't want union organizers crawling all over my house in Gloucester, Mass. But I knew it was no more likely than having union organizers crawling all over those Texas ranches. I knew that the "proposal" that Jimmy Carter favored actually referred to a proposition in California that Cesar Chavez favored and Jimmy Carter supported for local political reasons. It had nothing to *do* with Texas.

I felt that Carter should have been hit with his right-to-work flip-flop. And because I felt that his "fuzziness" on the energy issue was one of his political maneuvers, I didn't feel too guilty about those spots.

But there was something else wrong, basically wrong, with all the commercials, and it went against my grain as an advertising man. Our research had told us that John Connally was not a great spokesman for us in Texas.

John Connally is loved by a great many Texans. There is no question that he has done a lot for Texas. Someday, I'm sure, there will be a giant statue of John Connally standing in some giant park. He will probably have solid silver hair.

But the people who loved Connally during the Ford-Carter campaign were not the people President Ford needed to reach. The people whom Ford needed to reach thought of John Connally as the man who left the Democratic Party to go to work for Richard Nixon. The man who talked Texas into voting for Nixon was now trying to talk Texas into voting for Ford.

John Connally was important to Ford in Texas. But not as a television spokesman. No doubt he helped Ford tremendously in the inner political circles. But I am just as convinced that he hurt Ford on television.

I feel that only two people could have helped us on television. One of them was Ronald Reagan. He did a couple of commercials on national defense and the Republican platform. They helped. But if he had been willing to really speak out for President Ford, really work for Ford, I feel convinced that we would have carried Texas. The same goes, of course, for Mississippi. He could have made the difference in both states.

The other man who could have carried Texas for Ford was Ford. We should have made a special pool of commercials featuring the President talking about the gut issues that concerned Texans. We didn't. The fault was ours. *We* lost Texas for Ford.

There's only one thing I'm pleased about when I think about our loss in Texas. When I got the film back to the editing room, I managed to come to the conclusion that the gun control spot and the property rights spot wouldn't get us any votes after all. Somehow they ended up on the cutting room floor.

29
AMIGOS
AND BANDITOS

In this business, as they say, you have to learn to take the good with the bad. In the week between October eighth and October fifteenth we had a good deal of both.

The Ford commercials were beginning to get excellent reviews. Almost all the state chairmen, who are usually the harshest critics, were reporting strong, positive reaction all over the country. A major poll showed that voter perceptions of Ford were changing. His approval rating had increased dramatically. Undecided voters were showing a more positive attitude towards him as a man and as a leader. We had to believe, with all the troubles we'd been having, that our commercials had something to do with this change. And we'd only just begun to advertise. Our man-on-the-street commercials were just emerging from the laboratories, and Doug Bailey, who had spent weeks cutting them, was rubbing his hands in anticipation. My anti-Carter commercials, though stalled in the legal department and delayed by money troubles, were on the track again.

But the Eastern Europe problem wouldn't go away. Carter ran full-page ads in all the ethnic newspapers the week after the second debate. I saw them, and I didn't have to know a word of Polish to understand exactly what they said. Betty Ford tried to solve the problem. She gave a ringing defense of her husband's long record of working on behalf of the people of Eastern Europe. But the newspapers and television stations reported only her last sentence. ''I know

Jerry's position on Eastern Europe," she said, "but I certainly don't know where Jimmy Carter stands!" Well, she had tried.

The people from our ethnic desk were going around the Washington office wringing their hands. The Polish vote, the Hungarian vote, the Yugoslavian vote—something had to be done about them, or there would be disaster on November second. Stu Spencer arranged a White House meeting with the President and ethnic leaders from around the country. It calmed the storm. We took a large chunk of precious advertising money to run a full-page ad in major cities with large ethnic populations. I felt that a good offense was the best defense. The ad attacked Carter for distorting Ford's position or Eastern Europe. Fortunately, Carter *was* distorting the President's statement, and that gave us a target. We kicked. And it worked. But once again we'd wasted time and money overcoming a problem. That is no way to build momentum.

But more good things were happening, and for three straight days I thought our roller coaster was on the rise again. Somewhere I found a new burst of energy, and commercials started flying out of my typewriter. They were mostly radio commercials to be used in all the key states. Each one concerned specific issues, and I used appropriate spokespeople for most of those. That meant jumping into cabs and heading for the Senate Office Building to record important political people. I found that the cabbies of Washington aren't impressed when you say, "Take me to the Senate Office Building."

"You lookin' to get laid?" one of the drivers replied. The memory of Elizabeth Ray will die hard in Washington.

Senator Lowell Weicker of Connecticut did an enthusiastic endorsement of the Ford Presidency, and I felt that it would definitely help in his state. Our research told us that he had an extremely high rating among Democrats and Independents.

Senator Richard Schweiker of Pennsylvania, Reagan's chosen running mate, didn't seem to be at all bitter about his Kansas City defeat. He did two commercials for us, one for the western part of Pennsylvania, the other for Pittsburgh and Philadelphia. If you can judge by the election results, his western commercial was a hit, but the other one was a bomb.

Senator Paul Laxalt of Nevada touched on issues dear to the heart of Nevadans, including Carter's proposed closing of the nuclear testing site.

While we were making those commercials, Woody Hayes, the coach of the Ohio State football team, offered to help us in that key state. He made two effective radio spots for us. He had only one condition. He was willing to say that President Ford had been a football player, but he absolutely refused to mention the school that he played for. Apparently the word "Michigan" never crosses the lips of Woody Hayes.

At this point regional ads, brochures, and commercials were being churned out of our Washington headquarters at an incredible rate. Our staff in New York was starting work on the half-hour film for the last night of the campaign and re-editing other commercials. Barry Laffer, the man who had to keep track of it all, put his head in my office one day and announced, "We hit three hundred!"

"Three hundred what?" I asked.

"Three hundred different job numbers have now been issued."

"Let's go for four," I suggested.

Meanwhile, Phil Angell talked continuously into two telephones at once. He seemed to be the only bridge between the White House, Baker and Spencer, Deardourff and Bailey, the media department in New York, the traffic department in New York, and me. There were logjams at the bridgehead, but surprisingly few.

But we needed help, and once again the right person turned up at exactly the right time. Dennis Roehl, who had been account supervisor on Pepsi Cola at Batten, Barton, Durstine, and Osborn, joined us just as it looked as if everything was going to fly off into a thousand little pieces.

As soon as he had helped us straighten out some of the production difficulties on our regional ads, we put him to work on Amigos for Ford.

The Spanish-American vote is not an easy target in a national election. It is made up principally of three completely different groups. The Mexican-Americans, the Cuban-Americans, and the Puerto Rican-Americans. The Mexican-Americans are concentrated in Texas and California; the Cuban-Americans are in Dade County, Florida; the Puerto Rican-Americans are principally in New York and New Jersey. You can reach a part of all three communities in Chicago.

We had a little more than $200,000 to spend on all three voting groups. The cost of media was relatively cheap, but production was high because separate commercials were needed for each group. We had to do more than simply translate our ads into Spanish.

I wanted to use appropriate celebrities: Vicki Carr for Mexican-Americans, Tony Orlando for Puerto Rican-Americans, and Cesar Romero for Cuban Americans. My scripts called for them to speak, in both English and Spanish, about specific things that President

Ford had done for each of their communities. We didn't have a great case, but we certainly could show that President Ford had done more than any of his predecessors.

Vicki Carr backed out at the last minute, claiming other commitments. We wound up using a Mexican version of our musical commercial, "Feelin' Good." From the results, I feel we can conclude that Mexican-Americans weren't feeling good about America. Using the song was a mistake.

Tony Orlando didn't want to do a Spanish version of his commercial. For Spanish-speaking stations, we wound up with a Spanish version of "Feelin' Good." I feel that we can now safely conclude that Puerto Rican-Americans weren't feeling too good about America, either. Another mistake.

Cesar Romero, however, was just right for the Cuban-American commercials. He glared into the camera, his white moustache fairly twitching, as he spoke with deep Cuban pride:

"We Cubans know the importance of standing tall and being tough. President Ford has condemned the Cuban dictatorship, refuses to deal with it, and says it is not fit to belong to the Organization of American States. President Ford has fought against those who would cut the nation's defense budget. That is why so many Cuban-Americans support President Ford."

I had found a little zinger to put at the end of that commercial. One of Jimmy Carter's aides had told a *Washington Star* reporter that the Cuban-American vote wouldn't make any difference in the Florida outcome. Carter had shown us a tiny bit of his ass. We gave him a tiny bit of a kick.

"Aides to Jimmy Carter have called the Cuban-American vote 'insignificant,' " Romero thundered angrily. "Let us prove them wrong on November second."

It turned out that Jimmy Carter's aide was right. We got the Cuban-American vote. It *was* insignificant.

In retrospect, our whole approach to the Spanish-American vote was wrong. First of all, Jimmy Carter spoke directly to the people in Spanish. President Ford couldn't speak two words of Spanish. We couldn't possibly have topped Jimmy Carter's act with spokespeople. Instead, I feel, President Ford should have talked to them directly in English, speaking to them as Americans. He should have pointed out that though he didn't speak their native language, he understood their present problems. He should have spoken to them about those specific problems and told them, specifically, what he planned to do to solve them. These were the commercials we had wanted to make. But there never was time to make them.

Our mistakes in the Spanish community were as nothing compared to our disaster in the black community. We utterly failed to communicate with the black voters of America. No matter how I look at the final results, I have to conclude that this failure was the biggest single factor in our defeat. American blacks voted ten to one for Jimmy Carter. They elected Jimmy Carter.

We had hoped to get about thirty percent of the black vote. That's what a Republican Presidential candidate can normally expect. We were also hoping that the black turnout would be low. Based on polling data, and on the constant talk about voter apathy in the press, that seemed to be a relatively safe bet. One Ford staff member claimed to have made a poll of black taxicab drivers in Washington. He said the vote was two for Carter, zero for Ford, fourteen not voting.

We dreamed on and let Lionel Hampton, of all people, carry our banner. Lionel Hampton is a wonderful, cheerful man. He is a friend of President Ford's. He came into our offices with a song he had written about the President. It was called "Call Ford Mr. Sunshine." He had recorded it with his full orchestra and chorus. When he discovered that we didn't have a record player, he rushed out and bought an expensive one so we could hear his song. He left the record player behind, and we put his song on black radio. The listeners, apparently, did not sing along.

We made no serious effort to communicate with the black community. Perhaps we never could have overcome the Butz problem and the Republican problem, but I would feel better today if we had tried.

On the thirteenth, fourteenth, and fifteenth of October we were hit with the bad, the good, and the bad again—bang, bang, bang, in three consecutive days.

The worst blow that was dealt us in that traumatic time came from the skilled hand of John Dean. He sneaked up behind us, whacked us with a karate chop, and took off before anyone could catch him.

He appeared on the "Today" show on the mornings of those three days. He was there to publicize his book, aptly titled *Blind Ambition*. NBC was interested in publicizing his book, too. They had just bought the television rights to it.

In the course of his first interview John Dean blandly announced a new "fact" about Watergate. House Minority Leader Gerald Ford, at President Nixon's instigation, had successfully squelched the Patman investigation of the Watergate break-in.

Dean was asked whether he realized the seriousness of his allegation. He was asked why he had chosen the closing weeks of the campaign to make the charge. He was asked why he had not mentioned the matter before. He was asked why he hadn't even made an important issue of the matter in his book. Through it all, Dean stared blandly at the questioner and allowed as how he didn't think anything was unusual.

What Dean did not say was that the paperback rights to his book were being auctioned that very week. What he did not say was that the publicity from the interview could put enormous sums of money into his pocket, as the bidding went up.

The people Dean mentioned as the so-called intermediaries between Nixon and Ford in the squelching of the investigation heatedly denied his charges as soon as they could get to a telephone. They said flatly that Dean had been lying. But denials don't make headlines. Facts can't possibly compete with the innuendos of a John Dean. We were helpless, once again, in the face of a groundless charge.

There was no question in my mind that his charge was opportunistic. Five days later, on the "Panorama" show in Washington, Dean was again interviewed about his attack on President Ford.

The moderator asked, "Why now, John?"

Dean admitted that "there was a problem" in the timing. He blamed it on his publisher.

The moderator looked incredulous. "You've torpedoed the man's campaign," he said. "Why didn't you bring it up in June?"

Dean's answer was, "I'm in the business of telling the truth."

The moderator asked again why he didn't bring it up in June, when there was ample time to investigate the charges. He again pointed out that "you've torpedoed the man's career."

Again Dean had no answer.

The moderator then talked about the Butz incident. "The two most embarrassing moments of the man's campaign," he pointed out. "Why you?"

Dean replied, "Totally done by accident. If I'd wanted to, I couldn't have done it."

The moderator then asked if Dean, *Rolling Stone,* and Capricorn Records were all part of a Carter plot.

"Why did you cover the Republican convention for *Rolling Stone* and not the Democrat convention?" the moderator asked.

"I didn't want to go to New York City," Dean replied.

Were there motives other than greed behind Dean's last-minute allegations against Ford?

I don't know. I still find it strange—these repeated, evenly spaced allegations, all unproven, about the President's honesty. I don't know. I do know that John Dean raised serious doubts about the integrity of President Ford. If that was part of his goal, he succeeded.

You take the bad with the good. The very next day Charles Ruff, the Watergate prosecutor, publicly cleared President Ford of all charges in the investigation of illegal campaign financing. That cloud had been over our heads for over a month.

You take the good with the bad. The day after that Dole debated Mondale. I thought Dole lost. The polls said I was right.

30
CUTTING CARTER DOWN TO SIZE

I think that some of our best advertising in the last campaign was the ads and commercials that most outraged the idealists.

They got Jimmy Carter so mad that he twice complained to the media about our "misleading" advertising. We were delighted. On both occasions, Jimmy Carter's complaints gave our ads free national exposure. And on both occasions he looked a little silly.

His first yelp came after our *Playboy* ad appeared. Newsweek had done a cover story on "The Ford Presidency." It was by no means a "puff" piece. It was an honest appraisal of what Ford had accomplished in office, and what he had not accomplished. It inspired me to write a very simple newspaper ad. I showed a picture of the cover of *Newsweek* and a picture of the cover of *Playboy*. I wrote no copy, just a headline: "One good way to decide this election. Read this week's *Newsweek*. Read this month's *Playboy*."

It took so long to get approval of the ad from Baker, Spencer, and the President, that I finally had to change the headline to: "One good way to decide this election. Read last week's *Newsweek*. Read this month's *Playboy*."

We ran it as a full page ad in about three hundred cities. No large cities. People in large cities might think that Jimmy Carter came off pretty well in that *Playboy* interview. We ran it in places like Memphis and Baton Rouge and Sioux City and Waco, Texas. Places where you are most likely to find people who think that Presidential candidates shouldn't appear in magazines that have naked girls on the cover.

Jimmy Carter complained about the ad; most television stations showed the ad when they reported his complaint; we wound up with a nice bonus circulation.

He complained again when our man-in-the-street commercials appeared, and he again gave us some free advertising. It is very easy to criticize our man-in-the-street commercials. It's quite true that anyone can go out on the street with a camera and find people who are willing to praise one candidate and criticize another. Give me a week and I can probably make a film full of people praising Adolf Hitler.

But when Doug Bailey went out into the street with Lee Kenower, cameraman, and Michael Goldbaum, sound engineer, he was not just trying to find people who would say nasty things about Carter. He was trying to make commercials that accurately reflected an existing national attitude towards Jimmy Carter.

Our research showed that despite all his campaigning, most Americans had many unanswered questions about Jimmy Carter. People didn't know where he stood on the issues. People didn't know what he would do as President. Over thirty percent of the people who were supporting him in early October confessed serious reservations about him. They were supporting him only because they wanted a change, only because, in their opinion, he was the lesser of two evils. The purpose of our man-in-the-street commercials was to voice these feelings.

Doug and his crew went to five different cities. One of them was Atlanta, Georgia. Nothing was staged. The people were not selected in advance. Doug simply asked people questions, Lee turned on the camera, and the people said exactly what was on their minds.

We edited about a dozen different television commercials and over twenty different radio commercials from those interviews. My particular favorite was the one made up entirely of Georgians. Six different people allowed as how Jimmy Carter hadn't been much of a governor. At the end an attractive woman looked directly into the camera and said, "I'd like to have someone from Georgia become President—but not Jimmy Carter." It was a great television commercial. And it *accurately* reflected the feelings of most of the people who were interviewed that day in Atlanta.

Another of my favorites was the "wishy-washy" commercial. During the course of the interviews, several different people said that they thought Jimmy Carter was a bit "wishy-washy." It was a simple matter to string them all together into one commercial. "He seems a little wishy-washy to me," says a man in Dallas. Cut to a lady in Chicago: "I think he's wishy-washy." Cut to a man in New York: "Wishy-washy, that's how I'd describe Jimmy Carter." Cut to a woman in Atlanta trying to think of the word that best described Jimmy Carter: "It seems to me that he's . . . well . . . I'd say he was wishy-washy."

Those commercials worked. They worked because they reflected existing feelings that many people had. Lots of people who were interviewed had much worse things to say about Jimmy Carter. We didn't use them, because they wouldn't have worked. They wouldn't have expressed the feelings that most viewers of the commercials had.

One of Jimmy Carter's early commercials bragged, for five minutes, about what he had done as governor of Georgia. I felt that we should do a commercial about what he had done as governor of Georgia, too. It was a thirty-second spot. Our commercial literally began where his left off. It opened on a television set tuned to the end of the Carter commercial. An announcer read the last line of the Carter commercial: "What Jimmy Carter did as governor of Georgia, he will do as President of the United States."

We then proceeded to show, graphically, three things that Carter had left out of his own commercial.

Over a map of Georgia we superimposed the words "Government spending increased 58%." We cut to the words: "Government employees up 27%." We cut again to the words "Bonded indebtedness up 20%." Then we cut to a map of the United States and the words: "More Big Government." Over the visuals, the announcer read the litany of things he had done as governor and closed with the words: "Don't let him do as President what he did as governor."

Carter gave us a nice fat target on the right-to-work issue, and we kicked as hard as we could. I found a photograph of Carter with a big toothy grin. We turned the TV screen into a simple, graphic illustration. At the top we put the words "RIGHT-TO-WORK LAWS." On the left hand side of the screen we put the word "FOR." On the right hand side of the screen we put the word "AGAINST." The grinning photo of Carter appeared on the left side of the screen while the announcer talked about his favoring right-to-work laws as governor of Georgia. We then flipped the photo to the right side of the screen when the announcer talked of his agreement to sign the bill that would do away with state right-to-work laws. We mentioned the fact that the unions supporting him were behind such a bill. We then flipped the picture back and forth as the announcer said, "this is not just another flip-flop . . . this is a betrayal of the American working man.''

We ran that commercial only in states that had right-to-work laws. I think it will be interesting to see whether Carter *does* sign the bill doing away with right-to-work laws.

It's impossible to judge the effectiveness of advertising in a political campaign. It is only one part of the communications effort. But during the two-week period when we ran our anti-Carter commercials, we jumped six points in the polls. That may or may not say something.

We made two negative ads that we know were not effective. One never ran. The other ran in the South—and you know what happened to us in the South.

The ad that never ran was a commercial on Carter's income taxes. We opened on a clip from a Carter commercial that showed him saying he thought tax loopholes were ''outrageous.'' We then cut to his own 1976 income tax return. He earned over $120,000. After all his deductions, including a $41,000 tax credit for a peanut machine, he wound up paying the same tax as a family of four making $15,000 a year. We were a little afraid of that commercial. Sure it was hypocritical of him to make a commercial saying how ''outraged'' he was at ''tax loopholes.'' But he was, after all, entitled to use those loopholes. We were afraid that our commercial might backfire on us, so we tested it among a panel of undecided voters. They didn't understand it. It's bad enough when a commercial backfires on you. It's even more humiliating when it goes right over people's heads.

Somebody from South Carolina decided that the man to carry our banner in the South should be Strom Thurmond. I didn't know the South, and I didn't know Strom Thurmond, so I didn't argue too vehemently.

''Isn't he something of a curmudgeon?'' I asked.

''But they love him,'' the man from South Carolina told me. He had even written a script for Strom Thurmond. Among other things, it referred to Jimmy Carter as a ''scalawag.''

I laughed when I came to that word.

''But that's what he is,'' the man from South Carolina drawled. ''A scalawag. A no-good scalawag.''

Only Southerners should be allowed to use that word. When it comes rolling out of a Southerner's mouth it sounds more descriptive than the most colorful obscenity ever invented.

I told him that ''scalawag'' was a trifle strong for our purposes. I wrote two new scripts, a thirty-second and a sixty-second TV spot.

I tried to give my typewriter a Southern accent. Some words just sound better when they're delivered in a deep drawl.

When you read this, try to imitate Strom Thurmond:

"I'd like to have a Southerner for President, but not just somebody who's *from* the South, somebody who is *for* the South.

"I don't think Jimmy Carter is *for* the South / when he talks about cutting our *defense* effort by $7 billion; or when he offers a *blanket* pardon to all draft dodgers; or when he says he'll sign the bill that would do away with our right-to-work laws.

"Jimmy Carter is not *for* the South / when he comes out for gun registration; or for programs that mean more federal control / over our businesses, our schools, and our lives. He's not *for* the South / on bussing, on welfare, on taxes—on any issue I can name.

"President Ford may not have a Southern accent. But when he talks about the issues, he sure sounds *more* like a Southerner than Jimmy Carter.

"On November second, Southerners are going to vote their beliefs, not their geography. They're going to vote for President Ford."

Strom Thurmond has a huge corner suite in the Senate Office Building. His walls are literally covered, inch for inch, with photographs of Strom Thurmond with Presidents and other important people, and plaques honoring him for one thing or another. When I arrived, there was an aide, a pleasant middle-aged gentleman, standing in the hallway outside his office puffing away on a cigarette. He told me he would take me in to see the Senator just as soon as he finished his cigarette. Senator Thurmond didn't want people to smoke in the office.

When I met him, I decided that my vague impression of him had been surprisingly accurate. Old. Mannerly. Very, very Southern. I looked at his wavy brown hair and the word *toupee* popped instantly into my mind. I looked at his thin, tanned face, with touches of red on his cheeks, and the picture of a sunlamp popped into my head. There were three aides in the room. I gave copies of the script to Senator Thurmond and the three aides. The senator asked them what they thought of it. All three said that they weren't sure. He said he liked it very much. They agreed, almost in unison. The same thing happened when I presented the shorter version.

The senator scrawled a few minor corrections on the scripts, and summoned a young woman into his office.

"Have these put on the teleprompter," he said, handing her the scripts. She literally ran from the room.

I saw that girl three more times that morning, and all three times

she was running full-tilt down the corridors of the Senate Office
Building. I was standing outside the senator's office when I spotted
her, a good two hundred yards down the corridor, racing back with
the news that that copy was being put on the teleprompter. I saw her
again, a few minutes later, as she roared past me and announced
cheerfully that the senator wanted to change a few words. I missed
her sprint back from that particular mission. But about half an hour
later I was in a little TV studio in the basement of the Office Building,
and I knew she was on her way. I could hear the slap of her sandals
racing along the cement floor. This time I was a little worried. The
last fifty yards of the corridor leading to the TV studio goes downhill
at a rather steep incline. I heard her rounding the corner, and I could
tell she wasn't slowing down. The cameraman and I stood open-
mouthed at the studio doorway. She was bearing down on us, hair
flying, faster and faster. I'm sure she wanted to stop, but it wasn't up
to her now. It was up to us. The impact knocked us back a few steps,
but we managed to keep her from crashing into the television
camera.

"Thank you," she said, breathing heavily. "They're on their
way."

You've got to say one thing for those senatorial aides. They hustle.

The senator arrived a few minutes later at a leisurely pace. He was
accompanied by the three men who had been in his office. I had been
told that he didn't see very well, and that he didn't want to wear
glasses. I had him sit behind a small desk, and moved the camera
with the teleprompter just as close as possible.

"He'll do these in one take, you just see," one of the men told me
confidently. I asked for a rehearsal. "Don't need a rehearsal," the
man said. "Just let her rip. The senator will get it perfectly. You just
see." The senator beamed.

I decided to take his word for it. The first commercial was the
thirty-second version, and maybe they were right—maybe he was
another John Connally.

The teleprompter was located directly below the camera lens. It
slowly rolls inch-high letters up towards the lens, so you can read the
script but look as if you're talking directly into the camera.

We started the camera, I announced that this was "Take One,"
and I gave the cue to the senator.

He leaned forward, then he leaned even farther forward. He
squinted at the teleprompter. He read the words one by one, his head
moving from side to side as he followed the sentences. I watched the
performance on the TV monitor. Thurmond reminded me of a skin-

nier, older Mr. Magoo. He was so intent on making out the words, that he couldn't possibly turn them into meaningful sentences. It sounded a little like a seven-year-old reading one of the shepherds' parts in a Christmas pageant. But he got through it all—he didn't quit.

"Not bad," one of the men said. "A little long, maybe."

"It was forty-five seconds," I said, trying to be pleasant. "We have to do it in thirty seconds. I'll cut some of the copy."

"It was terrible," Senator Thurmond admitted. "I know it was terrible. I couldn't read the damn thing."

This time he agreed to a rehearsal. We rehearsed long enough so that the teleprompter was just an aid, not a crutch. After about forty-five minutes, we got two pretty fair commercials. He was still a little stiff. But he had the right amount of fire in his eyes when he said, "Jimmy Carter may have a Southern accent, but he sure doesn't talk like a Southerner to me."

The commercials ran for a week all over the South. We stopped running them when people outside South Carolina started to complain.

"Why the hell are you running that Thurmond commercial down here?" one campaign worker complained. "We don't give a damn for Thurmond in Alabama."

Three weeks before Election Day we started to watch Jimmy Carter's commercials seriously. We had seen all of them from the very beginning, of course, and had them recorded on TV cassettes so we could play them back at our leisure. But we knew that he was about to launch a whole new series of commercials, and we had reason to expect some strong attacks on President Ford.

We were particularly worried about the commercial on the Nixon pardon. That was our weakest front; the enemy's commercial had been made, and we could expect the attack any day. Finally it began. But it was hardly Normandy beach. We heard that it ran in a few small stations in the South, then stopped running. Our intelligence reports indicated that it was a test. The test must have showed that the commercial was too strong for people to accept. It would have backfired if run nationally. The commercial never appeared again. Jimmy Carter, after all, was still well ahead. He couldn't afford to take chances.

But we knew that our commercials were hurting him, and we had the best proof of this in the world: he called in a new advertising consultant. His name was Tony Schwartz.

I had done business with Tony Schwartz in the past, so I had an idea about what to expect. He seems to specialize in negative advertising—harsh, head-on attacks on the opponent. He admits that he created the most controversial television ad in political history, the "Daisy Girl" commercial that was used to attack Barry Goldwater in the Johnson-Goldwater campaign. The commercial opened with a pretty little girl picking daisies and suddenly switched to an atomic mushroom cloud. The implication, apparently, was that Barry Goldwater intended to blow up all the little girls who picked daisies. The public outcry was so loud that it was immediately yanked off the air.

I was hoping he'd try something like that against Ford. I figured it would be worth four points overnight. But we had no such luck. Rafshoon was still in charge of the advertising, even though Tony Schwartz had been hired to make the new series of spots. He had steered a safe and basically sound course until now, and I doubted very much whether he and Carter were going to gamble their lead on a completely new creative direction.

The Schwartz commercials turned out to be not *that* much different from some of Carter's earlier spots. They showed him talking directly into the camera for thirty seconds. Instead of dungarees, he was wearing a business suit. I thought that was a smart change. And instead of talking about the issues without mentioning Ford, Carter was now reeling off a laundry list of things that "The Nixon-Ford" administration—had done wrong.

I thought they were a little too harsh, a little too strident for Carter's own good. I thought they should have concentrated on one thing Ford had done wrong instead of rattling off six or seven of his mistakes. The mind boggles at so much malfeasance in thirty seconds. We continued climbing in the polls while those commercials were running. Carter won the election, but I haven't seen any evidence that he owes his victory to Tony Schwartz's commercials.

I was most seriously concerned about New York and the "Drop Dead" issue. New York was absolutely vital to us, and three weeks before the election it looked as if it would be close. If we could only lose New York City by a respectable margin, we could carry the state. One of our biggest problems was a headline that had run a year ago in the *Daily News*: "FORD TO NEW YORK: DROP DEAD."

It was a brilliant headline. And it might very well have cost us the election.

Ford had not, of course, told New York to drop dead. He had told New York that he wouldn't grant them a multi-billion-dollar loan until the city cleaned up its fiscal act. Subsequently, after New York had cleaned up its act, the Ford administration loaned the city $2.3 billion. It saved the city from bankruptcy.

In politics, however, it's not what you did that matters. It's what people think you did. Marie Antoinette probably never said, "Let them eat cake." But I'd like to see her try to deny it now.

To find out how serious the problem was, I called a friend of mine in New York, Charlie West. He was as close to New York politics as any non-political person would ever want to be. And he was a consultant on municipal financing. I figured he knew more about the city and state's real fiscal situation than anybody in New York.

"I don't think Carter could get away with using that issue now," Charlie told me over the phone. "Hell, Ford did the right thing. Everybody who understands the situation knows that. Beame knows it. Carey knows it. Ford saved New York City."

I felt better when I hung up. Carter wouldn't dare attack us on that issue.

Two days later a large, thin package arrived on my desk in Washington. It had been sent air mail special delivery. I opened it up. It was an enormous subway poster. There was a large rip in the right hand corner. And a note was attached: "Thought you might be interested in this." It was signed "Charlie."

At the left of the poster there was a picture of Jimmy Carter looking serious, determined. The message was set in large bold type against a black background:

"If I am elected President I guarantee that I will never tell the greatest city on earth to drop dead."

It was signed, in nice, crisp handwriting, "Jimmy Carter."

I flew into a rage. If I had known how to say the word "scalawag" with the right accent I would have called Carter that. While Carter had been pompously criticizing our playful little *Playboy* ad, he had been running this underground graffiti in the subways of New York. The poster was so blatantly false and misleading that I marched into Stu Spencer's office and suggested that we accuse Carter of reinstating the "stink tank" that he had reportedly used in his 1970 gubernatorial campaign. The "stink tank" was a dirty tricks group that had been guardedly reported in *Newsweek* and mentioned in Leslie Wheeler's biography of Carter. I didn't really believe it existed, but I was pretty mad.

Spencer, who never gets upset by anything that happens in a political campaign, laughed when he saw the poster. His only suggestion was that we hire a bunch of people to cross out the word "never" on all the posters that were up.

I was still a little mad when I got back to my office, but my anger disappeared when I showed the poster to the head of our print production.

"How the hell did you get that poster?" he asked.

"A friend sent it to me."

"Must be a pretty big guy," he said. "He must have ripped that thing out of a steel and glass shadow box. They're supposed to be vandal-proof."

The idea of Charlie West, who *is* a big guy, vandalizing a crowded New York subway car to get at the poster improved my mood immensely. I could easily imagine the expression on people's faces as they watched a tall, bespectacled businessman in a dignified three-piece suit, tearing the Carter sign off the subway wall.

We never did successfully rebut the "drop dead" charge, and I think that was a serious mistake of ours. We considered having Rockefeller tackle the issue for us, but we had two problems with the Vice-President. Too many people in New York thought he was responsible for the financial crises. And he had made an unfortunate gesture towards a heckler a month earlier. It appeared on the front page of the *New York Post,* the distinguished Vice-President of the United States giving his finger to the camera. I have to admit that he did it well. His head was hunched forward, his eyes were squinting fiercely, his arm was fully extended, and you could see that his index finger was quivering in anger. It was done in the best schoolyard style. It looked like something he had wanted to do all his life. I was glad for him that he got it out of his system, but it meant that for all practical purposes Nelson Rockefeller couldn't help us much in New York.

We nearly got Telly Savalas to be our New York spokesman. He would have been marvelous. He said that he wanted to do a commercial for Ford, and I immediately wrote a script and set up taping time in a New York studio. The script included a very simple, rational rebuttal of the "Drop Dead" charge, and coming from one of New York's favorite people, it would have had a lot of impact. But the day before the taping, Telly Savalas suddenly seemed to disappear. We tried all day to reach him. Finally we got word that he couldn't do a commercial for Ford.

We had one more serious problem in New York and throughout the Jewish community. Shortly before the election, General Brown was quoted as stating that supporting the Israel defense effort had been a "burden" to the United States. It was much more than a quote in the *New York Post*. The *Post* decided Brown's remarks deserved a typeface usually reserved for national emergencies and declarations of war.

When I saw the story, the phrase "dirty tricks" again popped immediately into my mind. First of all, General Brown had been quoted entirely out of context. Not even Moshe Dayan could read his full statement and consider it an attack on the Jewish nation. The timing looked even more sinister. His supposedly anti-Jewish remark had been made more than a year earlier. It seemed more than a little strange that it didn't become news until two weeks before the election. As they had done when FBI Director Kelley installed some curtains and Earl Butz told a lousy joke, the columnists and the outraged Democrats were again demanding that the President fire the man.

The President silently told the columnists and the outraged Democrats to go to hell.

It was one more cross to bear as we headed towards the third debate, six points down.

31
JOE AND PEARL

We seemed to be drifting now. Our last burst of momentum seemed to have stopped six points short of Carter. Our last hope was the last debate, and that was a willowy hope to cling to. The President was campaigning hard, and making strong speeches everywhere, but the press and the evening news still reported only his gaffes. And there were still too many to report. In an exhausting swing across Nebraska he had gotten three out of six towns wrong. And in a major speech at the University of Iowa he had said that it was good to be back at Ohio State. To make matters worse, there was a sudden shortage of money. Phil Angell had to cancel our first week's worth of advertising in Texas. The Texas people got furious at me, and I, in turn, rushed into Phil Angell's office to berate him. Tempers were getting a trifle frayed for the first time in the campaign.

I was still shuttling between Washington and New York, and there were so many last-minute things to be done in both places that I was hard put to know where I was at any one minute, much less where I would be the next.

Our sports desk had lined up dozens of new sports celebrities who were willing to do commercials for Ford. Our problem was that we didn't have the time or the money to make the commercials. Mickey Mantle had agreed to do a spot. Chrissie Evert agreed to do a spot. Joe Green, star of the pennant-winning Cincinnati Reds, agreed to do a spot. Bob and Al Unser wanted to do something. So did Richard

Petty, who, I was assured, was the secret to sweeping the whole racing-mad Midwest. Meanwhile, several politicians agreed to do commercials for Ford, including two who could be very helpful, Jim Thompson in Illinois and a congressman named Bill Cohen who, I was assured, was "dynamite in Maine."

We couldn't possibly do separate commercials for each of the sports celebrities who wanted to support Ford, but a pretty good idea occurred to me. Joe Garagiola. I wanted to get Joe Garagiola to announce that he was supporting President Ford, along with "several of my friends." He would then reel off a list of his "friends." About fifty of the biggest names in sports. My only problem was getting to Joe Garagiola, who was in Cincinnati broadcasting the first game of the World Series.

On a long shot, I called the hotel where I knew the NBC crew was staying during the Series. Joe happened to be walking through the lobby when I called. I had him on the phone in a minute. It was that easy.

"Hey, I'd love to do it," he said. "I love Jerry Ford. Helluva guy." There was a pause. "But wait a minute," he said. "I'm not sure NBC will let me. I don't think they like us announcers mixing in politics. I'll have to ask them and call you back."

My hopes were not high. A few weeks earlier Bud Wilkinson, the former Oklahoma coach and now an ABC announcer, had almost begged to do a spot for Ford. He was one of Ford's biggest boosters. But ABC refused to let him make a commercial for us. They said they had a policy. When he was announcing the Oklahoma-Texas game, ABC wouldn't even let Wilkinson announce over the air that the President was tossing the coin before the kick-off.

But a few minutes later the phone rang. It was Joe.

"I'd love to do it," he said. "I thought about it a few minutes and decided I wouldn't even ask NBC. Hell, it's my life. I never supported a politician before, but in my book Jerry Ford is no politician. He's just a damn good President. When do we make the spot?"

We made a date to record the spot the day he got back to New York to broadcast the next games from Yankee Stadium.

And that was a day I shall long remember. I flew to New York from Washington and didn't arrive at the studio, where we were to record several new radio spots and change several more, until ten o'clock in the morning. The receptionist had a stack of pink message slips waiting for me.

"Everybody's been trying to find you all morning," she said. "And they all say it's urgent."

I soon found that almost all the messages concerned one problem. Betty Ford had been trying to get hold of me. They had apparently sent a posse out to find me.

I called her office in Washington. Her secretary answered.

"Thank God we found you," she said. I felt as if I had been playing hooky. "Pearl Bailey told Mrs. Ford that she would do a television commercial for the President. She wants to do it today."

She gave me Pearl Bailey's number and I agreed to call her immediately. It's not easy to make a television commercial in New York without any notice. Studio time is hard to get. Pat Barnes was with me, and I put her to work trying to locate a studio that was free. I saw no point in calling Pearl Bailey until I could tell her where to go and when. To complicate matters, Joe Garagiola was about to walk through the door and I still had some changes to make in his script.

But before I could do anything, I had to answer one more of the urgent messages. Joe Bartlett, my lawyer and one of my best friends, was calling me from Boston. He had never left me an "urgent" message before, and I figured that either I was in trouble with the income tax people or something terrible had happened back home.

When I got his secretary on the phone, she seemed as relieved to finally hear from me as Betty Ford's secretary had been.

"He's in a meeting right now," she said. "But hold the line. I'll get him out."

While I was waiting for him to come to the phone, the receptionist handed me a note. Pearl Bailey's office was on the line. I told her to tell them I'd call right back. Bartlett finally came on the phone.

"Hey, MacDougall," he said, in the low, whispery voice he uses when he doesn't want anyone else in the room to hear what he's saying. "You've got to get me a gorilla suit."

"A what?"

"A gorilla suit. There aren't any in Boston. You've got to get me one in New York."

"Why do you need a gorilla suit?"

"I'm giving a party Saturday night and I feel like dressing up like a gorilla."

While he was talking, Joe Garagiola walked into the room. I waved hello and indicated I'd be right with him.

"Mimi said you'd be coming up Saturday," Joe said. "You can bring the gorilla suit with you."

"Gorilla suits aren't easy to find," I said. "It's almost Halloween."

"You can do it, MacDougall. This means a lot to me. One gorilla suit. Large. I don't care what it costs."

"I'm a little busy right now," I said. "The Ford campaign keeps me kind of busy."

"You can't help Bozo," he said. Bartlett's a Democrat. For the past six months he'd consistently referred to our President as "Bozo." "The gorilla suit. That's what's important. I'll cancel one of my bills that you haven't paid if you get me that gorilla suit."

When I hung up, Pat Barnes was waiting to tell me that she had lined up a TV studio for two o'clock that afternoon. I told her to rehearse Joe Garagiola while I called Pearl Bailey. I handed Joe the script without the changes I had wanted. It would have to do.

Joe went into an adjoining booth with a glass partition. While I was calling Pearl Bailey, I could see him reading the script and hear his voice over the studio loudspeakers.

Pearl Bailey's secretary was furious that I hadn't called sooner. After she berated me for keeping Miss Bailey from a U.N. appointment, Miss Bailey herself got on the phone.

"I understand you're the young man who's supposed to do the TV spot," she said. "Today's the only day I can do it." Her voice was definitely a little angry, but it was still that wonderful Pearl Bailey voice.

I told her that we had booked time for two o'clock.

"Can't do it then," she said. She reeled off a long list of appointments that she had that day. It didn't sound to me as though there was any time when she could do the commercial. Suddenly her voice softened.

"I'll be honest with you, honey. I'm just giving you a hard time because you didn't call me back right away. The truth is, I don't really want to do it here in New York because I know there'll be all these people hanging around. I want to do something for President Ford. But I want it to come from my heart. I don't want any scripts. I don't want a lot of people hanging all over me. Do you know what I mean, honey?"

I told her I did. She told me that she was going to Williamsburg for the third debate, and would be in Washington the next day. I told her that I'd reserve a TV studio for her that day in Washington.

"There'll just be you and me. I promise." I said.

She gave a perfect imitation of Pearl Bailey's laugh. "That sounds sexy as hell, honey. Only I'm a little too old."

While I was talking, Joe Garagiola had not only been rehearsing but had also recorded two spots. We played them back, and I thought they sounded great. We chatted for a while about baseball, and what was wrong with the Yankees, and he left. He again told me how much he wanted the President to win this election.

About two minutes after the elevator door closed behind him, I had another phone call. It was from John Deardourff. He was calling from the White House.

"Do you know how I can get in touch with Joe Garagiola?" he asked. I told him that he'd just left, and I hadn't the vaguest idea where he would be until game time.

"The President wants to talk with him directly," John said. "We've decided to do some live shows, and the President wants to do them with Joe."

"Well, if Cincinnati wins four straight, Joe should be a free man," I said. I told John that I'd try to get hold of Joe. It gave me one more thing to do that day. I still had ten radio spots to complete. But first things first. I called Mimi at our hotel room in New York.

"You've got to get a gorilla suit," I said. "I'm too busy to do it myself."

"Is the President planning to wear it for the third debate?" she asked.

"It's for Bartlett, and don't be a wise ass. He has to have a gorilla suit. You can get one at Brooks Costume."

Life must go on, even in a tight Presidential race. I got four more calls that day on the gorilla suit issue. Joe's wife, Apple, called:

"You've got to get Joe a gorilla suit," she said as soon as I came on the phone.

"I've already got the message," I told her. "Straight from the gorilla."

The other three calls were from Mimi. The first time she said she'd found a head but no costume. Would that do? I told her to keep looking. On her second call she'd found a complete suit but it cost a hundred dollars for a weekend rental. I told her to take it. On the third call she informed me that it weighed fifty pounds and she was goddamned if she was going to lug it all the way to Boston.

I finally took it to Boston on the shuttle Saturday evening. Mimi had gone down earlier, and she was meeting me at the airport with her three children. I decided that it would be fun for them to see me walking through the baggage claim area with a gorilla mask on my face. By the time I reached them Camilla, aged twelve, was laughing. Sammy, aged seven, was half-laughing. George, aged four, was screaming. When I took the mask off, I realized that several hundred passengers were staring both at me and at the briefcase in my hand. It was covered with FORD-DOLE stickers. I got into the car as quickly as I could.

The third debate was not a disaster. Nor was it a triumph. It was a stand-off by almost everybody's measure. It seemed a little more subdued than the other debates, and it seemed to be conducted on a higher level. I thought that the best assessment of all the debates came from Bob Gardner, who called me as soon as the third debate was over.

"You know what I think the debates proved," he said. "I think the debates proved that Jimmy Carter is every bit as boring as President Ford."

The next day we taped Pearl Bailey. On the drive back from Williamsburg she had planned what she was going to say. She had scribbled some thoughts on a yellow piece of paper. But she had no idea what she would say or how long it would take. Length was important to me. I needed a sixty-second commercial and a thirty-second commercial.

Her first commercial turned out to be the most interesting anti-Carter spot of the campaign. I still think that it's a pity we never ran it:

"Hi, Honey. You know I was sitting here thinking about something. You know when I talk to you or meet you on the street or anything and I smile at you, you know somehow you always kind of smile back at me. And that makes me feel good. I feel the same way as you. When I walk down the street and somebody smiles, I want it to bounce back from their eyes and from their heart. You can feel that kind of thing. But you know, when Mr. Carter smiles, I get the funniest feeling. I don't want to smile back. And I got to be honest with you. It bothers me. It really bothers me. I mean it. It bothers me."

She shook her head slowly during her last four sentences. It made you feel pretty damn bothered about Jimmy Carter's smile.

The trouble was, it left me a little bothered, too. Bothered about something else. This commercial was going to run on the last day or two of the campaign. I thought it would be more appropriate for Pearl Bailey to do a pro-Ford commercial at the end of the campaign. She agreed. And after a few takes, she came up with this spot. It makes no sense whatsoever if you just read the words. But when Pearl Bailey speaks to you, you don't just pay attention to the words. You listen to her heart talking.

"Hi. This is Pearl. I'm here to ask you to please vote for Gerald Ford. Now . . . you know . . . I've never done this before in my life. I'm not here to judge people. The Bible says I'm not to judge. But . . . I do hope you will think before you vote, use all the goodness that's within you. A couple of years ago, our country was truly shaken and a man was put at the head of it named Gerald Ford and I really believe in his heart . . . oh . . . he's made some mistakes, honey, you better believe he has . . . I wouldn't sit here and try to tell you he didn't. But I'll tell you what. If a man is trying and a man has more than dreams. If he has something I like very much in every human being—simplicity and honesty—'cause I really believe he's an *honest* man. That's why I like Gerald Ford, and that's why I hope that, I don't know—please think about it. It's so important. It really is.''

part seven

The Blitz

32
TUESDAY

"I think we're going to win," John Deardourff said quietly.

It was the first time I'd heard anyone say it without false enthusiasm.

We were alone in his office, the door shut against the chaos of our Washington headquarters. It was the Tuesday before the election, three days after the final debate, seven campaigning days to go. The morning newspapers were showing polls that proved Carter had won the final debate, other polls that showed Carter with a five-point lead.

"I think we're going to win," John repeated. "And I think the advertising is going to do it."

"I hope you know something I don't know," I said. "I just bet a hundred dollars on Ford—to boost my own morale."

John had just returned from California, where our ten-day cross-country blitz had begun. The New York and Washington papers had reported enthusiastic crowds. The first live half-hour TV show in Los Angeles had received good reviews.

"The President has never been better," John said. "He's strong, he's relaxed, he's sure of himself. The ads are working. People are responding to them. And the show was better than I ever thought possible."

"What kind of ratings do you think we'll get?" I asked.

"I don't think they'll be too bad," John said. "People are getting interested in this campaign all of a sudden." John leaned back in his chair and allowed himself a little smile of self-satisfaction. The Joe and Jerry shows had been his idea, after all. "No matter what the ratings are," he said, "we reached at least a million more people than we would have reached with live campaigning."

"How's Joe Garagiola doing?"

John laughed. "Joe is our secret weapon. He's fantastic. He does something none of us have been able to do in this whole campaign. He relaxes the President."

John talked about Joe's opening line in the California show. The President had looked tense, as usual, waiting for the red light on the live camera. The lead-in to the show was a tape of the highlights of the President's day in California. The final scene showed the President at a rally, and the sound had been boosted considerably to make the crowd seem more enthusiastic. When it was over, and the live cameras turned on, Joe had a great opening line.

"Mr. President, I haven't heard cheering like that since they took me out of a ball game."

"It broke the President up," John said. "For the rest of the show, he was just a guy having a good time. The President loves Joe Garagiola."

We talked about the new Carter ads. John had seen the new Carter five-minute commercial and he agreed with me. It was by far the most effective ad Carter had run.

"But it's not as good as 'Feelin' Good,' " John said.

I agreed with him there, too. I told him about some of the response I'd already gotten on the commercial, including a midnight phone call from an advertising friend in Boston who said he and his wife had just seen it and she was still crying.

"It's going to run seventeen times between tonight and Election Eve," John said. "I think it will do the job. I really do."

John hadn't seen the new Tony Schwartz spots.

"I don't think they'll hurt us," I said. "Carter looks too intense. I don't think people like those fierce eyes staring at them. And as usual, he reels off a laundry list of problems instead of concentrating on one thing that Ford's done wrong. I think our stuff is better. I *know* our stuff's better."

"We'll know Tuesday," John said.

I felt like complaining about the Texas fuck-up and some of the radio commercials that had been held up by Phil Angell, but I held myself in check. It was too late for complaining. We'd lost a week in Texas, but we hadn't necessarily lost Texas.

John and I talked about the final newspaper ad. Our last million dollars. By now I had written seven versions of the ad, one for almost every contingency. Now we had to decide which ad was the right ad to run the day before the election. We couldn't wait for another poll; we had to bet our instincts.

If we were going to be five or more points behind on Monday, I preferred the toughest ad, "Which Jimmy Carter Is the One on the Ballot?"

If we were going to be about three points back, I felt that "What Do You Really Know about Jimmy Carter?" was the ad to run.

If we thought we were going to be way ahead, what the hell, we could run the giant smiling picture of Jerry Ford, with the caption from his acceptance speech: "You've Done a Good Job, Jerry—Keep Right On Doing It."

But now it looked as if it would be neck and neck on Election Day, with the momentum slightly in our favor. And that gave us two choices. The tough ad, comparing the two men: "What You Still Don't Know about Jimmy Carter—What You Know about President Ford." And the softer ad: a quote about the earning of trust, set in huge type, and signed by the President.

It was an all-type ad based on one of the best passages from his speech at the University of Michigan. It was headlined "One final thought:" and the copy ran down the entire page.

> It is not enough for anyone to say "trust me."
> Trust is not having to guess what a candidate means.
> Trust is not being all things to all people, but being the same thing to all people.
> Trust is leveling with the people before the election about what you're going to do after the election.
> Trust is saying plainly and simply what you mean—and meaning what you say.
> Trust must be earned.
>
> President Gerald R. Ford

It wasn't a very powerful ad. But it was a safe ad. And the word "trust" was in every sentence. That one word was the heart of our final sales message to the American people. Trust the man. Earlier in the campaign Carter had said "trust me." But somehow it didn't work. Now it was our turn to run on trust—and I had a strong gut feeling that the word really belonged to Ford. People *did* trust him. Even I trusted him.

The soft ad won. The decision meant that Campaign '76 had officially declared that President Ford had a fifty-fifty chance of winning the election.

John had to hurry off to Chicago, to prepare for the next big Joe and Jerry show. Then they were going to Pennsylvania, Ohio, and Texas. The final show was scheduled for Sunday night in New York. I would be through preparing the last-minute surrogate commercials by then. And I was pleased when John asked me to work with him on the final show. I didn't think we could win New York, but it would reach New Jersey and Connecticut and could do some good there. Win or lose, my last hurrah was going to be a big one.

When I went back to my office, I was feeling good again. Bob Teeter passed me in the hall, and there seemed to be a new spring in his step. He knew, better than anyone, how genuine his smile should look. And he had a genuine smile on his face.

"How ya feelin'?" he asked.

"That depends entirely on how you're feeling."

"I'm feelin' good," he said.

"Then I'm feelin' good," I replied.

I sat down behind my cluttered desk and decided not to answer any of my calls just yet. I opened my briefcase and took out the plan we had written in Kansas City. It was the first time I'd looked at it in two months.

I went over our original list of objectives. I wanted to compare our goals with our accomplishments. I knew we'd done a lot of ads and commercials that we'd never planned to do. But I had a feeling that for the most part we'd gone pretty much by the book: the book in my hands.

The feeling was reinforced when I reviewed the first objective that we had written in Kansas City: "Strengthen the human dimension of President Ford."

We'd certainly done that. When we'd started, the country knew Jimmy Carter better than the President. Thanks in part to our five-minute commercial on the family and our five-minute biography, America knew just about all there was to know about Jerry Ford. Grand Rapids . . . Eagle Scout . . . football hero at Michigan . . . war hero in the Pacific . . . student working his way through Yale Law School . . . Congressman Ford . . . Minority Leader Ford . . . Ford the good father . . . Ford the good husband . . . Ford the good churchgoer . . . Ford the President who listens to people . . . Ford the non-imperial President. People now had a much better picture of Jerry Ford. They knew him better, they knew his family better. We'd done a pretty fair job on our first objective. And if people really *were* going to vote the man and not the issues, as we'd originally stated, then this was a pretty significant accomplishment.

I felt equally good when I reviewed our second basic objective: "Strengthen the leadership dimension of President Ford." That had been one of our biggest problems. Most people had considered Ford a pretty weak leader. Jimmy Carter had been harping on that every day of the campaign. But the perception of his leadership qualities had definitely improved. Our "Leadership" commercial must have had something to do with that.

I had forgotten our third objective: "More clearly portray President Ford's compassion for less fortunate Americans." When I'd written that, I'd been thinking of the problem that every Republican has. The "screw the little guy" image. Had we overcome that problem? I didn't think so. We'd tried. We'd avoided the word "Republican" like a disease. The only time the word had been used in advertising was when Ronald Reagan had refused to read his script if we took it out. Our commercials showing Ford with the elderly and Ford with children had been filmed with the "compassion strategy" in mind. But today, over two months later, I had to admit that we'd failed to portray President Ford as a compassionate man. Maybe this is one political area where action has to speak louder than words.

I felt better about our next objective: "Portray his accomplishments in office in a believable way." By God, we'd done this. We were right in Kansas City when we decided to tone down his accomplishments. We never claimed that he'd accomplished miracles in his two years as President. Our two major "accomplishments" commercials, the five-minute and the sixty-second spot, merely stated that things were terrible when Ford took over, and things are a lot better now. But I had to admit to myself that we had come dangerously close to crossing over the line of believability. Our slogan had been a gamble. "He's making us proud again." When I had put that slogan into the plan, I had secret visions of people hooting and laughing all over America. But for some strange reason, people accepted the slogan. Even Carter hadn't ridiculed it. Here we were, seven days before the election, and people were saying, "What the hell, Jerry's doing a pretty good job." That's exactly what we had hoped they'd be saying.

I looked at our fifth objective. And our biggest mistake of the campaign stared back at me. "Present his program for the future." In Kansas City it had seemed so important to us. We had known that we could never sell Jerry Ford as one of America's visionary Presidents. America didn't expect him to be Thomas Jefferson. We had wanted to present a program for the future. We'd even devoted two pages of our advertising plan to "A New Dimension of Freedom." It

was to be Ford's "New Frontier." I remembered arguing with Doug
Bailey for most of one night: should we call it " The New *Dimension* of
Freedom"? Or "The New *Generation* of Freedom"? What did it
matter now? The program had never gone beyond our advertising plan.
Not one of the President's speeches had offered a program for the future. Not one of our two hundred ads and commercials had so much as
hinted at what he might do for America in the next four years. This had
been worrying me for some time. But not until now did I fully realize
that we'd been basing our entire pitch on what he had done . . . not a
word about what he would do. I had written one brochure titled, "A
Program for the Future." But it was filled mostly with new words for
old programs. And the President had given us a peek at his vision for
America in his Ann Arbor speech. He spelled out a program to make
it easier for people to own homes. But the idea hadn't caught fire.
The commercial I had written on the subject died. Had we made a
serious mistake? We had run this whole campaign as if there were no
tomorrow. Would the voters enter the booth next Tuesday and suddenly realize that they hadn't the foggiest idea *where* President Ford
intended to lead us? The thought made me nervous. But too late
now. I made a mental note to ask Doug and John if our final live ten
minutes on Election Eve couldn't at least be a *little* bit visionary.

I looked at our next objective. "Cut Jimmy Carter Down to Size."
Had we really done that? We'd produced a few hard-hitting commercials. They had undoubtedly helped close the gap. But I began to
wish that we had hit him harder where I thought it might have hurt
the most. Throughout the entire campaign Jimmy Carter had tried to
be all things to all people. In one twenty-four-hour period he had accepted the Liberal Party endorsement in New York, and then rushed to
Alabama to have his picture taken with his arm around George
Wallace. He had sold himself as a champion of the civil rights movement, yet he had eagerly pursued the support of the South's leading
segregationists. After saying that we should elect him because he was
not part of the political establishment, he had proceeded to put together the strongest coalition of unions, bosses, and old pols that the
old political establishment had seen in decades. We let him get away
with it. We had the ammunition, but we never fired the gun.

We had written one final objective. "Help boost momentum when
needed." Until now, every time we had gotten momentum, we had
been stopped dead in our tracks. Gulf Oil, Earl Butz, the golf outings, the Watergate prosecutor's investigation, Eastern Europe,
John Dean, General Brown, one red light after another. But now, at
last, it looked as though we had it. Momentum. The most important

word in politics. Did we have the right advertising to boost it and maintain it?

I closed the blue book and leaned back in my chair. We did have the right advertising, and we had it at precisely the right time. We had the Joe and Jerry shows for five of the key states and a five-million-dollar spot campaign for all the key states. The blitz was on. And it was hitting America just as a sleeping electorate was beginning to wake up to the Presidential election. Best of all, we had the "Feelin' Good" commercial. Five minutes of sheer momentum marching into America's living rooms seventeen times between now and Election Day.

I had a cassette of "Feelin' Good" in my desk drawer. I had to see it again. I went to the conference room, turned on the TV, inserted the cassette. A marching band came right at me, trombones and trumpets swinging back and forth, as a full chorus belted out our song:

> *"I'm feelin' good about America*
> *I feel it everywhere I go.*
> *I'm feelin' good about America*
> *I thought you ought to know*
> *That I'm feelin' good about America*
> *It's something great to see*
> *I'm feelin' good about America*
> *I'm feelin' good about me!"*

Then the music went under as people from all over the country gave good, solid reasons why they felt good about having President Ford in the White House. Then came the best, most emotional scenes that had been filmed of President Ford. To see them was to love the guy. The commercial was right, every second of it. I could feel it in my bones. Doug and Ed Deitch had done a masterful editing job. Every scene, every frame was perfect. Doug's script said everything that should be said in the last week of the campaign. Bob Gardner's song, played in three different tempos, held the commercial together and gave it a tight, emotional impact. I thought it had to be one of the finest political commercials ever produced. It just might be good enough to do the job.

33

WEDNESDAY

Three times in my life I've had a song imbedded in my brain and I couldn't turn it off. The first time I was about ten. "Mares eat oats and does eat oats and little lambs eat ivy, a kid'll eat ivy too wouldn't you?" It was torture. It was worse than hiccups. For weeks I was helpless—mares eat oats and does eat oats going endlessly around and around in my brain. Then, when I was fifteen, I saw *Casablanca*. For weeks wherever I went, whatever I did, one melody was spinning around in my head, complete with all the words, all the music, and that gravelly voice,

> *Moonlight and love songs never out of date,*
> *Hearts full of passion, jealousy and hate;*
> *Woman needs man and man must have his mate,*
> *That no one can deny.*
> *It's still the same old story, a fight for love and glory,*
> *A case of do or die!*
> *The world will always welcome lovers,*
> *As time goes by.*

I still know every word—over thirty years later.

Six days before the election "Feelin' good about America" became trapped in my mind. I woke up at three in the morning with the marching band version parading through my mind. By four o'clock I was mentally dancing to the Mexican version, the Spanish lyrics keeping me wide awake. By five I was silently singing the rock version. By six my brain was running through twenty or so verses with the oboe and guitar accompaniment. By seven I was standing in the shower singing out loud, "There's a change that's come over America/It's something great to see/We're living here in peace again/ We're going back to work again . . . It's better than it used to be/I'm feelin' good about America."

Mimi came in to see if I'd lost my mind. I admitted that I had.

"That goddamned song. It's taken over my mind. It's stuck. I can't turn it off."

"Try to think of something else," she said sensibly.

"I can't," I argued. "I can't hear myself think over the goddamned music."

"I know what you mean," she said. "Like Stayfree maxi-pads. That song was with me for ages."

I closed the shower door.

The song stayed with me for the next six days. To all outward appearances I was a normal human being. I could talk naturally. I even made a speech in Columbus, Ohio, without once breaking into song. I could make decisions and act businesslike in meetings. I was even able to sleep a little. No one suspected that all through the last six days of the campaign I was a walking jukebox, playing the same song over and over and over again, a song that only I could hear. It added to the torture of the last week of the campaign.

I had thought my work would be done by this time. In fact I'd planned to spend the last week at our agency in Boston, gradually easing back into the real world. Just five days before Phil Angell had been screaming at us to stop producing commercials; we'd run out of money.

But now that we were slowly beginning to creep closer to Carter, the money was magically turned on again. The Joe and Jerry shows were costing twenty thousand dollars each to produce, and a lot more than that in TV time. The shows had never been planned or budgeted. But the money mysteriously appeared.

Then, on Wednesday, Phil Angell popped into my office with a big grin. "I just got a hundred thousand dollars more for network radio," he said. "I don't know where it came from, but Baker said, 'Spend it.' We're buying a heavy schedule for weekend radio."

I could forget Boston. We were still running. It was good news for me. It meant we could undo the foul-up on the Joe Garagiola commercial.

That particular problem had been bothering me more than almost any other. The sports desk had spent a month lining up over a hundred great athletes for Ford. It had been pretty much a waste of good energy. With the exception of our Woody Hayes, Bear Bryant, and Tom Landry commercials, we hadn't used any of our stars. I wasn't sure it would mean a lot of votes, but I felt bad about the people on the sports desk.

But now at last their day had come. The Joe Garagiola spot, which had been sitting uselessly in my briefcase, could finally be aired. I had figured out that it would have cost me well over half a million dollars to produce that spot for an ordinary client. Testimonials from people like Mickey Mantle, Arnold Palmer, Roger Staubach, Al and Bob Unser don't come cheap. We had forty or so names like that, as many as Joe Garagiola could rattle off in a sixty-second commercial. All voting for Ford.

Phil thought we should have four or five different commercials ready for our weekend on the networks, and we had a little trouble trying to agree on the other spots. By now we had over fifty completed radio spots to choose from.

A strange phone call made the decision easier. It was from one of the thousands of people who'd been advising me on the advertising throughout the campaign.

"Hello? Mr. MacDougall? My name is Bednarik." The accent was Eastern European. I hoped he wasn't going to help us solve our Polish problem.

"Any relation to Chuck Bednarik?" I asked. By now I'd learned to be pleasant to my advisers.

"Wish I was," he said. "Hey, I'm callin' from Brooklyn, so I got to be quick. My crew was sitting around talkin' about the Presidential campaign today. We're all Democrats. But we didn't know what we were going to do next Tuesday. And then one of your radio ads came on the air. The one with the bunch of Democrats sayin' they didn't know what they were going to do but Carter hadn't showed 'em anything. I just wanted to tell you that that ad really got to us. We all decided to vote for Ford. I think you ought to put that on the air a lot more."

I thanked him profusely. When I hung up I told Phil about the call.

"That settles it," he said. "We'll go with the Democrats spot."

That's how the best political decisions are made.

Doug Bailey arrived while we were still trying to decide on the fourth commercial for the package. He had just flown in from New York, where he'd completed the Georgia newspaper spot.

"I don't think Mr. Carter is going to like this," he said.

Like most of our best commercials, this was deceptively simple. No tricky graphics to distract from the message. A crawl rolled up the screen as the announcer recited the words on the screen.

"The people who know Jimmy Carter best live in Georgia," the announcer said. "And so we think you should know this."

For the rest of the sixty-second commercial he simply read a list of newspapers in Georgia supporting President Ford. The names of each newspaper appeared on the screen. A strong spot.

Doug then showed the thirty-second version of the commercial. The announcer read the names faster, and at the end it sounded as though there wasn't enough time to read off all the newspapers supporting Ford. The list was endless. I thought it was an even stronger spot than the sixty.

"And it's not all that misleading," Doug said proudly. "Those are genuine newspapers. Over half the newspapers in Georgia have come out for Ford."

"It figures," I said, smiling. "Most newspapers everywhere are owned by Republicans."

"Not in Georgia," Doug said. "A lot of people in Georgia don't like Jimmy Carter. And they don't mind saying so."

It suddenly occurred to me that the Georgia newspaper spot would be perfect as our final radio ad. Doug agreed.

"We don't have time," Phil said. "I have to get the spots to the network by tomorrow afternoon. To make a radio commercial out of that we'd have to add the President's voice, re-edit the track, put on the disclaimer. We don't have time. And it will cost money. They didn't give me any money for production, only for the air time."

"Let's do it," said Doug.

On the way to New York I read the *Washington Post,* the *Washington Star,* and the *New York Times.* I was covered in newspapers. And it seemed to me that the columnists, all the columnists, had been banging their typewriters pretty fiercely that morning.

As usual, almost all the columnists were pro-Carter. But today they seemed unusually strident in their attacks on Ford. It was a funny thing. The two candidates had toned down their attacks on each other. But their supporters were becoming more venomous every day. The editorial in the *Times,* and almost all the columns on the Op-Ed page, carried slashing attacks on the President. It bolstered my morale somewhat. They had to be getting worried.

The news stories about Ford and Carter were not surprising. Carter was drawing big crowds in New York. Ford was knocking them dead in Ohio. His campaign seemed to be picking up. But there were no polls to indicate that he was closing the gap.

I turned to the stock market. It was up ten points. Those shrewd Wall Streeters; they smell something in the air. My mood improved still further.

I turned to the sports pages. Jimmy the Greek had switched his odds. It had been six to five Carter. Now it was even money. I'd placed my bet with Lenny Zelick in Boston. I wondered what odds the bookie had given him.

Denny and I finished the radio spot in less than an hour. I'd been a little worried about the mandatory use of the President's voice. We had twenty-two short passages from various Ford speeches, but none of them seemed to fit the spot about the Georgia newspaper endorsements. But we got lucky. We found a tape of the President's Ann Arbor speech in which he had said the words we were using in our final ad, "Trust must be earned." We cut ten seconds of the "trust" passage into the spot. We put it at the tail end of the commercial over the announcer's voice reading the laundry list of Georgia newspapers backing Ford. It sounded just right. The President's voice booming into the list of papers in Carter's own state: "It is not enough for anyone to say 'trust me.' Trust must be *earned*."

Then we had another stroke of luck. Richard Petty had finally found time to record our radio spot, and he had recorded it word for word as I'd written it. It arrived by messenger as we were still doing the Georgia newspaper spot. His deep Southern drawl was perfect. The racing nuts of America would love it. Especially the ending: "Ah don't always agree with Mario Andretti and Bob and Al Unser and ol' Andy Granatelli, but ah can tell ya we're tigither on one thing raht now. As they come around the final turn in this election race, we're all sure hopin' the checkered flag goes to a Ford."

Of course it was corny. We ordered thirty tapes to be air-shipped to the Southwestern states.

After the taping, I wandered back to our offices at Forty-second Street. It was six o'clock. For the past two months, six o'clock in the evening had been about the middle of the day at Campaign '76. But now the penthouse was almost deserted. I wandered down to the editing rooms. All four Steenbecks stood quiet and empty. No more film to edit. No more awkward Fordisms to splice onto the reel of "ummms" and "er-ahs" and awkward pauses. The circus was over. It had ended as abruptly as it had started. Overnight we had created an instant advertising agency and an instant TV production company. And overnight they had both gone out of business.

I walked back down the empty hallway to the offices that John and Doug and Bob Gardner and I had shared, without ever determining who belonged to which office. Only the receptionist was there. She had several messages for me. One of them, she said, was fairly urgent. Some girl from the *New York Post* had been trying to get hold of me all day. The *New York Post*. No good could possibly come from that, I thought. The Post had been murdering us for weeks. I considered the *Post* the most viciously irresponsible newspaper outside of Manchester, New Hampshire.

I called the girl at the *Post*. You have to be nice to reporters.

She sounded pleasant enough. "I'm doing a story on the advertising for Ford," she said. "And I have a few questions about your people."

"They're not *my* people." I said nicely. "We all work for Campaign '76. Deardourff and Bailey head up the operation."

"But you're listed as the creative director."

"Right. Merely a title."

"Well, did you hire the TV and radio producers?"

"Not really."

"Well, have you ever heard of Vivian Productions?"

"No."

"Have you ever heard of Michael Goldbaum?"

"Sure. He's a sound man."

"I understand he's a producer. He produced your man-in-the-street commercials."

"He did the sound for them. He's a terrific sound man."

"How much do you pay him?"

"I don't know how much we pay him. He's got some kind of contract to edit and ship some of our radio spots. The man-in-the-street radio spots. I'd guess he does about a third of our radio work."

"He does it through Vivian Productions," the reporter informed me.

"Okay. If you say so. May I ask you a question?"

"Certainly."

"What are you leading up to?"

"I told you. I'm doing a story on some of the advertising people."

"Why don't you do a story on Doug Bailey; he actually produced the man-in-the-street stuff."

"I know about him. I'm interested in Mr. Goldbaum."

"Well, I want to know why you're asking. After your preposterous story last Friday, I think I have a right to ask."

"What preposterous story?" she asked innocently.

"The front-page headline that said, "How Ford Blocked the Watergate Investigation."

"The story was accurate," she said firmly.

"I think we both know that the story was nothing but a rehash of John Dean's discredited and disproven innuendos. Dean has since admitted that he brought the thing up on the "Today" show because his publisher wanted to hype his book."

"Well, that's your opinion."

"And that's why I'm kind of wondering why you suddenly want to do a story about Michael Goldbaum."

"How long have you known him?"

"I met him in Kansas City. He was one of the sound men with our film crews. That's all I can tell you about him."

"Okay," she said firmly. "Thank you."

I hung up. I had a feeling that I hadn't been as nice as I should have been. Why shouldn't she do a story on Michael Goldbaum? He was kind of a strange guy. But he was a helluva good sound man.

34

THURSDAY

Five days before the election my hands began to shake. Dennis
Roehl pointed that out as I tried to sip a casual beer in a friendly bar.

"Why are your hands shaking?" he asked, in a voice loud enough
to catch the attention of the bartender and the guy on my right.

"They're not shaking," I said firmly.

"Hold your hand straight out," he said.

I put down my beer and held my hand straight out in front of me. I
tightened the muscles of my arm as tight as I could but I couldn't
control the obvious vibrations of my fingers. I tried relaxing my
muscles, but the fingers kept on shaking. They seemed to have their
own electric current.

"You must have had a rough day," the bartender said.

I put my hand down and ordered another beer. The fact was it had
been a good day. I couldn't understand why I felt so tight inside.
Maybe my body was trying to adjust to the shock of the sudden
possibility of victory.

I had just seen a poll that showed we'd moved ahead of Carter in
almost every Western state. Carter was now writing off California,
I'd been told. The Joe and Jerry show was continuing to knock 'em
dead—Texas, New York, Ohio were beginning to swing our
way. And we'd saved the final push of the big blitz for Texas, New
York, and Ohio. It was now an even race in Illinois. Maybe that was
why my hand was shaking. My system couldn't adjust to success.

There was another possible explanation, but I didn't want to think about it. It meant that I was vulnerable to the one thing that everyone in politics should steel himself against. I was letting the press get to me.

Up until now I'd been lucky. I'd been interviewed several times during the course of the campaign, but always by friendly reporters from the advertising trade press, or by Boston reporters who wanted to write a local-boy-makes-good story. The story and picture in *Time* Magazine had been so nice I had sent a copy to my mother. I'd had a few tough questions thrown at me during the flap over the *Playboy* ad, but I had apparently fielded them fairly well.

But now, as the campaign was nearing its climax, the wolf pack seemed to be starting to sniff at my heels. I was beginning to worry about what the lady from the *Post* had up her sleeve. Why was Michael Goldbaum so important all of a sudden? Other reporters had been calling about some anti-Carter brochures that were being circulated in the South. I knew nothing about them and said so. They didn't seem to think I was lying. They seemed to *know* I was lying. And just before Denny and I had gone out for the beer, I'd been interviewed by a Boston radio talk show.

I'd expected to have softballs lobbed up to me. It was my hometown calling, after all. The first question came at me like a knife in a dark alley:

"Mr. MacDougall, a lot of people think it's wrong the way you package political candidates. They feel that your slick Madison Avenue approach obscures the real issues in the campaign. Do you think it's in the best interests of the electorate to sell a candidate the way you sell a soap or a cereal?"

I started out by answering the third part of the question. By the time I'd stumbled through that, I'd completely forgotten the first two parts of the question. He then went on to question the propriety of our *Playboy* ad, the honesty of our commercials, the spending of millions and millions of dollars in the final TV blitz.

There was no question that I was shaking inside when I hung up. I had decided then and there that I'd never be a politician. They spend their lives answering those same aggressive, antagonistic questions. I have one live interview and have to make my way to the nearest bar.

I looked at my shaking hand, curled around the beer, and thought about the press and TV coverage of this campaign.

It seemed to me that the most debasing part of the whole political process was the fear of the press, the playing to the press, the ass-kissing of the press. I'd only seen it from afar, but I didn't like what I had seen. I felt that the TV and newspaper journalists had made a circus of the campaign.

That's what this campaign had become. A three-ring circus: ABC, NBC, CBS. A show every night. Complete with rallies, parades, pratfalls, balloons, softball games, and Rose Garden interviews. The two candidates were the leading clowns. With a new act almost every week. Of course we had had most of the headliners: the Gulf Oil show, the Earl Butz show, the Watergate prosecutor show (held over two big weeks), the Polish show, the John Dean show, the bumbling President show, the TV blitz show. But I had to admit that they had saved the really big one for Jimmy Carter. He had the *Playboy* show. That had to be the hit of the campaign as far as the networks were concerned. That was in the highest traditions of the Greatest Show on Earth.

I hadn't had time for drinking during the long campaign and three beers made me sad. I thought about the young people in both campaigns who had worked to make this a better campaign.

I thought of the stacks of mimeographed papers that made it so hard to move around our Washington headquarters. They were our position papers. A lengthy document for every issue that might concern the people of America. Each paper had been researched by teams of specialists. I remembered the young Harvard assistant professor who came up to me one day while I was leafing through a paper on foreign policy.

"I just want to tell you," he said with a wry smile, "that you are the first person who has ever asked to see one of our position papers."

Now that was sad. And it was true. The Jimmy Carter campaign had issued a truckload of documents defining their position on every conceivable issue. Our people had topped them. We had issued boxcars full of documents. There was not a shred of evidence that a single reporter had read a word in any of those papers.

Of course President Ford and Jimmy Carter knew the game. They knew that they could talk brilliantly about the issues all day long. And they knew that when they turned on the television that night or read the newspapers the next morning the only news would be that President Ford had said it was nice to be in Davenport, Iowa, when he really was in Lincoln, Nebraska, and that Jimmy Carter did not really think President Johnson was a cheat and a liar.

35
FRIDAY

I still had to check the Pearl Bailey section of the final half-hour film, and I was supposed to be in New York Sunday night for the last Joe and Jerry show, but there was no real work for me to do.

I'd been invited to give a talk about the campaign to a Columbus, Ohio advertising club. I figured Ohio would be a good place to feel the pulse of America, so I went.

The pulse seemed strong. My taxi driver survey, conducted to and from the airport, showed that Ford would get a hundred percent of the vote. And the Columbus Advertising Federation was clearly a landslide for Ford. The fact that the audience didn't represent a perfect cross-section of the Ohio electorate didn't dampen my enthusiasm in the least. A Carter advertising man had appeared before the same group a month earlier, and after my talk I was assured that our advertising was far superior to his. Rafshoon, I thought, eat your heart out.

My confidence climbed still higher when I read the Columbus newspapers. They headlined glowing reviews of the Joe and Jerry show that had wowed them in Cleveland the night before.

Our momentum was still building, the columnists said. Ohio could go to Ford after all—Ohio could be the state that crowned the political upset of the century. I didn't pay much attention to a small article about a union spokesman who promised the best organized get-out-the-vote drive in Columbus history.

I had time to kill before my plane, so I took a little walk around

Columbus. It was a warm, sunny, optimistic day. The building next to the hotel was practically covered with FORD-DOLE posters. A girl was outside the building, handing out leaflets. I took one and thanked her. "Monster Ford Victory Rally Monday Night," the leaflet announced. I wondered whether I should come in the gorilla suit. I had forgotten that Ford had chosen this city for the very last hurrah of his campaign. He had been scheduled to stop at Columbus on his way to Grand Rapids. I hoped that he'd still be able to stand up after the extraordinary ordeal of the ten-day blitz.

I had seen a poll that showed that if the vote was reasonably close in Columbus, we would definitely carry the state. Close? Hell—we were going to *win* Columbus. I could feel it. I could see it. This was Middle America. This was Ford country. These people had just two things on their minds: they had to cheer for Ohio State on Saturday and vote for Jerry Ford on Tuesday.

When I got back to the hotel, the red light on my telephone was flashing. It was a message to call Phil Angell in Washington immediately. As I dialed his number, I guessed that he'd received still another financial windfall and wanted a new, last-minute commercial.

"What did you tell that woman from the *New York Post?*" Phil's voice was controlled, but there was a note of panic.

"Oh, her," I said. "She said she was doing a story on the advertising."

"What did you tell her about Michael Goldbaum?"

"I'm not sure," I said. "I couldn't figure out why she was so interested in Goldbaum. I think I told her that he was our sound man on the man-in-the-street spots. That's what he was."

"Did she ask any questions about Vivian Productions?"

I thought a moment. "Yes, as a matter of fact. I'd never heard of Vivian Productions. What is it?"

"Well, I'm going to read you the headline in today's *New York Post*." Phil paused. "You'd better sit down," he said.

"Read it," I said. I remained standing but I was beginning to feel apprehensive.

"FORD AD MAN LINKED TO PORN."

I sat down.

"Want me to read you the article?" Phil asked.

"Is it as bad as I think it is?"

"Worse. Much worse. They describe Goldbaum as the three-hundred-dollar-a-day media expert behind the Ford campaign. He's our chief producer."

"And he really is making a porn movie?" I asked weakly.

"According to the *Post* he's been shuttling between interviewing the President and casting for a hard-core porn film."

"What does Goldbaum say?"

"He says it's not a hard-core film. It's an art film. We fired him last night. This is going to cost us New York."

"People aren't going to believe that shit," I said.

"Every newspaper, every wire service, every television station in the country is after us for the story."

"But they all know what the *Post* is up to, for Christ's sake," I said. "They know what kind of a paper it is. I just can't believe anyone else will play up this insanity." My stomach was beginning to tighten up in anger. I thought about the sweet-voiced woman who said she wanted to do a story on our advertising. I now knew what writers meant when they described their characters as being "weak with rage."

"This isn't just a phony news story," Phil reminded me. "It's part of the campaign now. There's nothing we can do about it."

"People aren't that dumb," I said hopefully. "They're going to read it for what it is. They're certainly not going to link Ford with porn."

"They'll link Ford with stupidity," Phil said. "That's worse."

"We should have done the same thing to Carter," I said. "I'm sure there were people in his film crews who were making porn movies. There aren't ten people in the film business who haven't tried to make a pornographic movie at one time or another."

"But I doubt if Carter's people would be stupid enough to hold auditions in front of campaign posters."

"Goldbaum did that?"

"He had the girls strip and talk about their sex fantasies in front of a Ford poster. It's all in the *Post*. With pictures."

I pictured the naked girl in front of our poster. "He's Making Us Proud again." I groaned. "What are we going to do about it?" I asked weakly.

"Nothing. Except say that Goldbaum's been fired. Can you think of anything else we can do?"

I thought for a moment.

"Nope."

I said good-bye and hung up slowly.

I stared out the motel window, remembering when I worked for the *Boston Post* while I was going to Harvard. One night a bunch of drunken Southerners had burned a cross in the Yard in front of a dormitory where several black students were living. I knew about the story but decided not to report it. Unfortunately, the campus newspaper wrote an editorial about the incident. My editors saw the editorial and told me to write a short piece for the *Post*. I wrote as mild a story as I could, including a quote from one of the black students who thought the incident was ridiculous and meaningless. He made a special point of talking about Harvard's enlightened attitude towards minority students.

The next morning there was a screaming headline across the front page of the *Post:* "Burning Cross Seen at Harvard."

The editors had completely rewritten my story. They had omitted the quote from the black student. It read like the report of a campus race riot.

I had spent three years in the newspaper business. I fully expected to make it my career. But when I saw that headline I called up the *Post,* quit my job, and left the newspaper business forever.

Now I felt that same, sick anger all over again. The Goldbaum story was exactly like the burning cross story. The *New York Post* was carrying on the same tradition as the long gone *Boston Post.*

I picked up the telephone. I knew that what I was doing was the worst thing I could possibly do under the circumstances. But I went ahead and dialed New York information, got the number of the *New York Post,* hung up and called the *Post.* I asked to speak to the person who had written the Ford porn story. I heard the sound of the newsroom as I waited for her to come on the line. The clicking of typewriters, the ringing of telephones took me back twenty-five years.

I hadn't planned what I was going to say. The question I asked came from somewhere deep in back of my mind.

"Do you think you'll be able to sleep well tonight?"

"What are you?" she asked politely. "Some kind of nut?"

"Sort of," I answered, introducing myself. "I just wanted to call and find out from you how you really felt about the story in today's *Post.*"

"I feel fine," she said. "Why?"

"Do you think your story is really front-page news? Do you think it's the most important thing that happened in the world today?" My voice was calm, almost pleasant.

"I don't decide what goes on the front page," she said. "The publisher does."

"Well, how do you feel about working for a newspaper that uses its news columns for its own political purpose?"

"Why do I have to sit here and listen to you?" she asked. She was beginning to sound upset.

"Obviously I'm angry about the story. That's why I'm calling you. But I also wanted to know if you, personally, had any regrets about it."

"No, I don't," she said firmly. "Do you think there's anything about it that isn't true?"

"I'm sure it's accurate," I said. "I just don't think it's front-page news."

"That's not for you to say."

"No, of course it isn't," I admitted. "But don't you think it's too bad that Presidential elections are sometimes decided by stories like yours?"

"It was news. I'm a reporter. I wrote it as news."

"It's supposed to look like news and seem like news, but I think you and I both know that it's really something else."

"Complain to the publisher," she said angrily. "Don't bother me."

"But you still haven't answered my question," I said pleasantly. "How do you, personally, feel about the story?"

"Christ!" she said. There was a long pause. I knew she was trying to think up something devastating to say to me. And from the way she had said "Christ!"—almost like a cry for help—I felt that she was pretty upset.

"You people don't understand the working person!" she said finally. And she hung up the phone.

I let the phone hang in my hand for a minute. I had gained absolutely nothing. I had been completely unprofessional. But still I felt a little better.

36
THE LAST WEEKEND

I thought about the Ford-ad-man-linked-to-porn story on the way to Boston. After two bourbons I decided it was one of those things you laugh about in the morning.

I was right.

In fact Mimi started laughing about it as soon as I got home that night. I had picked up a copy of the *Post* at Logan Airport. I held it in front of my face when she opened the door.

"I have something to tell you," I said in my guiltiest tone of voice.

At first she wouldn't believe the headline was real.

"You had that made up in one of those phony headline places," she insisted.

When I convinced her that the paper actually was the *New York Post,* she howled.

"I'd give anything to see Mother's face when she sees that headline," she said. "Her worst fears about you will be confirmed."

Early Saturday morning my friends started to call.

"Congratulations on making the front page." "Did you persuade President Ford to star in your movie?" "I understand your film is called 'The Making of the President' starring Linda Lovelace."

It also cheered me up to discover that the *New York Times,* in spite of its outspoken Carter leanings, had shown the good taste to bury the story. In fact the only story any of the other news media seemed to be carrying was the fact that we had fired our sound man.

I had no idea what damage, if any, the story had done to our campaign. But at least no one else was blowing it out of proportion. It wasn't another Butz. It wouldn't slow our momentum. And the Saturday polls showed that we were definitely still moving.

"I know things are getting better," Mimi told me. "They only ripped two Ford bumper stickers off the car all week long."

In Boston that was a good sign. The week before six stickers had been ripped off the car. Political feelings run high in Boston.

"And Camilla's class at Shore Country Day just had a key vote," Mimi announced.

Camilla is Mimi's daughter. She's in the fifth grade.

"Who won?"

"Landslide for Ford," Mimi said. "The vote was forty-one to one."

"Who was the little brat who voted for Carter?"

"It was the teacher," Mimi said.

I was back in the real world for a day. I watched my son Mal play soccer and he played magnificently. I was with my daughter Leslie again. I felt guilty when I realized that she had grown since I last saw her. Soon, I thought. Soon life will be normal again. I forgot about politics until the evening news. And that was mostly good news. Ford had knocked them dead in Texas. I went out to dinner with Mimi and the kids and nobody mentioned Jimmy Carter or President Ford once. It was a wonderful dinner.

The next day I flew to New York under about twenty-five pounds of Sunday papers. As I read the *Boston Herald,* the *Boston Globe,* and the *New York Times* I began to wonder if there had ever before been so many words written to make a single, inconclusive point. The campaign was too close to call.

On page two of the fourth section of the Sunday *Times* I found something I had not seen before in this long election. A report on how the two candidates differed on the issues. It was a rather sketchy report by David Rosenbaum. The *Times* gave Mr. Rosenbaum only half a page, a third of it dominated by a cartoon. It's not easy to discuss both sides of sixteen vital issues in that much space, but Mr. Rosenbaum, I thought, did a creditable job. Of course I thought it was slanted towards Carter. Especially when I read his handling of the housing issue. He covered Carter's plan for more federal subsidies in one sentence, and didn't mention the housing program Ford announced in his Ann Arbor speech.

But I was fascinated by the article. Here, at the very end of the long campaign, buried deep in the world's thickest newspaper, was

the essence of what could have been an exciting, interesting, reward-
ing, uplifting Presidential election. Both men had actually taken chal-
lenging positions on every issue. But no one had bothered to take up
the challenge. It occurred to me that not one voter in a million would
be going to the voting place with a clear idea of the differences
between the two candidates. They would know far more than they
had ever wanted to know about campaign strategy, and campaign
blunders; about Butz and lust, abortion and *Playboy*. But they would
know nothing about things that truly separated the two Presidential
candidates. The debates had helped. But they had been mostly show
business, with the candidates spending so much time attacking each
other that they never attacked the issues.

The plane landed and I came down to earth. I hailed a cab and
headed for my last job in the real-life Presidential campaign. The Joe
and Jerry show.

"President Ford's Flying TV Circus" was in full flight when I
arrived at the studio where they were editing the tape for the New
York show. That was the name Bob Gardner had given the film crew
that accompanied the President during the TV blitz, and who put
together, in record time, a four-to-five-minute localized introduction
to each of the shows. Gardner had issued T-shirts to the dozen crew
members with the name of the group emblazoned on the back and
"Feelin' Good" stenciled on the front. Most of them were wearing
the T-shirts when I entered the studio.

They had been traveling from one end of the country to the other.
They had already put together five shows. They seemed to be a
pretty smooth-running team by the time they got to New York City.

When I entered the editing room, Bill Caruthers, the crew's director, was staring at a battery of TV monitors. Whenever he saw a
scene that he thought should be included in the final tape, he would
snap his fingers furiously and shout an unintelligible command. The
tape editor would then electronically transfer the scene to a cassette
containing only the best footage. As I noted before, editing tape is a
tedious, nerve-shattering process. The electronics of tape is nowhere
near as precise as the mechanics of film. But watching Caruthers in
action made me realize that tape can be tamed if you shout loud
enough, point hard enough, and snap your fingers with enough authority. He was the Führer of the editing room. As a result, a full
day's work was accomplished in two frantic hours.

The crew had taped President Ford going to church in Buffalo.
They had taped him at rallies in upstate New York and on Long
Island. They had taped him in a parade, in a motorcade, in his

helicopter as he took off and landed at various places throughout the city. They had taped him diving into crowds in his shirt-sleeves. They taped him with Smokin' Joe Frazier and other celebrities. At the same time, they had taped Betty Ford as she made her way through enthusiastic crowds in downtown New York.

The various crew members would rush the tape cassettes to Caruthers in the editing room as soon as they finished shooting the various scenes. A young man rushed in with the tape of Betty Ford shortly after I arrived at the studio.

"Sensational stuff here," he said as he handed the tape to one of the engineers. "The crowd was fantastic. They pushed Mrs. Ford down three times."

"Terrific," said Caruthers.

"No, it was really great," the young man went on. "We shot her at Ratner's—eating blintzes. They loved her."

The engineer had racked the tape up while he was talking. A button was pushed. A picture appeared on the screen.

"Holy shit," Caruthers shouted. "It's out of focus."

The screen was a fuzzy blur.

"Holy shit," echoed the cameraman quietly.

The blur rolled on.

"Fast forward the fuckin' thing," Caruthers commanded.

The engineer pushed another button and the picture disappeared while the tape was speeded ahead. He stopped it well into the reel and snapped the picture on again. Mrs. Ford was still an unrecognizable blur.

"Holy shit," Caruthers said again.

"Fuckin' camera broke," the cameraman explained.

"Who else was there?" Caruthers barked. "ABC? CBS? NBC?"

"ABC had a crew."

Caruthers shouted to an assistant in the other room. "Get ABC. See if we can buy their Betty Ford stuff."

He went back to editing the footage he had. Another runner came in with tape of a Long Island rally. The engineer racked it up. The sound was bad.

"Fuck it," Caruthers said after listening to about thirty seconds of the garbled tape. "We'll go with another helicopter scene." The engineer jammed another cassette into the Sony. I disappeared into another room with Bob Gardner.

"This the way it's been every night?" I asked.

"No," he said. "This one's going smoothly."

It took a couple of hours to pull together a four-and-a-half-minute tape of the highlights of the President's day in New York State. Bob dashed off a script that Joe Garagiola was to read while the tape was rolling. ABC wouldn't sell us the Betty Ford footage, but it didn't matter. She was going to be on the live part of the show anyway.

While Caruthers was finishing his editing I checked the Pearl Bailey insert for the half-hour film that was to run nationally Monday night. Pearl's introduction, by Joe Garagiola, had been filmed aboard Air Force One. It was a nice introduction but I thought it looked about as contrived as show business can get. A film of a sportscaster aboard the President's plane introducing a film of Pearl Bailey that was shot in a Washington studio. It lacked warmth, it lacked spontaneity, but it's all we had, folks.

While we were putting it together, one of the crew members rushed in.

"Just heard a news bulletin," he said excitedly. "Jimmy Carter's church had to close down today because they didn't want to let some blacks in."

My first reaction was sheer elation. Now we had the son of a bitch where it had to hurt most. I remembered Stu Spencer's words, "When it comes time to vote, a lot of blacks are going to say 'He comes from Georgia, and that's the bottom line.' "

Well, here was the proof that Georgia was still Georgia, that racism was still racism, and a lot of blacks were now going to see that right on the evening news. Our biggest problem, the black vote, might have been solved. Now the Pearl Bailey spot would really hit home.

That was my first reaction. It took about five minutes for the second reaction to set in.

I began to realize that this was the last Sunday of the campaign. I began to suspect that somebody just might have put those blacks up to forcing a racial issue in Carter's church. If *I* was suspicious, what would the rest of the country be thinking right now? The Republicans are up to their old dirty tricks, I see.

I could see this one backfiring right in our face, whether or not we had anything to do with it.

It made me realize that I had become a very cynical man.

The "Flying Circus" crew finished their edit less than an hour before air time. We rushed across town to the ABC-TV studio. We literally ran into the studio. We had to transfer the cassette to two-inch broadcast tape. Bob had to put the script on cue cards so Joe could read it. Caruthers had to rehearse the studio crew and Joe Garagiola. Bob had to rush back to the audio booth to insert background music in various portions of the tape. To add to our anxiety, the President arrived late. John Deardourff had been waiting at the studio. He had hoped to have at least an hour to brief the President, Mrs. Ford, Garagiola, and the two other stars, Democratic Congresswoman Edith Green and Senator Jacob Javits. By the time they all arrived there was less than half an hour to air time. I sensed impending disaster. And the look on Caruthers' face didn't alleviate my fears.

He was Mussolini now, jaws set, screaming orders and gesturing wildly.

"I want more cheering!" he screamed, throwing his pointed finger at an audio engineer.

"That's as loud as I can boost it," came a desperate voice from a sound booth.

Caruthers whirled in his director's chair. "Bob, you're late on the goddamned music."

"You were early with the goddamned film," came Bob's voice over a studio loudspeaker.

I looked at my watch. Five minutes to seven. There would be no time for another rehearsal. I walked into the main studio where the live show was going to take place. It was a nice set. Five regal but comfortable-looking chairs in a semicircle. Behind the chairs was a large, blue Presidential seal. There was only one trouble with the set. The only member of the cast who was on the set was Joe Garagiola. He was on his knees, his back to the cameras, scribbling new words on the cue cards. Three minutes to air time. It looked to me as if we were going to have the damnedest show opening in the history of television.

Joe looked up, smiled, and said hello to me. He placed the cue card in front of the camera and sat down in the middle seat. Just then the President walked in, a little hurriedly, followed by Mrs. Ford, Senator Javits, Edith Green. The President made a circle with his thumb and forefinger and gave me a little "Everything's A-OK" salute. I couldn't tell whether it was a campaign gesture, or whether he recognized me. But I was pleased. He was calm. *I* wasn't. But he was. John Deardourff took a position behind one of the cameras. He looked calm, too, I glanced at the studio clock. My watch had been fast. There were still three minutes to go. But I was still nervous. Did they have any idea what the hell they were going to say when the camera started turning? Suddenly the President got up out of his chair. I heard a voice yell "Quiet in the studio" over a loudspeaker. The President walked directly to one of the cameramen. He clapped the man on the shoulder and shook his hand. The studio was becoming quiet and I was standing close enough to hear the President say to the cameraman that he'd known his father . . . he was a great guy. The cameraman looked as if he were about to burst into tears.

"Stand by," came the voice over the loudspeaker.

The President hurried back to his chair.

Suddenly Joe Garagiola was talking. I stood stock-still. We were on the air, for Christ's sake. If I sneezed, it would be heard all over New York State. Joe was talking smoothly, casually, about the President's day in New York. I glanced at the studio monitor. I tried to do it without moving my head. I thought that might make a noise. I could see Caruthers' tape on the monitor. I could hear Bob's music giving body to the show, giving great tone to Joe's flawless reading.

I turned back to the stage. They were on live now. Joe was laughing about something with the President. I had never seen the President so relaxed.

Joe lobbed some softballs at the President: "What are the main differences between you and Jimmy Carter?" "What do you feel have been your major accomplishments in office?"

The President used the same words I'd heard before. But now they didn't sound stiff. He sounded warm and real.

Joe asked him about the headline in the *Daily News*. "Did you tell New York City to drop dead?"

The President laughed. He explained the headline. He explained what he had done to help the city. He casually pointed out that the *Daily News*, the paper that had carried the headline, was now supporting him for the Presidency.

Joe turned to Mrs. Ford. "What kind of husband is this man? What kind of father?"

Mrs. Ford clutched her husband's hand. The President smiled shyly. Her answer oozed with all the warmth of a well-loved woman. It was nice.

Joe turned to Edith Green. "You're a Democrat. Why are you supporting President Ford?"

I had heard that Edith Green had been terrific on the previous shows. Tonight she was brilliant. She had to put her country above her party. She knew what a good, decent man President Ford was. She would remain a Democrat, but she could never vote for Jimmy Carter.

Could Senator Javits top Edith Green?

He could. He told things about President Ford that I had never heard before. It was far more than a fellow Republican praising his

President. It was a tribute from the heart. Maybe Jacob Javits was just a brilliant politician, but I found myself being deeply moved by what he said.

A man held up a sign: "Last question."

The President began talking earnestly about the importance of the election.

The man held up another sign: "Thirty seconds to go."

The President picked up his tempo imperceptibly, like an old pro. He closed with a warm tribute to the spirit of the American people. The light on the cameras went off at the precise instant his voice hit the period on his last sentence.

I didn't know whether anyone had been watching, but it had been a fine show.

The studio doors flew open and the entire "Flying Circus" crew started marching in. As they walked towards the stage they started taking off their shirts. The Secret Service men looked startled. The President, who was chatting on stage with Senator Javits, started laughing.

This was the time for the team picture. The President, Mrs. Ford, and Joe were supposed to pose with the entire crew right after the show. Someone had neglected to tell the Secret Service. They started to form a ring of protection in front of President Ford. The President quickly straightened the problem out, and the crew climbed onto the stage. They were now all wearing their "Flying Circus" T-shirts.

First they posed facing the camera, the "Feelin' Good" slogan on their chests. Then they turned their backs to the camera while the President, Betty, and Joe stood smiling straight ahead.

37
THE LAST HALF HOUR

The decision as to who was to get the last half hour of advertising was made with a flip of the coin shortly after Kansas City.

The networks had decided that they were going to give each candidate an equal crack at all the best available commercial time. To do it, they held the equivalent of a professional football draft. They gathered representatives of both candidates in a room. They flipped a coin to decide who would get first pick. Our team won. We chose the last half hour on all three networks. We wanted to have the last word in this campaign. It meant that our final commercial would run at eight-thirty on ABC (just before Monday night football); nine-thirty on CBS; and ten-thirty on NBC.

The Carter people were delighted. They had wanted the half hour preceding ours, apparently thinking that no one would sit through an entire hour of political commercials.

So both sides had gotten just what they wanted. And now, over two months later, it was time to watch the last hurrahs. I was with Mimi in our Boston apartment when the appointed hour arrived.

And I was very nervous.

I had seen our half-hour film in most of its many stages. I had gone by editing room three, night after night, and Ed Spiegel had always been there, tearing it apart and putting it back together again. It had undoubtedly been the most fussed-over film of the campaign. The final version, with the Pearl Bailey insert and the Air Force One footage, had been completed only the night before.

I felt that it had the look of a film that had been created by a committee. And in its final form, that's exactly what it was. It wasn't the film that Ed Spiegel wanted. It didn't *look* like an Ed Spiegel film. It wasn't the film Doug Bailey had wanted. The narration wasn't as inspiring as a Doug Bailey film. It wasn't the film John Deardourff had wanted. It wasn't as politically sharp as a John Deardourff film. And it certainly wasn't the film that I had wanted. I hadn't wanted a film at all. I'd wanted a live half hour, ending with the President delivering an inspiring talk about the future of America.

I was also nervous about what I *didn't* know of Jimmy Carter's last half hour. We had heard a rumor that he would be using the same half-hour show that had been broadcast in one of the Southern markets a week earlier. That show, as described to me, sounded like the old Nixon half-hour format: various people from around the country, stooges all, ask corny questions. The candidate answers them, with a warm, end-of-campaign smile from a studio.

If that's really all he's got, I figured, we have him beat. But if we only had something great. Then we could *kill* him.

I knew that it would be impossible for Mimi and me to view the two films objectively. I decided that we'd have to watch them as two other people.

We were still arguing about who she should be when we suddenly realized that the Jimmy Carter show had already begun. I quickly ordered Mimi to become a grade school teacher in Lubbock, Texas. I decided to become a New York taxi driver. I handed her a pen and some paper and said we would compare notes in an hour.

It looked as if the rumors had been correct. Rafshoon had chosen the old Nixon format. Mr. "Average American" was looking into the camera.

"I don't think I'm going to vote," he was saying. "Ford pardoned Nixon: I certainly can't vote for him. And I'm not sure I know enough about Mr. Carter."

Cut to a deeply concerned Jimmy Carter saying how important it was for this man to vote (he called him by name, as if they were old buddies). I noticed that Carter had gotten out of his dungarees and changed into a suit. Tony Schwartz's influence, I thought. I tried to stop thinking those thoughts. New York taxi drivers don't think about Tony Schwartz. Carter was saying that "this Republican administration has really been terrible." He went through the old laundry list: over seven million people out of work, cost of living going up every day, etc., etc., etc., and it's time for a change. Everything in America was terrible, disgraceful. Would a New York taxi driver buy that?

It occurred to me, as another Average American was asking him the next question, that Carter had never *addressed* the first question. And obviously he had never intended to. It was the old one-two punch. The question was a way to hit us with the Nixon pardon. The answer was his way of reminding voters that Ford was a Republican. Very tricky. Very neat.

But would the New York taxi driver see through it?

I wasn't sure.

A man named Bob Gary asked a question about tax reform. It sounded like a real question. "Is it true that you want to eliminate the home mortgage interest deduction?"

Jimmy Carter smiled like a man who's now heard it all. "That's a perfect example of how the Republicans are distorting my positions. Our tax laws are a disgrace. The Republicans are scared because they know I want to eliminate those hidden loopholes for big shots. Those laws are designed for Republicans and their friends who don't want to pay taxes. The average worker pays the taxes for them. That's a disgrace. If I'm elected we're going to have comprehensive tax reform for a change."

I had to admire the man. Not a word about the mortgage deduction—which indeed he once *had* wanted to eliminate. Not a word about the Democrats who had written those "disgraceful" tax laws. Not a word about the comprehensive tax reform bill that had just been signed three weeks ago. And certainly not a word about the eighty-five thousand dollars' worth of "hidden loopholes" that he himself had taken on his own tax return just last year.

Now the Average American Senior Citizen was asking him about the problems of living on Social Security. Did he understand those problems?

Carter offered us his senior citizen sympathy smile. "My mother Lillian is over seventy," he said, with a little glance towards heaven. "She doesn't let us forget about Social Security."

The answer was short but sweet.

He was asked some foreign policy questions. He talked about the "terrible mistake" of the grain embargoes . . . selling crops instead of guns . . . the Republicans' robbing the farmers. He thought that the President, not the Secretary of State, should be America's spokesman. He felt that the President should express the moral tone of the American people, develop a foreign policy that makes us proud and not ashamed.

Well, I thought, you couldn't argue with that.

A tough-looking Average American asked him about the defense budget.

"I was in the Navy," Carter answered. "I've seen waste in the Defense Department. I'm trying to cut out waste. The Republicans are defending waste. We need tougher management to maintain a strong defense. That's number one." He said it with a clenched fist. The fighter for a strong defense.

The Average Farmer asked him why farmers were going broke.

"As a farmer," Carter answered, increasing his drawl almost imperceptibly, "I've seen firsthand how Republican promises haven't helped us farmers." He said he thought it was a disgrace that farmers were going broke trying to produce food that people couldn't afford to buy. What we need, he said, is "stable production—stable prices."

I tried to think about that, but it kept slipping off my mind.

The Average Woman's Libber asked, "What would you say to your wife if she said she wanted a job?"

Carter gave us his "I love Rosalynn" smile. "I had to face that problem during this campaign," he said. "Rosalynn wanted to work full-time. We couldn't always be with each other." He felt that the experience had brought them closer together.

The Average Mexican-American asked, in broken English, what he would do for Mexican-Americans.

"Everybody has been hurt under this Republican Administration," Carter said, "but the minorities have been hurt most of all." He then launched into a new laundry list of things the Republicans had done to hurt minorities.

Then I nearly fell off my chair.

Carter suddenly started speaking in Spanish, and English subtitles began crawling across the screen.

Now if he'd just said a few words in Spanish, and let it go at that, it would simply have been another little bit of political silliness. But this earnest Berlitz monologue. Those English subtitles!

I turned to Mimi and laughed. Mimi was laughing too. Even the New York cabbie was laughing.

The Average Street-Wise New Yorker had a question for Mr. Carter: "Would you have the guts to handle crime in New York?"

Carter thought our criminal justice system was a disgrace.

"Why, in Georgia," Carter said, "we had a man who'd been indicted fifty-five times and never gone to jail. Well, I put him in jail!"

The whole trouble, Carter explained, was that "the powerful don't go to jail. The average family goes to jail."

While I was forming a picture of "the average family" sitting together behind bars, Carter told us that crime starts at the top. "We've had two Attorneys General convicted of crimes," he explained. "We've had a President and a Vice-President who had to resign in disgrace!"

Well, I thought, *that* ought to take care of the New York crime problem.

The Average Black Workingman (the last of several Average Blacks) had a final question. He had heard too many promises, he said. Why should he think that Mr. Carter would keep his promises?

Jimmy Carter thought that it was a tragedy that so many Americans had lost confidence in the system. The reason, he explained, was the years of government incompetence, insensitivity, mismanagement—even betrayal in high office. He told us that he was not part of the Establishment (something I hadn't heard since he had joined forces with Mayor Daley and George Meany). He said that now we needed someone who had not been there before. Someone who could make the people part of the decision-making process.

It is time, he said in conclusion, to restore the greatness that we have lost and prove once again that we live in the best country on earth.

The instant it was over I turned to Mimi.

"What did the school teacher from Lubbock think?" I asked.

She held out her right fist and turned the thumb down.

"How about the cabbie?" she asked.

I held out both fists and turned both thumbs down.

I knew in my heart that I had failed to throw myself into the role of an undecided cabdriver. It occurred to me that there was no such thing as an undecided cabdriver, anyway. It was a contradiction in terms. But even from the totally biased viewpoint of President Ford's creative director I felt that Jimmy Carter had put on a pretty lousy show.

Mimi was even more positive about that than I was.

"It was boring," she said. "Boring, depressing, and contrived. "In fact," she said, warming to the subject, "it was a stinking show. It was down, down, down—too down. It was grating. This country isn't that awful. And he didn't answer anything. He didn't answer anything at *all*."

I felt that it was always helpful to have an unbiased, outside viewpoint in these things.

When our half hour began, I couldn't even pretend to be anybody but me. I was just too close to every foot of film that flickered across the screen.

The film opened with a magnificent shot of Air Force One slowly banking a turn into a bright blue sky. It was beautiful. It was Presidential as hell.

But, I wondered, would too many taxpayers begin to ask who pays for the props in our commercials?

Joe Garagiola came on, talking to us from a comfortable seat aboard Air Force One. He was very friendly, very smooth; you just knew that he really meant every wonderful word he had to say about the President.

But, I wondered, does anybody care whether the President has a pal named Joe Garagiola?

Joe introduced Pearl Bailey with just the right amount of warmth and genuine respect. Pearl seemed even more emotional, even more convincing than she had seemed when we had made the tape. It sent chills up my spine when she said, "I do hope you will *think* before you vote—use all the goodness that is in you." And at the end, when she looked at us and asked us, "Please vote for President Ford. It's important. Its . . . I don't know . . . it's . . . so important," well, there was a lump in my throat.

Then Joe introduced the special film about President Ford.

Isn't it a little silly, I wondered, to have a film introducing a film?

There was that same old footage again. A new narrator. A few new scenes. But the same Eagle Scout . . . captain of the high school football team . . . most valuable player at Michigan. Then Willis Ward, the black judge, came on the screen. He reminisced again about the Michigan-Georgia game, when someone from Georgia had chided Jerry Ford for liking "(bleep adjective)—meaning people like me." He told of Jerry's block "that ended that fellow's participation in the game. Jerry said he dedicated that block to me."

I wondered if America would catch the significance: Jerry Ford of Michigan knocking out the guy from Georgia, and dedicating his block to his black buddy.

No, I decided, America *wouldn't* get the significance.

Then, right on cue, there was Scranton again, talking about how Jerry Ford had worked his way through Yale Law School and still managed to graduate in the top third of a class made up almost entirely of Phi Beta Kappas. This was followed immediately by Lieutenant Commander Ford once again shooting down those two Jap torpedo bombers. I wondered how many people who had seen our commercials would decide that this is where they came in.

Suddenly it began to dawn on me that this last half hour was no more than a recap of most of the commercials that we'd made during the long campaign. Scenes from the family commercial. Scenes from the biography commercial. Scenes from the accomplishments spot. Scenes from the leadership spot.

I couldn't imagine anyone watching it as a film. It was just a batch of scenes from old Ford commercials haphazardly spliced together. The Best of the Ford Advertising Campaign. The Worst of the Ford Advertising Campaign.

I was depressed and disoriented as those same old scenes sped across the screen. This had been a time for something new. This had been a time to add a new dimension to the campaign and to President Ford's character. *This* had been the time to present America with the New Generation of Freedom.

Instead we showed reruns of tired commercials.

I felt even more depressed as I realized what was coming up next.

It still could have been saved if, after this awful film, President Ford had come on live and delivered a fiery, original speech for the last ten minutes of the campaign.

But I knew what was coming. And on he came. President Ford sitting awkwardly in Air Force One. His voice so hoarse you could barely make out his words. And that might have been a blessing. For his words were the same tired clichés. We've cut inflation in half. More people are at work than ever before. Truth is the glue. . . . Trust is something that must be earned. . . . Our long national night-mare is over. . . . People shouldn't go broke to get well. . . . I was well aware that you hadn't elected me with your ballots, so I asked that you confirm me with your prayers. . . . Now I ask for your ballots as well as your prayers.

Thank God for the finale, I thought. Thank God for the marching bands and Bob Gardner's inspiring song. "I'm feelin' good about America—I'm feelin' good about me."

As the bands played, as the chorus sang, as Air Force One was shown banking away into the sunset, I wondered if anyone was still tuned in.

I turned to Mimi, not really wanting to know the verdict.

She held out her right fist and firmly turned her thumb up.

"It was wonderful!" she said. She seemed to be fighting back tears. But then, I thought, Mimi cries over *Ozzie and Harriet*. "It was fun, it was up, it was honest! It gave me a warm feeling, it made me feel good. Those Bicentennial shots were happy and so attractive! That Jimmy Carter must be scared to death!"

Yes, I thought, it is helpful to get an unbiased, outside viewpoint.

After the show the news came on. I was only half paying attention.

What difference did the news make now?

Suddenly I found myself sitting straight up in the chair. The final Gallup Poll was being announced.

It was prefaced with several disclaimers. There could be a statistical variation of two to three points. There were still a surprising number of undecideds. It was, of course, really too close to call.

But the last Gallup Poll had President Ford *ahead* by one point: forty-six percent to forty-five percent.

I laughed. I knew that it didn't really mean anything. But it was damned significant to me. The Sunday it all began the Gallup Poll had had us thirty-three points behind. It felt good, no matter what tomorrow would bring.

38
ELECTION DAY

Because they are both religious men, I feel certain that the candidates got on their knees to pray before they went to bed on Election Eve, Jimmy Carter to ask for sunshine from Massachusetts to Mississippi, Jerry Ford to ask for blizzards in the Northeast and tornadoes throughout the South.

When I woke to a clear, sunny view of Boston Harbor, I had my last creative thought of the campaign: why not hire airplanes to seed the clouds over Detroit, Philadelphia, Cleveland, and Harlem?

There was something else in the air that morning besides warm, Democratic sunshine. I think it disturbed most of us in the Ford campaign. When it was all over, Bob Dole told a television news team that, "It just didn't feel right."

I knew exactly what he meant. It *didn't* feel right. The late surge had been exhilarating. It was nice of Mr. Gallup to give us a one-point lead in his final poll. I was delighted to see in the morning papers that we had the momentum. But somehow the "whoosh" was gone. It had been there when I went to bed, but it was gone when I woke up.

I took the dog for a long walk shortly after the polls opened and all the people I saw looked as if they had just voted for Carter. I wanted my dog to growl at them. But he just wagged his tail. I went all the way to the North End looking for clues. Our liquor dealer is in the North End. He had assured Mimi that he was voting for Ford—that everybody in the North End was voting for Ford. That had seemed important, even though I knew that Massachusetts would go for Carter. If the Italian North End, good Catholics all, voted for Ford, it could tell the story of the close, crucial Northeastern states.

The people in the North End love to display political signs. They all seem to put them in their living room windows. "Vote Lo Presit." "Keep Langone." "Turco for School Committee." I looked down the rows of brick three-story apartment buildings and saw half a dozen green Carter signs. It was the first time I'd ever seen a Wasp name in the North End. There was a young Italian boy on the corner, straight out of a Prince Macaroni commercial, passing out Carter-Mondale leaflets. Every passerby seemed to be taking one.

There was the biggest crowd I'd ever seen at the polling place. Just as I entered the building, someone tried to thrust a Carter leaflet in my face. I told her she was violating the law. There were a few people inside who looked like Ford supporters. They were wearing suits. I waited in line for half an hour, grimacing every time I heard the ker-thunk of the lever that racked up another one for Carter. It wasn't like the last time, when Massachusetts was the only state in the union to vote for McGovern. That year we emerged from the booth a little sheepishly. This time when the curtains parted, out stepped a voter with the confident grin of a person who's voted in a winner.

Finally it was my turn to close the curtain behind me and stand alone before the printed names on the voting machine. What I saw made my heart sink. I saw what every undecided voter would see all day long. Not President Ford next to one lever and Jimmy Carter next to another. That would be a tough decision for that confused undecided voter. No. He had help. The little cards said Ford and Dole versus Carter and Mondale. By golly. He didn't have to choose between Ford and Carter after all. They were both nice men. He could choose between Dole and Mondale. That was easy. Click. Mondale.

It would go the other way in Kansas, I thought. And in the West. Maybe even in Texas. But Ohio, Pennsylvania, Illinois, New Jersey, New York—I left the booth more depressed than ever.

A politically savvy friend called me around two in the afternoon. "Congratulations," he said cheerfully.

"For what?"

"I just heard."

"Heard what?"

"You mean you haven't heard?"

"Carter voted for Ford?" I asked hopefully.

"The odds just changed. Now it's seven to five, Ford."

"That's nice," I said. "But do you think Jimmy the Greek understands precinct politics?"

My friend wasn't sure. I hung up feeling no better. I was beginning to identify the discouraging feeling in the pit of my stomach. I was beginning to form a picture of it.

It had a black face. It had a Southern drawl. It was carrying a Bible. It had a union card.

We had given up on the black vote even before Mr. Butz's remarks. We'd bought a few spots on black radio so the media couldn't report that we'd given up. Lionel Hampton singing "Call Ford Mr. Sunshine." The only black vote we got out of that was Lionel Hampton's. Before the campaign began, the Democrats were working on the biggest black registration drive in history. We weren't worried. They wouldn't vote anyway. Now even I could sense how wrong we had been. Of course they would vote. Right now there was an army of disciplined union Democrats working every black precinct in the country. Right now millions of dollars of "walking around" money was walking around Harlem, Detroit, Philadelphia, Cleveland. The blacks would vote. They had something to vote for. Jobs. They would vote ten to one for Jimmy Carter. They weren't going to be impressed by our last-ditch plea from Pearl Bailey. Pearl didn't need work. They weren't going to be shaken by the fact that four blacks were turned away from Jimmy Carter's church. They knew that for what it was. Two months ago I had been assured that the black vote had never affected a Presidential election. We had ignored one little fact. There had never been a Southern Baptist in a Presidential election.

Maybe it was so ironic—a Southerner with a black mandate—that we had missed its significance. I had little to do on Election Day except think about that irony.

I could sense that today, in spite of all our efforts, the South would rise again. We had tried to paint Carter as a liberal scalawag. Strom Thurmond: "He may have a Southern accent, but he doesn't sound like a Southerner to me." Our commercials showing his flip-flop on the right-to-work laws. Our efforts to remind Southerners of his mediocre record as governor of Georgia. I could clearly sense that they hadn't been forceful enough to dent the Southern pride in their own Jimmy, the Southern desire to have one of their own in the White House, the Southern Democratic tradition. We had hoped for Louisiana and Texas, prayed for Virginia and South Carolina, but now I could feel no real basis for our hopes and prayers. The South would probably be his. The election would be half over when the Southern votes were counted.

And then I thought of all those people from coast to coast who would pray before they voted. That had been one of the very first things I had learned about this peculiar election. For months I had been amused by the columnists and commentators who had talked of Carter's "religious handicap," who had wondered whether a reborn Christian could be elected President. I had been worrying about his religious *advantage*. I had been wondering whether it was possible to *beat* a reborn Christian. Carter had turned the strongest religious movement in America into a political base. I had no idea how strong that base would turn out to be. We had tried desperately hard to crack it, and he had certainly booted part of it away in his *Playboy* interview. But when they go into the booth, and say their prayers? The most frustrating thing about Carter's religious vote is that it came from people who were politically closer to Ford than to Carter.

That's why it "just didn't feel right" on Election Day. He had the South. He had the biggest religious vote that had ever marched to the booths. All he needed was a strong showing in just a few of the Northern industrial cities. I knew that the unions were working the precincts as they'd never been worked before. I knew that the blacks were united as they'd never been united before.

Mimi tried gallantly to bolster my sagging confidence.

When she returned from a trip to the Sunny Corner Grocery Store, arms laden with bulging paper bags, she let out a hoot of triumph as she entered the apartment.

"I won the last debate!" she said proudly.

She and the young college guy at the cash register had been holding a series of short, sometimes vituperative debates throughout the campaign. Carter had clearly won their debate on the economy—Mimi had left the store fighting back tears. I suspect Mimi had lost their foreign policy debate as well—she'd been rather glum that night. But on Election Day she was clearly the victor.

"He admitted that Ford was going to win," Mimi said. "And he admitted that he wasn't too bad a President."

"That's good," I said. "I hope you were statesmanlike."

"I was humble," Mimi said. "I didn't want him to lose his spirit. I told him that his man had put up a darn good fight."

A few minutes later Mimi was back with another piece of good news.

"Now I *know* we're going to win," she said, after hanging up from a long, serious conversation on the telephone. "Helen has just decided to vote for Ford."

"Who's Helen?"

"The lady who's doing the slipcovers."

"That could do it," I admitted.

"You don't understand. She made up her mind after watching both half-hour shows last night. She thought Carter was boring. She thought the President was wonderful."

That did make me feel good.

"She's Polish," Mimi added.

Maybe we've licked that problem after all, I thought.

"And she's deeply religious. Every other word is 'God.' "

The Catholic vote, I thought. What if we *win* the Catholic vote?

"And her son's a cop," Mimi said. "He's voting for Ford too."

Helen was our only hope, I thought.

The day seemed to be filled with people trying to boost my morale.

Peter Caroline, one of our writers at Humphrey Browning Mac-Dougall, called from a pay phone near a voting booth. Peter was the only strong Ford supporter I'd found in our office. He had decorated his office with Army surplus furniture, painted it olive drab, and put camouflage netting across the windows instead of curtains. He collected guns and was spending the day at the polls working to defeat a gun-control referendum on the ballot.

"I've got good news," he said.

"They're voting for Ford?" I asked hopefully.

"Can't tell," he said. "But I have just read your Chinese horoscope."

"Oh."

"It says that this year you are going to achieve enormous success in either war or politics."

"Well," I said, after absorbing the full impact of this news. "If we lose tonight, there's still plenty of time for you and me to start a war."

I had avoided the office all day because I knew that I was too nervous to be useful there. But about three-thirty in the afternoon, just as Mimi and I were leaving for Washington, and "The President Ford Victory Party," the office came to me.

I heard our phone ring just as I closed the front door. I should have known better, but I returned and picked up the receiver. It was our account executive on Acushnet, one of our largest accounts.

"We've got to see you right away," he said. "Emergency on Acushnet."

"Can't. I'm heading for the airport."

"We've *got* to see you. Our presentation is tomorrow. We can't agree on the copy."

"You can't, dammit." I was getting angry. The old advertising tension was coming back. Too much to do, too little time. It wasn't like the political tension I'd been feeling for the past two months. I'd had only one product to worry about. It had almost been a vacation.

"I've got less than half an hour to get to the plane," I said firmly. "I'm *not* going to miss that plane."

"Then we'll ride in the taxi with you," he said pleasantly. "We can go over the copy on the way to the airport."

It was an odd meeting. The copywriter and the art director sat in the back seat with me. The account executive sat up front with Mimi and the driver. By the time we had reached Logan, we had set the Acushnet copy strategy.

We crawled out of the crowded cab. As Mimi and I headed for our plane, I felt more depressed than ever. I realized that I wouldn't be as lucky as President Ford. He would have a nice, easy transition period from one job to another. But me?

39
ELECTION NIGHT

Quite a few people, trying to be nice, have suggested that we might have won if only we'd had a couple more days.

I don't think so. I think we ran out of gas just before the finish line. By November second, our money was gone, our drive was gone, and the President's voice was gone.

We arrived at our Washington apartment at six o'clock. As usual, I turned on the television set before I turned on the lights. There it was on the six o'clock news, clear evidence of where we stood at the end of the long campaign.

Jimmy Carter came on first, his garment bag slung over his shoulder as usual. Carter was beaming into the cameras with that famous toothy grin. His voice was caressing the microphones; he was humble; he was grateful; he only hoped for a greater America. He looked strong, he sounded strong, he was strong.

Mimi looked discouraged. "I don't think America can survive four years of seeing that man with his garment bag slung over his shoulder," she said.

Then President Ford came on. He was unveiling a mural, depicting his life and his family, at the Grand Rapids airport. His voice was cracked and hoarse, barely audible as he said how pleased he'd be to see the mural whenever he returned to Grand Rapids. Then he mentioned how much he owed to his mother and stepfather. Tears filled his eyes. He couldn't go on.

I wished, for all of our sakes, that the polls had been closed.

At that moment I wasn't certain we'd lose the election. But I was sure that if it turned out to be a tie, we couldn't survive the sudden-death overtime.

Mimi was still trying to cheer me up. The *New York Times* had published a score sheet listing all the states and their electoral votes. She tried to predict the states we'd win. She did a pretty good job. She checked off all the states that we actually thought we had a chance to win if everything—*everything*—went our way. They added up to two hundred seventy-four electoral votes. Four votes over the top. It didn't cheer me up.

She tried again. She gave me a strong bourbon. And then she recited all the logical reasons why Ford would win. People trusted him. People liked him better than Carter. He had done a good job. He was a decent, honest man. Why should people vote for the unknown when they already had a perfectly good President?

I let her talk until she ran down. Then I looked up from my bourbon and turned to her.

"Don't you feel it?"

She gave a big sigh, and finally nodded her head.

"I think I do feel it," she said. "I don't know why, but it just doesn't feel right."

That *did* make me feel better. At least I wasn't the only one who felt it.

The President Ford Committee had taken over the Sheraton-Park Hotel, and the Sheraton-Park is an enormous hotel. When Mimi and I entered the lobby, it seemed like Kansas City all over again. Camera lights, great surges of people, reporters fighting over credentials, politicians standing in bunches, hoping to be recognized, people asking directions from people who are lost themselves, posters and pictures and pretty girls in straw hats. Crowded confusion. It began like this. Now it's ending like this.

Jim Baker had invited "staff workers only" to a buffet reception in the Crystal Room. After several false starts, we finally found ourselves in a large room crowded with people.

I saw only three or four familiar faces. It seemed strange. Here we were at an office party—and after being on the job night and day for months, I knew only a handful of my coworkers. There was a giant television screen at the far end of the room, and a small group of people were clustered in front of it, quietly watching the early returns. A six-piece orchestra was playing bouncy, happy melodies loud enough to drown out the TV commentator's voice. I decided I needed a drink. I made my way to one of the bars.

The bartender was standing in front of the rows of unopened bottles with his arms folded across his chest. I hadn't noticed that I was the only one at the bar.

"Bar's closed," he said.

I'd forgotten. No drinking until the polls closed. There was over half an hour to go.

The situation reminded me of the greatest political concession speech ever given. Jimmy Breslin had delivered it the night he and Norman Mailer had been defeated in a wonderful New York mayoralty campaign.

"I am personally mortified," he had said, "to have actively participated in a situation that caused the bars of New York to be closed for the entire day."

Why was I thinking of concession speeches? Why did it seem so important to have a drink in my hand?

I grabbed Mimi by the elbow and forced a path through the quiet, unsmiling crowd to a post near the television screen. We were looking at the giant electronic NBC map of the United States. The states that the NBC experts predicted would go Ford, based on key precincts, were to be shown in blue. The Carter states were to appear in red.

We couldn't hear the announcer. The music was too loud. But suddenly the first state of the night lit up. It was Indiana. One of our key states. It was blue. A cheer went up. A completely new feeling swept over me for the first time that day. It was hope. We had won Indiana. We were ahead. Eleven electoral votes to zero.

I strained to hear the commentator. I wanted to hear him say that the Indiana vote was significant. All I heard was the orchestra. Jack Frost came over to me. He didn't look too happy.

"I dunno," he said. "Is Indiana important?"

"Vital," I said. I suddenly realized that I was trying to cheer him up. What was *I* doing trying to cheer *him* up? I hadn't the vaguest idea what the Indiana vote meant.

I steered Mimi to the buffet table. We waited in a line. At the end of the line a waiter was putting cold roast beef on salad plates. That seemed to be all there was to eat, except for some crackers and cheese. The very last of the campaign funds, I decided. I managed to spear a large piece of rare beef with my fork. The man next to me had been going for the same piece, and he looked angry. There wasn't much cheerful camaraderie at this office party.

I walked back to the TV set, trying to cut my beef with the fork.

There hadn't been any knives. The beef kept slipping off the plate. I was just bending to catch the falling beef with my left hand when the second state lit up. South Carolina. It was red.

I put the meat back on my plate and started sawing away again.

"Goddamned Southerners!" It was Jack Frost at my elbow again. "We should have split the Confederacy up when we had the chance."

I wanted to laugh, and make Jack feel better, but the meat had infuriated me. I thought about Strom Thurmond, and that infuriated me even more. Who were the idiots who thought that curmudgeon could help us in South Carolina? I hated myself for having made the Strom Thurmond commercial. I went back to my meat, ignoring Jack.

I couldn't cut it. Too tough to cut. Another state lit up as the blob of red meat slid across the plate one more time. It landed on the floor. I was picking it up as Kentucky turned red. Before I had straightened up, Alabama turned red.

I put my salad plate with the dusty, uneaten meat on a nearby table. I grabbed Mimi by the elbow, and again steered her through the crowd.

"Let's find a restaurant," I said as I reached the edge of the crowd. "I've never traveled so far to go to such a lousy party."

We ate alone in a coffee shop. We had steaks, without conversation. It was almost pleasant. I told the waitress to bring us bourbons the minute the bar opened. They arrived with the coffee.

I had planned to watch the returns in the Campaign '76 suite on the seventh floor. But I was feeling antisocial, so I wandered into the pressroom instead. Six television sets were going at once. Everything seemed so abnormal anyway, that it wasn't at all strange to have two Barbara Walterses, two Walter Cronkites, and two David Brinkleys speaking to me simultaneously. I adjusted right away. The Cronkites were saying we'd lost Florida; the Walterses were saying that Ohio was incredibly close; the Brinkleys were saying that New Jersey looked good for Ford.

I wandered out again as the Cronkites were saying something about Texas. It was nothing I wanted to hear—not that early in the evening.

As Mimi and I worked our way past the entrance to the Grand Ballroom I saw hundreds of people waiting to get in. They didn't look cheerful. They didn't even look hopeful. They just looked determined to get in. Most of them were young people.

We shoved our way through the packed lobby, waited ten minutes for the elevator, and finally made it to suite D-700.

It was a good place to die. I was among friends, and they knew what the returns meant, and they sat quietly with their own gloomy thoughts. The room was elegant and comfortable. I had a large, squishy chair to scrunch down into. Bourbons kept being placed in my hand. And there were heaping bowls of glazed strawberries and fresh grapes on beautiful beds of lettuce and parsley. It wasn't quite so bitter, watching Texas turn red, with a glazed strawberry in my mouth.

Bob Gardner arrived wearing his "Feelin' Good" T-shirt under his tuxedo.

"Don't watch that channel," he said, waving his hand at Walter Cronkite. "Watch NBC. They're much more cheerful over at NBC."

Someone quickly switched to David Brinkley. Sure enough. Texas hadn't gone under on NBC. David Brinkley was saying that Ford looked strong in Michigan, New Jersey, and Connecticut. Ohio, Pennsylvania, Illinois were close. Too close to call. Texas was still too close to call. New York was still too close to call, but seemed to be moving towards Carter. I tried to remember all the signs I was supposed to be looking for, but the states and their electoral votes all seemed to be jumbled around. If we lost Texas and New York, we could still win with a combination of industrial states. Which states? How many states? Brinkley was saying Philadelphia had come in "better than expected" for Carter. Could we afford to lose Pennsylvania too? The returns from the rest of Pennsylvania would be in very soon, Brinkley assured us.

"Let's go down to the ballroom," Bob suggested. I pulled myself up from my chair. Good suggestion. I wanted to be out of the room before the Pennsylvania returns were announced.

There were several long lines of people waiting to get into the ballroom. Bob, with the air of a person who owned the place, led us quickly past the lines to the usher checking invitations. We moved right in front of a pleasant-looking elderly couple, flashed our invitations, and were inside immediately.

President Ford's Victory Party took place in a ballroom as big as an ocean liner. People were pressed tightly together from one end of the room to the other. I couldn't believe that so many people could stand so much discomfort just for a long-shot chance at being able to cheer for the President. No one was cheering when we entered. There was a large television screen against one of the far walls. We slowly pushed our way towards it.

We could hear music coming from the stage as we neared the TV screen. The music was drowning out the words coming from the television. I saw that it was Lionel Hampton and his orchestra. Lionel was playing under an enormous Ford-Dole banner. He was grinning happily as he tinkled the keys of his glistening vibraphone. I didn't recognize the tune, but it wasn't "Call Ford Mr. Sunshine."

When we reached the screen, the picture went off and words began to crawl across the screen electronically. "Ford . . . wins . . . New Jersey." There was a half-hearted cheer from the crowd. Most of them probably knew by now that New Jersey was old news. "Ford . . . wins . . . Iowa." Another little cheer. "Ford . . . wins . . . Connecticut." A louder cheer this time. I could tell that only the good news would be flashed across this screen tonight. And I could sense that the huge crowd knew it too. Give them something to cheer about. That was the strategy. And have Lionel Hampton play loud enough to drown out the television.

Bob Gardner decided that he was going to cheer the crowd up all by himself.

"Be right back," he said, pushing his way into the throng. "I'm going to get Lionel to play 'Feelin' Good.' We've got to get every-body singing."

I watched him make his way to the stage, as I made my way to the bar. I had lost him in the crowd by the time I got to a table with bottles. I gestured to the bartender. Somebody grabbed my arm.

"Hey, Buddy, who do you think you are? Get in line like the rest of us."

I looked back. There was a long, scraggly line leading away from the bar.

"Where does the line begin?" I asked.

"About half an hour from here," the man said. "But first you got to wait in the other line to get the tickets." He held up four tickets labeled $2.00.

I moved back to Mimi. She pointed towards the stage. Bob Gardner was on the stage talking animatedly to Lionel Hampton. Al Hirt joined them, trumpet in hand. Bob kept pointing to the crowd as he talked. Finally he climbed down from the stage, and was lost again.

It took him about five minutes to make his way back to our side. He looked dejected.

"They won't play it," he said. "They think I'm some kind of crackpot. They were *supposed* to play it, dammit. I saw the lead sheets." He looked back towards the stage sadly. "Let's get out of here."

s

As
fat'

star
man
shal
Win
white
had ma
advertisi.
ting thous.
country. I I

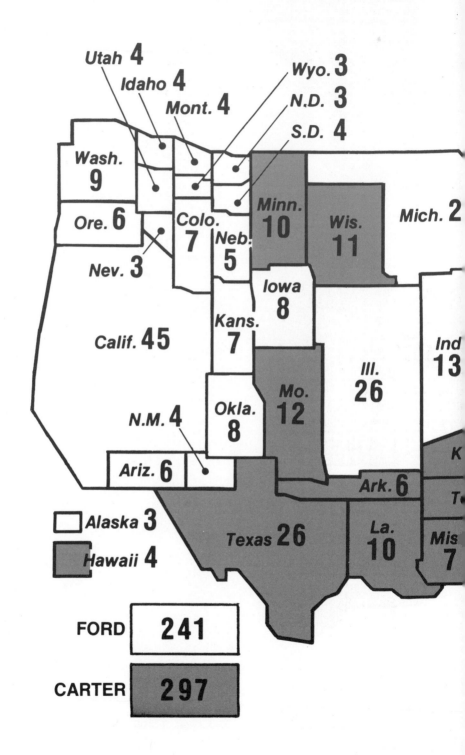